BTEC FIRST

Early Years

Kath Bulman and Neil Moonie

www.heinemann.co.uk
- ✓ Free online support
- ✓ Useful weblinks
- ✓ 24 hour online ordering

01865 888058

Heinemann

Inspiring generations

Heinemann Educational Publishers
Halley Court, Jordan Hill, Oxford OX2 8EJ
Part of Harcourt Education

Heinemann is the registered trademark of
Harcourt Education Limited

Text © Kath Bulman and Neil Moonie, 2004

First published 2004

09 08 07 06 05 04
10 9 8 7 6 5 4 3 2 1

British Library Cataloguing in Publication Data is available
from the British Library on request.

ISBN 0 435 46244 X

Designed by Carolyn Gibson
Typeset by TechType, Abingdon, Oxon
Original illustrations © Harcourt Education Limited, 2004
Cover design by Wooden Ark Studio
Printed in the UK by Bath Press Ltd

Acknowledgements
The authors and publishers would like to thank the following individuals and
organisations for permission to reproduce photographs:
Digital Vision page 61; Harcourt Education Ltd/Gareth Boden pages 58, 75 and 166;
Harcourt Education Ltd/Haddon Davies page 202; Harcourt Education Ltd/Martin
Sookias page 157; Sally and Richard Greenhill page 97 and Zefa (cover).

Crown copyright material on pages 31–3 is reproduced under Class License Number
C01W0000141 with the permission of the Controller of HMSO and the Queen's
Printer for Scotland.

We would also like to thank Sarah Horne for her invaluable, and very quick, input
into this book.

Every effort has been made to contact copyright holders of material reproduced in
this book. Any omissions will be rectified in subsequent printings if notice is given
to the publishers.

Tel: 01865 888058 www.heinemann.co.uk

CONTENTS

About this book

Welcome to your BTEC First Diploma in Early Years. This book is written to support students who are studying on the Edexcel, BTEC First Diploma in Early Years course – a National Qualification Framework Level 2 qualification. This book can also be used as a resource for any Early Years course of a similar level. For example, the knowledge requirements of this course are very similar to the underpinning knowledge required for successful completion of the NVQ level 2 qualification in Early Years.

Features of this book

This book is written in an accessible, easy-to-read format and divides the text into sections and sub-headings for easy reference. Throughout the text there are a number of features that are designed to encourage you to reflect on the issues raised, relate the theory to your practice and assist you to understand the relevant concepts and theories. These features are:

What you need to learn	a list of points that set the context of the unit in relation to Edexcel's standards
Think it through	questions designed to encourage reflection or discussion with others
Did you know?	information to act as a stimulus for discussion or reflection
Case studies	examples of real scenarios to help explain a concept or help to link the theory with real practice
Diagrams and tables	a list of practical suggestions for promoting good practice in an early years setting
Bullet points, diagrams and tables	some key points are expressed using bullet points, diagrams and tables to make a theory accessible and easy to use in case discussions or activities
Assessment activities	activities designed to support achievement in relation to unit outcomes
Glossary	There are key words that you will be expected to know and understand through your course. A list of these words and their meanings of these words can be found in the glossary on pages 278–9.

About your course

A BTEC First Diploma is a practical work-related programme resulting in a qualification at level 2. This means it is equivalent to four GCSEs at grades A* to C.

Success on this course will mean you will have the entry requirements to take a level 3 programme such as the Edexcel BTEC National Diploma in Early Years or an NVQ level 3 in Early Years Education and Care – both of these offer qualified nursery nurse status. With these qualifications you can take your training further and qualify to work in nursing, midwifery, other early years settings or as a nursery or primary school teacher.

During your course you need to complete six units – three core units and three specialist units. This allows you to study an aspect of early years care and education in depth.

The three core units are:

- Values and Interpersonal Skills
- Physical, Social and Emotional Development
- Good Practice in Child Care Settings

These units provide the foundation understanding needed to work in any early years settings. The material is further developed in the specialist units which are:

- Intellectual and Communication Skills
- Children's Activities and Play
- Care of Babies
- Working in Partnership with Parents
- Post-natal Care

Unit 8: Post-natal Care is suitable for anyone wanting to work with newly delivered mothers. If you combine this unit with Unit 6: Care of Babies and Unit 7: Working in Partnership with Parents you will have a firm grounding for working with young babies and their carers.

The first two specialist units, Unit 4: Intellectual and Communication Skills and Unit 5: Children's Activities and Play, provide complimentary knowledge and are suitable for people wanting to work in a nursery school or reception class. A suitable third specialist unit would be Unit 7: Working in Partnership with Parents or Unit 6: Care of Babies – if the nursery setting has a baby unit.

As well as learning the theory behind working in an early years setting, you will be expected to spend a considerable amount of time in an actual early years setting during your placement. This will not only give you valuable experience in working with children, help you make sense of the theory, but also help you to decide which of the different early years settings you find the most rewarding.

While you are in placement you can gather a lot of very useful material to help your studies, including:

- records of the activities you have helped children enjoy

- observations of children in different settings

- notes about incidents you observe, or are involved in

- copies of the work children complete

- any other material that you think might be useful.

How to succeed on your course

Training to work in the early years sector is not an easy option – it can be challenging and demanding, as well as highly rewarding. Young children are full of energy, curiosity, enthusiasm and have an unquenchable thirst to find out about everything around them – this means they need committed, energetic help from the people that care for them. As a result you will have very little time to prepare activities during your working day. You will need to balance your time so that you can plan and prepare the activities and sessions you carry out with children. Although time consuming, planning will become easier as you become more competent and involved.

It can be a little daunting when you consider the demands on you as an early years worker, especially when you think about the influence that you can have on a very young, developing child. This means you have a responsibility to always be professional in your behaviour and appearance, particularly when you are with children and their parents or carers. This is particularly important because children learn by example and copy what they see and hear, so be aware of the subtle messages you may be giving to a child.

This book has a range of activities that are not directly needed for the unit assessment, in the form of case studies and 'Think it through' activities, but completing them will help you to have a better understanding of the essential theory. The secret of success on the BTEC First Diploma in Early Years course is to work hard, be enthusiastic and gather as much as you can from your placement, and then use that to make sense of the theory.

Assessment

All of the units, except Unit 3: Good Practice in Child Care Settings, are internally assessed. This means that you have to provide evidence for the assessment criteria for each unit. Your tutor may set assignments for you to complete, perhaps using situations they know you are familiar with.

Unit 3: Good Practice in Child Care Settings is an externally set unit – assessed by your tutor and then re-marked by Edexcel examiners. To pass the whole unit you must provide satisfactory evidence to meet all of the pass criteria. To gain a merit you must do this as well as provide evidence for all of the merit criteria and likewise for the distinction criteria. Before you hand any part of the assessment in, read the assessment grid again and ensure you have covered all the listed requirements.

It is important that you read the criteria very carefully and make sure you understand what is required. The following is a list of the words you will come across in the assessment criteria and how you will be expected to answer them —using the choice of nappies a parent might make as an example.

List	simply write down the main points in 1- or 2-word points (e.g. a list of the types of nappies – terry nappies, nappy pads, shaped disposables, pull ups)
Identify	write a list with a little bit of explanation (e.g. terry nappies —reusable, washable, used with liner; nappy pads — unshaped rectangles for inside protective pants)
Describe	write short sentences going into some detail (e.g. using terry nappies requires access to a washing machine, as they need to be washed after each use. Disposable liners, with the soiled content, need to be flushed away. The nappies are then soaked in a bucket of solution)
Explain	write sentences giving reasons for why something happens (e.g. many parents are starting to use terry nappies, as using disposables has a damaging effect on the environment)
Discuss	write sentences that explore reasons for choices (e.g. many parents are starting to use terry nappies, as using disposables has a damaging effect on the environment. Disposable nappies use a lot of resources in their manufacture and many use damaging bleaches. After use they are often dumped on landfill sites and can pose a health hazard. In addition, many parents find them very expensive to buy)
Compare or contrast	explain the differences between two different examples (e.g. both terry nappies and disposables are effective in collecting the excreta of a baby and both need to be changed every few hours. Terry nappies use energy in their washing and do not wick moisture away from the skin. Disposable nappies do not need washing and often have a wicking layer that helps to keep the skin dry)

| Evaluate | explores the similarities and differences that have been compared and contrasted. You need to compare and contrast before you can evaluate (e.g. terry nappies are better for the environment because they can be reused. However the cost of washing has to be considered) |
| Analyse | this is a more in depth comparison than an evaluation. It considers the reasons behind a choice. This is a skill not often expected at level 2, but you will be required to analyse issues at level 3 (e.g. look at how users of disposable nappies might be persuaded to use terry nappies, or how the use of disposable nappies has become so popular). |

For each completed unit you will be awarded points that count towards the final grade you gain for the whole qualification.

For each unit	Internally assessed	Externally assessed
Pass	2 points	4 points
Merit	4 points	8 points
Distinction	6 points	12 points

The points for all six units are added together to give the final grade that is entered on your certificate and shows your college tutor, or a potential employer, the level you have achieved.

Final points	Final grade
32-42	Distinction
20-30	Merit
12-18	Pass

Integrated Vocational Assignment (IVA)

The IVA is the assessment set by Edexcel. It is used to test your knowledge and understanding of Unit 3: Good Practice in Child Care Settings. You will be given a scenario – about an early years setting – and asked to carry out a series of related tasks. There may be particular needs of the children or setting that you will need to consider when giving your answers. You will be given a set length of time to carry out the different tasks designed by Edexcel's examiners for each assessment criteria.

If you have been completing the unit activities and the end-of-unit assessments throughout this book, as well as applying this learning to your experiences in placement, you will not find the IVA difficult!

As you see from the previous chart you can gain double marks for the IVA compared to your internally set work. It is very easy to gain good marks if you follow the following suggestions.

- Ask your tutor if they have copies of past IVA assessments and practice doing an IVA yourself.

- Read all of the instructions very carefully, at least twice, before you begin.

- Ask your tutor if you are not sure about anything.

- Do all the tasks that are set – taking note of the marks awarded for each question. You do not gain extra marks for doing an entire page of work when only 2 marks are offered. Equally, if a question has 10 marks it will need a longer more in-depth answer.

- Remember to keep records of any involvement in group work or discussions that are part of the assignment.

- Provide all of the evidence for the task— see the 'Summary of your task and what you should hand in' and 'Materials to be handed in' sections in your candidate handbook.

- Do not hand in any extra work or additional evidence that is not been asked for.

- Before you hand your work in, check you have done all the tasks and covered all of the assessment criteria.

- Fill in all the required forms, remembering to sign them.

Finally...

You are entering a fascinating and very rewarding area of work. Working with children offers unlimited enjoyment and satisfaction – as well as hard work. You will learn as much – if not more – from the children you work with, as they will learn from you. Enjoy your course and your future career in early years education and care.

Good luck!

Kath Bulman, 2004

VALUES AND INTERPERSONAL SKILLS

This unit explores the social and political factors that influence child needs and the role of early years workers. The values, rights and responsibilities that are central to early years work are studied during this unit. The unit also focuses on the skills that early years workers need in order to be able to work effectively.

Ideas for evidencing the grading criteria are presented.

In this unit you will learn about:

- factors that influence diversity and equality
- skills required of an early years worker
- responsibilities of the individual early years worker.

Social care work is 'working with people' – and people are all different from one another. Examine your fingerprints – there are about 6000 million people in the world today and yet it is very unlikely that you will have exactly the

Figure 1.1 *There are approximately 6000 million people in the world, but each person's fingerprint is different*

same fingerprints as anyone else. Each person is different from other people physically, and each person also has different life experiences.

The great thing to enjoy about early years work is getting to know so many different people, with their different views of life. Although each person is special, there are patterns which mean that some people are similar in some ways to other people – they may share similar life experiences. This unit will explore some of the social and political factors that influence people's lives, making us different from each other but also creating patterns we can recognise.

Because people have different life experiences, it is very important that people are not treated as if they were all the same. Each person you will work with will have his or her own individual, social and cultural needs. If people are to receive a fair and equal service, their different needs have to be understood. This unit will explore the risk of discriminatory practice. Discrimination can happen when people are seen as being 'all the same'.

Factors that influence diversity and equality

The range of differences between people is called 'diversity'. It is important that people working in care should recognise diversity and treat people with equal respect whoever and whatever they are. Many factors make people different from one another. These factors include:

- social class
- geographical location
- culture
- gender
- financial viability
- family structure
- ethnicity
- age.

Figure 1.2 *Most people feel that they belong with groups such as their family and friends – but people also belong with other groups such as their social class, age group and ethnic group*

The groups we belong to can have a strong influence on how we think, what we value, how we act and what we do. When people are with their friends they will behave differently from when they are at work. People say and do different things when they are with family than when they are with people they have not met before.

The wider groups that people belong to also influence how they behave. It is important not to make assumptions that other people will have the same views, attitudes or needs that we do. Men often react to things differently from women. Older people do not necessarily see things the same way that younger people do. Ethnicity can influence your life experience, and social class can make a big difference to the experiences and opportunities an individual may have.

Social class

> **Case Study –** William, Mischel and Sean: Schools
>
> **William** is 16. His father works in the diplomatic service as a senior civil servant. He boards at a private residential school, which charges fees of £12,000 per year. In the holidays he stays with his parents on their five-acre estate in the country. He is studying four A-levels and has advanced skills in sailing. He is not sure about his career, but after completing his degree he may choose to take a post within the civil service. If he chooses this option he would expect to achieve a senior post by the age of 30.
>
> **Mischel** is 16. Her father is a senior teacher at a comprehensive school. Mischel attends a different school three miles away from the semi-detached home where she lives with her family. Her mother takes Mischel to school each day by car – and will do so until Mischel is old enough to take her driving test. Mischel hopes to stay on at school and take A-levels. She would like to get the qualifications to work as a journalist.
>
> **Sean** is 16. His father is currently working as a technician at a tyre-fitting company. Sean walks or catches a bus to school each day. Sean lives on a large housing estate in an urban area which is very congested with traffic. He is not sure what he wants to do when he leaves school, but hopes he can get bar work or some sort of hourly paid employment locally.
>
> These three people are the same age – yet they have very different lifestyles. One boards at school, one travels by car to the best school in the area, and one walks to the local school. Their lives will be different in many other ways. The friends they mix with, education, career opportunities and future income will probably be very different. Sociologists would explain these differences in terms of **social class**.

Social class is a way of classifying the social status that different occupations have. In other words, some jobs are seen as high status or high class, while other jobs have less status. Your social class is concerned with the way other people think about your job – not just about the money you have.

Social class is a term that has been used to describe different groups of people for a very long time in Britain. Mostly, people are used to the terms 'upper class', 'middle class', and 'working class'. Upper-class people have more power, influence and status than middle-class people, but middle-class people have more power, influence and status than working-class people. Before the 1960s, class differences were open and obvious. People usually wore different clothes which showed the class they belonged to and they usually only mixed socially with members of their own class.

Historically, social class was often seen as being like a pyramid, with the upper class at the top and depending on the work of the other classes.

Between 1971 and 2001 the official system for grading jobs contained five 'classes' in order to grade different occupations. The system was known as 'The Registrar-General's Social Class Index'. The five classes in this system are set out in the table below:

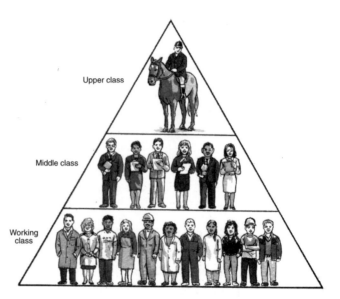

Figure 1.3 *The social class pyramid*

Class Level	Definition	Examples of occupations in each class
Social Class I (1)	*Professional occupations*	Company secretary, doctor, judge, lawyer, university teacher, solicitor, scientist
Social Class II (2)	*Intermediate occupations*	Aircraft pilot, police or fire brigade officer, teacher, manager, farmer
Social Class III N (3 Non-Manual)	*Skilled non-manual*	Cashier, clerical worker, estate agent, sales representative, secretary, typist
Social Class III M (3 Manual)	*Manual occupations*	Bus driver, bricklayer, carpenter, electrician, hairdresser, baker, butcher
Social Class IV (4)	*Partly skilled occupations*	Agricultural worker, bar staff, hospital porter, street trader
Social Class V (5)	*Unskilled occupations*	Road sweeper, kitchen labourer, refuse collector, window cleaner, office cleaner

Since the 2001 census, a new system for classifying social class has been used in all official statistics and surveys. This system uses eight classes to classify occupations and is called the National Statistics Socio-economic Classification. The whole system is very complex and can be viewed at www.statistics.gov.uk. The eight 'analytic classes' used in the system are set out overleaf.

The National Statistics Socio-economic Classification – Analytic Classes

1	Higher managerial and professional occupations. This class is split into: **1.1** Large employers and higher managerial occupations **1.2** Higher professional occupations.
2	Lower managerial and professional occupations
3	Intermediate occupations
4	Small employers and own account workers
5	Lower supervisory and technical occupations
6	Semi-routine occupations
7	Routine occupations
8	Never worked and long-term unemployed

Case Study – William, Mischel and Sean: Money

William comes from a wealthy family, and mixes with people who are used to taking money for granted. If William wants extra tuition to help him with his studies, the money is there. If he needs a car, it will be bought for him. William can expect to travel widely – expense isn't an issue. If he wants books or sailing lessons, he gets them. William mixes with other people who have very high expectations of life. William listens to people who have direct experience of how government and business work. He is very clear about the possibilities for his future. He works very hard – but he knows what he is working for. He would describe himself as middle class – but his father's occupation and his family's status would fit Class 1.

Mischel's parents are buying their house on a mortgage. Mischel can get the latest clothing and music and she has her own computer. She has a Saturday job which gives her a small income. Mischel's parents can pay for little extras, but money is always an issue that has to be talked about. Mischel mixes with people who do not know much about government or business, but she gets advice on careers from the local school. Mischel is interested in her future career and her parents put pressure on her to do well in exams, telling her that qualifications are very important. People similar to Mischel's parents are likely to fit Classes 2–4.

Sean's parents live on a crowded housing estate. Sean goes to a school similar to Mischel's, except that many of the students there do not believe that school is important. Most of Sean's friends say that school is boring and that what matters is getting out and earning money. Once you get some money you can be independent – you can do what you want. Sean hasn't got a job yet, but he is looking forward to getting the latest clothes, CDs, etc. when he can get one. Sean's parents often worry about money and are looking forward to Sean going out to work so that he can contribute to the household budget. Sean's parents might fit into Class 6 or 7.

THINK IT THROUGH

What are the differences in lifestyle for these three people?
What will happen to each person in the future?

Does social class matter?

Social class can make a difference to how people live their lives – whether they think about social class or not. One reason social class matters is that class can influence the attitudes and values that people have.

People whose work roles place them in Social Classes 1 and 2 often believe that they control their own lives. They expect to choose where to buy their own house or flat, they choose entertainment, what they eat and what they wear. People in classes 1 and 2, or children with parents in classes 1 and 2, may not see themselves as being wealthy, but often they do not worry too much about the cost of items, or about getting into debt.

Some people in lower status occupations feel that they cannot control their income, their jobs and housing needs. Some people in 'routine occupations' may feel worried about money. If you are short of money, you have to be careful what clothes and what food you buy. Money worries can limit where you can go out – where you can go on holiday and what social life you can have. If you have to rent a house or flat, you may feel that you have less choice of where to live than if you can afford to buy your own property.

Sociologists explain that people who belong to the higher social classes often feel they can choose their own lifestyle, whereas people in the lower classes may have less chance to choose how they live and what they do.

Does social class influence happiness?

Happiness is a very personal issue, and happiness comes and goes each day. In 1994, the psychologist Michael Argyle published a book on social class and happiness. He came to the conclusion that a large range of studies showed that people in the higher social classes are generally 'somewhat happier' than people in the lower social classes. Why does higher class lead to more happiness for many people?

- **Money** Lower social class jobs often don't pay very well. People in the lower classifications may have less to spend and less savings than people in the higher classes.

- **Enjoyable work** The more prestigious jobs, like lawyer or accountant, may often be more enjoyable than routine or boring jobs.

- **Respect** People with high-status jobs may be treated with more respect than people with low-status jobs.

- **Self-esteem** People who feel they have been successful and have developed their abilities may feel good about life.

- **Stress** People who have money worries, or who live in poor-quality housing – in areas of crime and so on – often feel that life is difficult and full of stress. Upper-class people may be more free of this stress.

- **Holidays** The higher classes take more holidays and more days out from home than working-class people.

- **Sport and exercise** Generally, people in the higher classes enjoy more sport, exercise and social activity than people with occupations lower down the scale.

- **Health** On average, people in the higher classes had less chronic (or long-term) illness, less sickness and even lived longer than people in lower classes during the last century.

- **Job security** Unskilled people are ten times more likely to be out of work than people with a high level of education and training.

Naturally, not every person who is in a job of high social class is happy, and not every person who is in an unskilled job is sad. All sorts of things can go right or wrong for anyone, but the evidence suggests that people with high-status jobs do seem to have more chances of being happy over their lifetime.

Lifestyle

In modern Europe, it seems that you are what you buy. Whenever you read a newspaper, watch TV, look at the Internet or just walk down the street, you see advertisements. Adverts don't just tell you about things you can buy – they often invite you to join in a way of life. Adverts offer a lifestyle.

Some sociologists say that it's not so much the work you do that matters, it's more how you spend your money – what lifestyle you buy into.

Many people now buy four-wheel-drive cars, yet rarely use them in the way they are intended to be used – in the country. Most of the time they may sit in traffic jams. But owning a four-wheel-drive says 'I'm part of the sporting outdoor set'. It's the image or lifestyle that people spend their money on.

When it comes to spending money, people are not equal – some have far more money to spend than others.

Figure 1.4 *People buy into a lifestyle*

DID YOU KNOW?

On average financial managers earn over five times more per week than people like hairdressers, catering assistants and bar staff. *(Source – Social Trends 2002)*

Financial viability

People who get less than 60 per cent of the income that an average person expects may be considered to be at risk of poverty and social exclusion. Financial viability means having enough money to live on. In 2001 an estimated 10.7 million people (18 per cent of the population) in Britain lived on or below the 60 per cent of average earnings poverty line; in 1979 only 4.4 million people were estimated to live in poverty. The number of people who can be considered to be poor increased dramatically between 1985 and the early 1990s. The proportion of people with low income (18 per cent of the population) has remained the same for the last few years.

Key groups of people who have to live on very little money include one-parent families, people who are unemployed, elderly people, people who are sick or disabled, single earners and unskilled couples.

People who are poor may have enough money for food, for some clothes and for heating, but poverty means that there is little money for interesting purchases and exciting lifestyles. People who depend on benefits have limited life choices. The latest clothes, nice reliable cars, the latest electronic equipment, digital TV and so on, may not be choices for people on low incomes. People with little money have to restrict what they can buy when they visit a supermarket or shopping centre.

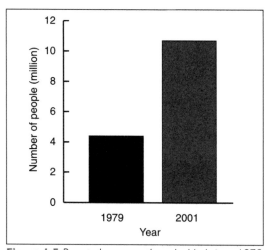

Figure 1.5 *Poverty has more than doubled since 1979*

Many lifestyles are not possible for people in poverty. Belonging to a sports club is not possible if you cannot afford the membership fees. Even jogging is not possible if you feel your neighbourhood is not safe to go out in.

In 1999 the government published a report called 'Opportunity for All'. In this report the government states: 'Our aim is to end the injustice which holds people back and prevents them from making the most of themselves'. The government says that their goal is: 'that everyone should have the opportunity to achieve their potential. But too many people are denied that opportunity. It is wrong and economically inefficient to waste the talents of even one single person'.

The 'Opportunity for All' paper states the following:

■ People living in households with low incomes have more than doubled since the late 1970s.

■ One in three children live in households with below half average income.

■ Nearly one in five working-age households has no one in work.

■ The poorest communities have much more unemployment, poor housing, vandalism and crime than richer areas.

The government report, 'Opportunity for All', says the following problems prevent people from making the most of their lives.

■ **Lack of opportunities to work** Work is the most important route out of low income. But the consequences of being unemployed go wider than lack of money. It can contribute to ill-health and can deny future employment opportunities.

■ **Lack of opportunities to acquire education and skills** Adults without basic skills are much more likely to spend long periods out of work.

■ **Childhood deprivation** This has linked problems of low income, poor health, poor housing and unsafe environments.

■ **Disrupted families** Evidence shows that children in lone-parent families are particularly likely to suffer the effects of persistently low household incomes. Stresses within families can lead to exclusion; in extreme cases to homelessness.

■ **Barriers to older people living active, fulfilling and healthy lives** Too many older people have low incomes, lack of independence and poor health. Lack of access to good-quality services are key barriers to social inclusion.

■ **Inequalities in health** Health can be affected by low income and a range of socio-economic factors such as access to good-quality health services and shops selling good-quality food at affordable prices.

■ **Poor housing** This directly diminishes people's quality of life and leads to a range of physical and mental health problems, and can cause difficulties for children trying to do homework.

■ **Poor neighbourhoods** The most deprived areas suffer from a combination of poor housing, high rates of crime, unemployment, poor health and family disruption.

■ **Fear of crime** Crime and fear of crime can effectively exclude people within their own communities, especially older people.

■ **Disadvantaged groups** Some people experience disadvantage or discrimination, for example on the grounds of age, ethnicity, gender or disability. This makes them particularly vulnerable to social exclusion.

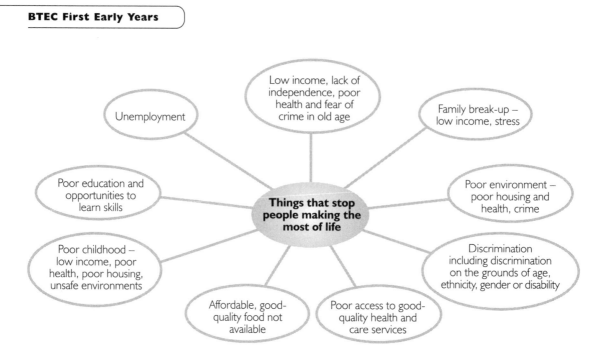

Figure 1.6 *Factors that affect whether people are able to make the most of their lives*

THINK IT THROUGH

Looking at all the problems listed above can you see how being poor might lead to a whole range of other problems? For example, if you have a low income, you might live in a poor neighbourhood; if you live in a poor neighbourhood you may experience more fear of crime.

Geographical location

People who feel confident about their future income and finances can choose their lifestyle. They can also choose where they would like to live. People in the higher social classes tend to live in more expensive housing areas with good facilities for travel and education. People with lower incomes tend to live in more densely occupied housing areas. People on lower incomes are often forced to rent rather than buy their homes. Different social class groups often live in different neighbourhoods. Marketing companies can use postcodes to work out what advertisements to send to different areas.

Does it matter what kind of location you live in? Many people would say that the important thing is to get on with the people you live with and that money, or the size of your house, does not matter. But there can be disadvantages to living in poor-quality or high-density housing. These can include noise, pollution, overcrowding, poor access to shops and other facilities, and stress from petty crime. When people are on a low income, household maintenance can become a problem. Poorly maintained housing can create health hazards.

If you live on a low income in a crowded block of flats or high-density housing, you may get:

- noise from neighbours

- more chance of being woken up in the night

- stress from neighbours' behaviour

- nearby busy roads where traffic fumes create pollution

- a number of children or relatives crowded into one bedroom

- more burglary, car crime and personal attacks

- poor car parking and travel facilities.

Door hinged outward to create space (safety hazard)

Windows kept shut to conserve warmth – resulting in poor ventilation

Damp patch on wall from broken gutters outside – risk of infection from fungal spores

Overcrowded bedroom – helps spread airborne infection when combined with poor ventilation

Poor lighting

Portable radiant electric fire (safety hazard)

Poor hygiene maintenance of bathroom facilities (lack of cleaning agents) – increased risk of skin and other contagious diseases

Poor maintenance of building – increased accident risk

Overcrowding may increase interpersonal stress and, coupled with other stressors, may lead to poor mental health

Figure 1.7 *Poor housing may contribute to a wide range of hazards to health and social well-being*

Low income and poor housing are a source of stress to many people. The table below lists the percentages of householders who said they had problems with the issues listed in the left-hand column. In general, people with money appear to have fewer problems compared with people who live in low-income areas. Living in the suburbs or in the country may also cause less stress than living 'in town'.

Problems in the area that you live	People in wealthy suburban or rural areas	People in council or low-income areas	People in wealthy urban areas	Overall percentages
Crime	49%	66%	59%	56%
Litter and rubbish	26%	58%	49%	42%
Vandalism and hooliganism	25%	58%	42%	40%
Dogs	22%	37%	25%	29%
Noise	16%	31%	35%	23%
Graffiti	11%	36%	32%	22%
Neighbours	7%	18%	17%	13%
Racial harassment	1%	8%	9%	4%

Source: Adapted from *Social Trends 2002*

THINK IT THROUGH

Explain what is meant by social class and the relationship to geographical location. Look at a map of your local area. Work out if the housing is different in different areas on your map. You may need to walk around the streets to note what kind of housing exists. What lifestyles do people have in the different areas? How do you think lifestyles and stress levels might vary between different housing in your area? What conclusions can you draw about social class in different areas?

Family structure

People differ from one another in the kinds of families or groups that they live in.

THINK IT THROUGH

Try watching the TV adverts on a typical evening. Many adverts for food products and cleaning products will show actors in a family setting. Just looking at these adverts, it would seem that most houses are occupied by 30-year-old couples with two children, and perhaps some cats and dogs. Is this image really how most people live?

Looking at the homes that people lived in in 2001, 29 per cent of homes were occupied by single people, 23 per cent of homes were occupied by couples with dependent children and 6 per cent were occupied by single parents with children. In 2001, 29 per cent of homes were occupied by couples with no children and only 1 per cent of homes housed more than one family.

Many people do live as couples with their children, but it would be a mistake to imagine that all people are born into and grow up in small families.

A family is a social group made up of people who are 'related' to each other. This means that other people (society) recognise that this group is related. In British society, 'family' is the word used to describe groups where adults act as parents or guardians to children. Belonging to a family can have many advantages. Family relationships can provide a safe, caring setting for children. Family groups can guide and teach children, and they can provide a source of social and emotional support for adults and older family members as well as children.

Modern sociologists identify four different types of family:

- extended families
- nuclear families
- reconstituted families
- lone-parent families.

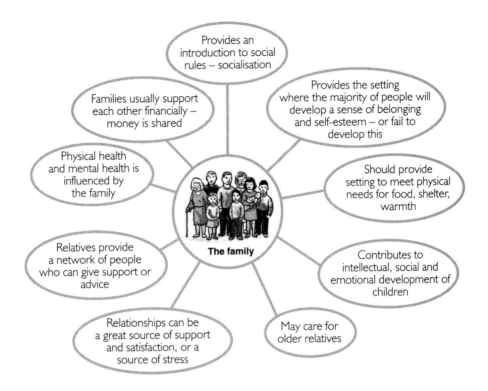

Figure 1.8 *What the family does for people*

Extended families

An extended family is where parents, children and grandparents all live together or near each other, so that they are often together. Between 1800 and 1900 in England, many families lived in this way. The extended family can have many advantages. Parents can work all day without having to worry about who is looking after the children – the grandparents might do this. If the grandparents needed care, then the parents or even the older children could help. The extended family provides a network of people who can support each other.

Ross lives with his brother and his mother and father on the top two floors of a very large semi-detached Victorian house near the centre of a city. Ross's mother's parents live on the ground floor of the building. They have their own bathroom and kitchen, although the whole family sometimes eat together at the weekend. Ross's parents were able to buy such a large house only because the grandparents sold their home to

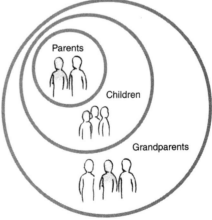

Figure 1.9 *The extended family*

make it possible. The grandparents own part of the new house, but they have left their share of the house to Ross's parents in their Will.

Nuclear families

A nucleus is the centre of a living cell, and the nuclear family is like the centre of the extended family on its own. By the 1950s, many people in Britain no longer lived with grandparents. The term nuclear family was invented to describe this new, smaller family. The original nuclear family was usually a husband who would go out to work, a wife who would look after the children while they were young, and the children.

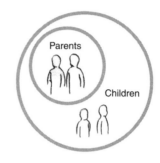

Figure 1.10 *The nuclear family*

Nowadays many couples no longer fit this description. Often both parents will have full-time work and the children are cared for by childminders, nannies, or nursery services. Male and female roles have been changing – men and women are now usually seen as equally responsible for household tasks. However, studies suggest that women still undertake the majority of child care and housework tasks.

Meena lives with her sister, mother and father in a three-bedroom, semi-detached house. Meena's grandmother (her mother's mother) lives in the Caribbean and she has not seen her for two years. Meena's father's parents live about eighty miles away, and she sees these grandparents about five to eight times each year. Meena's family moved to the house they live in three years ago when her father got a better job.

Reconstituted families

Approximately one marriage in every three now ends in divorce, and some people think this figure will increase. Many young people live together before marriage and have children, but there is evidence that a large number of these couples split up too. Over a third of marriages each year are likely to be re-marriages, and about one million children live with a step-parent. Roughly a quarter of children might experience their parents divorcing before the age of 16.

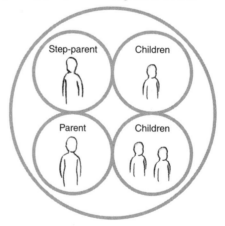

Figure 1.11 *The reconstituted family*

The reconstituted family is where the couple are not both the parents of each child in the family. One partner might have been divorced from an earlier marriage, and has now re-married to create a new family. Sometimes children from different relationships may be included in a new, reconstituted family. One partner may have been single but is now married to a partner who has children from a previous relationship.

Sarosh lives with his mother and stepfather in a modern terraced house in a small town. His mother and stepfather have been married for two years. Sarosh's 'real' father calls every other Saturday to collect him for a visit. Sarosh's mother and father divorced four years ago. His new stepfather has a daughter, Zara, who lives with her mother over two miles away. Sarosh has met Zara and they like each other, but Sarosh thinks his stepfather cares more about Zara than him.

Lone-parent families

Nearly a quarter of all families with dependent children are lone-parent families. Twenty per cent of families with dependent children are lone-parent families led by a lone mother, with just 2 per cent led by a lone father.

While some lone-parent families may be well off, many are disadvantaged. A family expenditure survey in 2000 showed that twice as many lone-parent families live on low incomes compared with couples with dependent children. Many lone parents rely on benefits or receive low income wages.

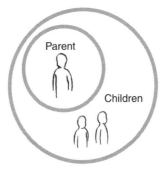

Figure 1.12 *The lone-parent family*

Janice is a single mother with an eight-year-old son, living in a fourth-floor flat on a large housing estate. Janice is looking for part-time work, but her son has an attention problem at school and the school often telephones her to ask her to come and collect him or to calm him. Janice depends on Income Support to get by. She doesn't have enough money for holidays or to take her son out for the day. Janice cannot afford leisure activities which cost money. At night Janice usually stays in and watches TV. There is a high drug-related crime rate on the estate and Janice worries that her flat may be broken into.

The type of family that a child lives in can change. An extended family can turn into a nuclear family if the grandparents die or move away. Families can become 'reconstituted' if one partner leaves and is replaced by a different person. Few people can guarantee a family style for life. When people leave their partners, divorce or die, a lone-parent family may be created. If the remaining parent finds a new partner, the lone-parent family becomes a reconstituted family. The same child might live in different family structures during childhood and adolescence. Some advantages and disadvantages of different family types are given overleaf.

Extended families

Advantages

Children	Parents	Grandparents
You have grandparents to look after you, as well as parents. You learn from a wider group of people. Security and stability. There is usually someone at home all day.	Grandparents can look after your children. Shared financial resources; parents and grandparents may be able to afford a bigger home. There is someone at home all day.	You feel that you belong and are needed. Both children and grandchildren can help you and talk with you. Shared financial resources.

Disadvantages

Children	Parents	Grandparents
Adults might boss children about. Children might feel they have less freedom.	You may have to look after your parents as well as your children. It may be difficult to move house and relocate for work reasons. Larger houses cost more to run. Smaller houses may become crowded.	You have to get on with your children. You may have less independence.

Nuclear families

Advantages

Children	Parents	Grandparents
Close relationship with parents. Security and stability.	Family can prioritise one parent's career. Family can move house to further a career. Family may have two incomes.	Independence from children. No unwanted pressure to look after grandchildren.

Disadvantages

Children	Parents	Grandparents
May tend to receive care from one person only (often the mother.)	The division of work may not satisfy both people. Child care may be needed if both parents work full time.	May lose contact with children and grandchildren. May become lonely or have insufficient social support.

Reconstituted families

Advantages

Children	Parents	Grandparents
Similar to nuclear family.	Similar to nuclear family – may have two incomes and financial security.	Few responsibilities.

Disadvantages

Children	Parents	Grandparents
May have difficulty making relationships with a new parent or with new brothers and sisters. May have to live in, or make visits to, more than one home.	Similar to nuclear family.	Possible feeling of being cut-off from grandchildren or from a child's family. Risk of isolation. May have to establish new relationships

Lone-parent families

Advantages

Children	Parents	Grandparents
Only one parent to relate to. Possible freedom from stressful or even abusive relationships.	Independence and control of own life.	Similar to nuclear family.

Disadvantages

Children	Parents	Grandparents
Only one parent to guide and help.	Generally more risk of low income. Responsibilities for home and child care fall on one person. Managing an independent lifestyle might be stressful on a low income.	Similar to nuclear family.

Changing family patterns

In the past 45 years there has been a gradual change in the way people live. Fewer people now live in extended families than at any time in the past century, and fewer people live in nuclear families than in the 1960s and 1970s. There are more reconstituted and lone-parent families with dependent children than there were 20 years ago.

There are many issues that influence people's lifestyles, but it is important to understand how money and economic factors influence family patterns. People do not simply 'choose' their pattern of family life like picking clothes from a catalogue.

When people worked on the land as farmers and farm labourers, the extended family was a very effective way to live. There was little reason for children to move away from the village when they grew up – the work went with the house where they lived. The more people that lived together, the more they could help each other and share the work.

When most people stopped working on farms and worked instead in businesses and factories, it was hard for young people to stay in the same area as their parents. If a new factory opened 20 miles away, it was best to move to the area where the new work had developed. Because younger people moved away from their parents to get work, fewer extended families existed and more nuclear families developed.

We live in an information age where each person may do individual work – men and women increasingly share employment opportunities. Running a home can be done much more easily than forty years ago. People may not need to live as a couple in order to cope with the dual pressures of employment and running a home.

Economic pressures no longer encourage or force people to live in traditional types of family to the same extent as in the past.

Culture

The way we behave, the language we speak, the diet we eat, the way that we dress and our lifestyle are all part of our culture. Culture includes the things which make one group different and distinctive from another.

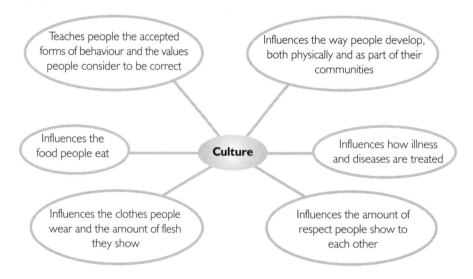

Figure 1.13 *How our culture can influence us*

Culture gives us a set of rules or expectations which help us to understand each other, and to know how to react in certain situations. Very often we do not even understand the culture we are surrounded by; we just do 'what is normal' and fit in. Because society is made up of different sorts of people, brought up in different circumstances or places, and following different beliefs and religions, different people's cultures can be different. We all tend to follow the way we were brought up and the influences of the people around us. Not everyone shares the same culture. There are many different cultures in Britain.

Ethnicity

For many people their race is of vital importance and it enables them to understand who they are. Race is not easy to define. In the past, people believed that different races of people were somehow biologically different. It is almost impossible to define racial groups in terms of genetic differences or features to do with skin colour or physical appearance. People do classify themselves and are classified by others in terms of the social and cultural groups to which they belong. A person's culture, religion, style of dress, way of speaking and so on may lead to classification in terms of ethnic group.

A key way in which people distinguish themselves is in terms of being black or white. Some people talk in terms of a black, white or Asian group. But there is no single black culture, and no single white culture.

A study of the British population by ethnic group is reported in *Social Trends* (2002). Details of the size of various ethnic groups are set out in the table below.

White	53 million people
Black Caribbean	0.5 million people
Black African	0.4 million people
Other black groups	0.3 million people
Indian	1.0 million people
Pakistani	0.7 million people
Bangladeshi	0.3 million people
Chinese	0.1 million people
None of the above groups	0.7 million people
All other groups – including people who refused to state ethnicity	0.8 million people

There has been law to prevent discrimination on the basis of race since 1965. The current Race Relations Act was passed in 1976 and amended (or updated) in 2000. The 1976 Act of Parliament set up the Commission for Racial Equality. This Commission seeks to investigate cases of discrimination based on racial and ethnic group membership.

Despite the law and the powers of the Commission, however, there is evidence of inequality between white and black groups in Britain. Black and Asian people are more likely to be victims of crime than are white people. The British crime survey in 2000 showed that black and Asian adults in England and Wales were roughly twice as worried about becoming victims of crime as white people. The table below shows the percentage of people in different ethnic groups who were worried about crime.

	White	Black	Asian
Theft of car	20	37	37
Theft from car	15	33	30
Burglary	18	37	41
Mugging	16	32	38
Physical attack	17	35	38
Rape	18	34	34

Source: The British Crime Survey published by the Home Office 2000

Unemployment rates vary between different black and white groups, but generally rates of unemployment are higher for black and Asian people than for white people. In 2001–2, 4 per cent of white people were unemployed. Among non-white groups, 21 per cent of Bangladeshi people, 16 per cent of Pakistani people, 14 per cent of black Africans, 12 per cent of black Caribbean people and 6 per cent of Chinese people were unemployed (Social Trends 2003).

More black and Asian families are likely to have a low income compared to white families. The table below shows the proportion of people from different ethnic groups who were in the bottom 20 per cent of the population for the amount of spending money that they have (spending money is called 'disposable income').

Ethnic group	Percentage of bottom 20 per cent of population
White	19
Black Caribbean	24
Black non-Caribbean	34
Indian	29
Pakistani / Bangladeshi	64

Source: Social Trends 2003

Many black and Asian people believe that they have poorer employment opportunities and are more likely to be victimised than white people.

Gender

It was only in 1928 that women were granted equal rights with men to vote in elections. Eighty years ago, women were considered to have a lower social status than men. Assumptions were made that women should look after children, do housework, cook and tidy, and do light jobs. Men did the more valuable administrative, management and labouring jobs that women were not seen as being able to do.

Great changes have come about in the nature of work and the nature of family life since 1928. Women are now generally given equal opportunities in education and employment – the Sex Discrimination Act of 1975 made it illegal to discriminate against women in education or employment.

However, the government's Women's Unit (2003) reports that: 'women who work full-time are paid on average just 81 percent of men's hourly earnings. Women still hold fewer top jobs and seem to profit less from promotion. Women far outnumber men in jobs like nursing and primary school teaching – often, these jobs are not highly paid. Men often get the more highly paid jobs, such as becoming head teachers, even within areas of work dominated by women. When it comes to domestic work, men still generally do less of the child care, washing and cooking, although they may do more gardening and maintenance jobs.'

THINK IT THROUGH

Look at the table overleaf. In general, it would appear that men and women still make assumptions about who should do what within the household.

Household task	Hours and minutes per week	
	Fathers	Mothers
Cooking/preparing meals	2:50	13:30
Cleaning	2:00	13:15
Washing and ironing clothes	0:55	9:05
Spending time with the children	5:05	8:45
Shopping	2:50	5:50
Washing up	2:00	3:40
Driving children to school	1:45	2:55
Gardening	3:00	2:00
Sewing/mending clothes	0:10	1:20
Other household tasks	2:25	1:40
All household tasks	23:0	62:00

Source: Social Trends 1997

How are tasks shared between men and women in households you know?

Age

Over 20 per cent (one in five) of people are over the age of 60. In 1900, if you were over 60 you would generally have been considered old. In 1900 the average life expectancy of a new-born boy was 55, and the average life expectancy of a new-born girl was 57. Today a boy might expect to live to 73 and a girl to 79. Far fewer people die young, and far more people live to be old. People live longer because of better food, better housing, better public health and better medical care.

DID YOU KNOW?

An Age Concern survey asked people when old age began. The average suggestion of 16- to 24-year-olds was 63 years. People aged over 75 suggested age 76, and were more hesitant to give an answer at all.

Most people want a long life, but people do not want to be old. In many black and Asian societies, being an elder is a very positive thing. As an old person you may not have the physical fitness you had when young, but you have developed wisdom instead. In Britain a large number of people seem to think that being old is a very bad thing.

ASSESSMENT ACTIVITY

Describe the ways in which people are different from each other.

1   Get together with a team of other students to design a quiz to test your knowledge of the ways in which people are different from each other. The quiz could consist of a series of cards with numbers and questions on one side. The answers to the questions could be kept on a separate sheet. Another team could design a similar quiz and both teams could 'play each other'. Use the sections on social class, financial viability, geographical location, family structure, ethnicity, gender and age to help you make up this quiz.

2   Working with the people in your team, imagine two different children. One of these children might live in a nuclear family, with professional parents, in a high-income neighbourhood. The other child might live with an unemployed single parent in a low-income neighbourhood. How do you think these children's lives might be different? How might being male or female, black, Asian or white affect the experiences of the two children? What values and beliefs would you expect the two children to have? Write a report which lists ways in which people are different because of the effects of social class, financial ability, geographical location, family structure, ethnicity, gender and age.

To achieve a **merit grade** you need to be able to explain the effects of employment, income, culture, values and family structures on individuals. At this level your report must explain some of the ways in which employment, income, culture, values and family structures influence people's lives. Use your discussions about the two different children to help you write this report.

Discrimination

Discrimination means telling things apart – knowing the difference between similar things. You can discriminate between, say, a sandwich filling that you don't like and one that you do. Telling things apart is a vital part of life – if we didn't do it we wouldn't be able to live independently.

Discriminating against people has a different meaning; it doesn't mean 'telling them apart'. It is important to realise that people are all different – with different life experiences. Discriminating against people means giving people an unequal service or treatment because of their differences.

If an employer did not want to appoint a woman to a job, because she might leave to have children, the employer would be illegally discriminating against her. The discrimination would not be simply that the employer realised she was female. The discrimination would be that she was treated differently from a man who might want to start a family. A man in the same situation would be appointed; the woman gets unequal treatment because the employer thinks she might leave the job or take maternity leave to have a baby.

Discrimination can take place against people who belong to any group. Common forms of discrimination are based on race and culture, gender, age, disability and sexuality.

How does discrimination come about?

People usually feel that they belong to certain types of group. We have friendship groups, families, and some teenagers belong to gangs or clubs. People get to feel that there are 'people like me who I belong with'. There are people who share the same views, who look similar to us, who think like us. But we all meet people who are different. There is a danger of seeing people who are not like us as being threatening, stupid or disgusting. Many people then divide their social world into us and them. 'Us' is the group we feel safe and OK with. 'Them' are the people who are different; people we don't like.

People who work in care have to be interested in learning about other people; interested in diversity and difference. Early years workers cannot divide people into 'types that I like' and 'types that I don't like'. Early years workers must never exclude people from receiving a good service because they belong to a different race, culture, religion, gender or age group, or because of their sexuality or abilities.

Seeing the world in terms of 'us and them' leads to certain kinds of thinking. Discrimination sometimes comes about because of assumptions that people make in their thinking. People will sometimes stereotype or label others.

Stereotyping

Life can feel very complicated. Sometimes people try to make life easier by using fixed ideas to explain 'what people are like'. When a person has fixed ideas that he or she uses to see a group of people as 'all being the same' this is called 'stereotyping'. Some adults might even have a stereotyped view of children. Every child is an individual person with his or her own personality, but some adults might think of children as a problem that has to be managed. Thinking of children as a problem might be caused by stereotyped assumptions such as the assumptions listed below.

Figure 1.14 *An example of stereotyped thinking*

People may make assumptions based on stereotyped thinking. For example, an adult might say: 'I don't know how you do your job – working with noisy children all day – they would drive me nuts'! This person might be making assumptions based on the stereotype that young children are all 'difficult, naughty and noisy'.

When people say 'all women are ...' or 'all black people are ...' or 'all gay people are ...' they will probably go on to describe a stereotype of these groups. Skilled caring starts from being interested in people's individual differences. Stereotyping lumps people together as if they were all the same. Thinking in stereotypes usually stops a person from being a good carer.

Labelling

Another way in which discrimination can be shown is labelling. Labelling is similar to stereotyping, but labels are brief and simple. Instead of having a set of fixed opinions about a group to which a person may belong, the person is summed up in just one word or term.

THINK IT THROUGH

Some years ago there was a school for children with learning difficulties. When it came to meal times, the children had to sit down for their meal. The 'slow' children were allowed to start first because they took longer. Staff would label children 'slows'. The 'slows' knew who they were, and sat down when 'slows' were called for. Some children were not very skilled with holding plates, etc., and these were labelled 'clumsies'. Children would describe themselves as 'slows' or 'clumsies'.

Figure 1.15

What effect do you think describing him - or herself as a 'slow' or a 'clumsy' would have on a child's development of self-esteem?

Labels can be words like:

- aggressive
- emotional
- disgusting.

These words might be used to describe ethnic groups, women or old people. Labels can be used to claim that a group of people are all the same. Labels may say that people are all only one thing, such as aggressive, emotional or disgusting. When individuals are labelled, it's almost as if they stop being people – labels take away people's dignity and individuality.

Prejudice

When people live in a world of 'us' and 'them,' it becomes easy to judge people who are different from us. People who are unemployed might be judged as lazy by people who have not experienced unemployment. People who do not follow healthy lifestyles might be seen as 'stupid' by people who can manage to do the right things. It can be easy to judge and label other people. Judging other people involves thinking that we are better or superior, our views are right and that people who do not meet our standards should be criticised or punished for failing to meet our expectations.

Prejudice comes from the term 'pre-judgement', and means judging other people without the knowledge to judge properly. No new information or understanding can alter such a judgement. If people believe stereotypes about groups, they may go on to make judgements about individuals. For instance, an employer who believes that 'women don't really care about work – they only care about their family', may develop a prejudice that women aren't suited for promotion to senior positions. Employers with such a prejudice might try to promote only men. Once people develop prejudices against groups of people they are likely to discriminate against them when in a position to make decisions.

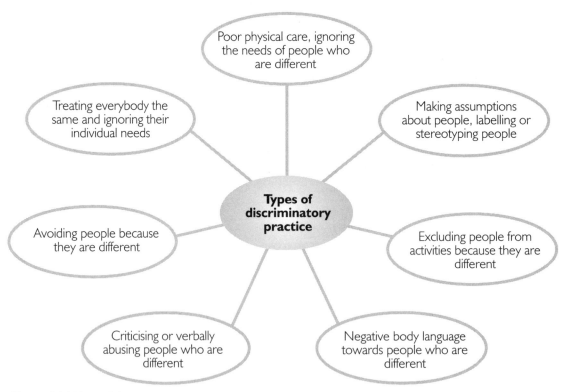

Figure 1.16 *Types of discriminatory practice*

The effects of discrimination

Early years workers have to make decisions about how to help others all the time they are working. If early years workers have prejudices or if they label or stereotype others, they may discriminate against some people in the way that they care. Some of the dangers of discrimination are listed in the diagram below.

Figure 1.17 *Effects of discrimination*

Sometimes people communicate in a way that does not show equal respect and value for others. A member of staff may not want to sit next to someone he or she has a prejudice about. People may use different body language when they have a prejudice towards someone.

Discrimination is not always obvious – very often carers simply make assumptions that everyone does or should think like they do, and this can come out in conversation.

THINK IT THROUGH

Imagine you went to a day care centre during November. The walls are full of artwork about Christmas. There are pictures of Jesus being worshipped by shepherds and artwork representing presents, Father Christmas, reindeer and the North Pole. All the people in the artwork have white faces. The children are learning to sing Christmas carols. There is no evidence of any other religion other than Christianity, and no evidence of any other ethnic group other than white people.

What would children learn from such an experience? Why does it matter that there is representation of diversity if all the children are Christian and white? How might a young child who belongs to a different ethnic group or religion be likely to be effected if he or she experienced such a day centre?

It is unlikely that you will ever find a centre like this nowadays, although older people may remember such things from many years ago.

THINK IT THROUGH

Imagine that you are watching children playing. Some of the children are calling other children 'scuzz' – 'You're a scuzz', etc. One child looks different from most of the other children and he seems to be 'picked on' most of all. This particular boy seems to be chased and shouted at by many of the other children.

If this boy does feel unwelcome and 'picked on' what effects could this discrimination have on him? Why is it important for early years workers to challenge exclusion and discrimination?

Challenging discrimination – anti-discriminatory practice

It is very important to recognise how discrimination can happen and to make sure that we do not discriminate in our own professional practice. Professional early years workers also have a duty to challenge any discriminatory behaviour that they see. Anti-discrimination means taking action to stop other people being harmed or having their rights ignored.

All Health and Social Care employers will have policies and procedures that will enable discrimination to be challenged. People have specific rights to be free from discrimination established by law. The main Acts of Parliament that have established rights are:

- The Sex Discrimination Act 1975 (amended 1986)
- The Race Relations Act 1976 (amended 2000)
- Disability Discrimination Act 1995 and Disability Rights Commission Act 1999
- The Human Rights Act 1998.

ASSESSMENT ACTIVITY

Identify discriminatory practice, with particular reference to early years settings.

1 Think about day nurseries or other care settings you have visited or worked in; try to imagine examples of what might happen if everyone was treated the same. What kind of discriminatory assumptions might be made about a child's ethnicity or gender? Write a report that describes some examples of the risks of discrimination that could exist in an early years setting.

What discriminatory assumptions might be made about ethnicity, gender and age if people are treated 'all the same'? Write a report which describes some examples of the discrimination that an individual child could experience if staff were discriminatory.

2 While you are on placement, arrange an interview with a senior member of staff. Ask him or her about the organisation's policies and procedures for preventing discrimination and maintaining the rights and well-being of children. Try to find out what a worker would be expected to do if he or she saw examples of discriminatory practice.

Find out how managers in the organisation try to prevent discrimination and encourage high-quality care.

To achieve a **merit grade** you need to be able to explain the effects of discrimination on individuals in early years settings. Your report must not only describe examples of discrimination but you must also explain how discrimination could harm children. For each example of discrimination that you describe, go on to explain its effects on the well-being of the child.

To achieve a **distinction grade** you need to explain how early years settings can promote anti-discriminatory practice. Your report should include details of an early years setting's policies and procedures for protecting the well-being of children and preventing discrimination.
You will need to explain how a person could go about challenging any discriminatory practice in this care setting. You should also explain how managers would support their staff in order to prevent discrimination.

The skills required of an early years worker

The relationship between early years worker, child and professional team members

Professionalism

A professional role is like being a character in a play. An actor has to do and say the things that their audience would expect them to do and say. Being a professional early years worker means that what you do and say has to fit the expectations of the people who have expectations of you.

THINK IT THROUGH

If you work as an early years worker, who will have expectations as to how you should behave? There may be a large range of people, but usually this will include the children, managers, other staff, relatives and other professionals who work with children.

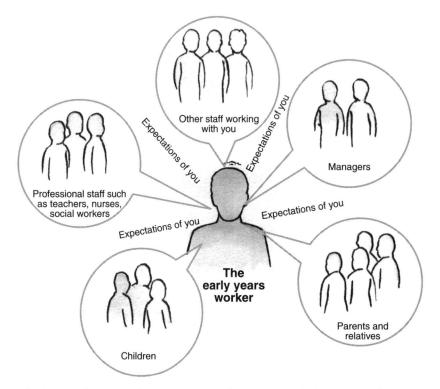

Figure 1.18 *As an early years worker, other people will expect you to behave as a professional*

Each role may involve different expectations. Not everyone will expect exactly the same things. The following are some general expectations of professional behaviour.

■ Early years workers must respect that people are different from each other or 'diverse'. Early years workers must be careful not to discriminate against people because of differences.

■ Early years workers must maintain confidentiality.

■ Early years workers must show respect for diversity and difference in children and parents.

■ Early years workers should develop good communication skills and make appropriate relationships with children.

■ While at work, early years workers have to work to meet the needs of employers and children rather than putting their own wishes first.

■ Early years workers should check and think about the work they do with people. Early years work is not always easy and it involves lifelong learning.

The Early Years National Training Organisation has produced a definition of the principles of good practice in early years work. These underlying principles are integrated into every unit of early years NVQ qualifications and describe the values that guide early years work. The underlying principles are central to the skills required of an early years care worker and are copied here in full.

The Underlying Principles of Early Years National Vocational Qualifications

These principles draw on both the UN Convention on the Rights of the Child and the Children Act 1989, and also take into account the delivery of the School Curriculum and Assessment Authority: 'Desirable Outcomes for Children's Learning'. They are based on the premise that the earliest years of children's lives are a unique stage of human development, and that quality early years provision benefits the wider society and it is an investment for the future.

1) **The welfare of the child**
    The welfare of the child is paramount. All early years workers must give precedence to the rights and well-being of the children they work with. Children should be listened to, and their opinions and concerns treated seriously. Management of children's behaviour should emphasise positive expectations for that behaviour, and responses to unwanted behaviour should be suited to the child's stage of development. A child must never be slapped, smacked, shaken or humiliated.

2) **Keeping children safe**
    Work practice should help prevent accidents to children and adults, and should protect their health. Emergency procedures of the work setting, including record keeping, must be adhered to. Every early years worker has a responsibility to contribute to the protection of children from abuse, according to her or his work role.

3) **Working in partnership with parents/families**
    Parents and families occupy a central position in their children's lives, and early years workers must never try to take over that role inappropriately. Parents and families should be listened to as experts on their own child. Information about children's development and progress should be shared openly with parents. Respect must be shown for families' traditions and child care practices, and every effort made to comply with parents' wishes for their children.

4) **Children's learning and development**

Children learn more and faster in their earliest years than at any other times in life. Development and learning in these their earliest years lay the foundations for abilities, characteristics and skills in later life. Learning begins at birth. The care and education of children are interwoven.

Children should be offered a range of experiences and activities which support all aspects of their development: social; physical; intellectual; communication; emotional. The choice of experiences and activities (the 'curriculum') should depend on accurate assessment of the stage of development reached by a child, following observation and discussion with families. Early years workers have varying responsibilities concerning the planning and implementation of the curriculum, according to their work role, but all contributions to such planning and implementation should set high expectations for children and build on their achievements and interests. Child-initiated play and activities should be valued and recognised, as well as the adult planned curriculum. Written records should be kept of children's progress, and these records should be shared with parents.

5) **Equality of opportunity**

Each child should be offered equality of access to opportunities to learn and develop, and so work towards her/his potential. Each child is a unique individual; early years workers must respect this individuality; children should not be treated 'all the same'. In order to meet a child's needs, it is necessary to treat each child 'with equal concern': some children need more and/or different support in order to have equality of opportunity. It is essential to avoid stereotyping children on the basis of gender, racial origins, cultural or social background (including religion, language, class and family pattern), or disability: such stereotypes might act as barriers to equality of access to opportunity. Early years workers should demonstrate their valuing of children's racial and other personal characteristics in order to help them develop self-esteem.

These principles of equality of access to opportunity and avoidance of stereotyping must also be applied to interactions with adult family members, colleagues and other professionals.

6) **Anti-discrimination**

Early years workers must not discriminate against any child, family or group in society on the grounds of gender, racial origins, cultural or social background (including religion, language, class and family pattern), disability or sexuality. They must acknowledge and address any personal beliefs or opinions which prevent them respecting the value systems of other people, and comply with legislation and the policies of their work setting relating to discrimination. Children learn prejudice from their earliest years, and must be provided with accurate information to help them avoid prejudice. Expressions of prejudice by children or adults should be challenged, and support offered to those children or adults who are the objects of prejudice and discrimination. Early years workers have a powerful role to play in ensuring greater harmony amongst various groups in our society for future generations.

7) Celebrating diversity

Britain is a multi-racial, multi-cultural society. The contributions made to this society by a variety of cultural groups should be viewed in a positive light, and information about varying traditions, customs and festivals should be presented as a source of pleasure and enjoyment to all children including those in areas where there are few members of minority ethnic groups. Children should be helped to develop a sense of their identity within their racial, cultural and social groups, as well as having the opportunity to learn about cultures different from their own. No one culture should be represented as superior to any other: pride in one's own cultural and social background does not require condemnation of that of other people.

8) Confidentiality

Information about children and families must never be shared with others without the permission of the family, except in the interest of protecting children. Early years workers must adhere to the policy of their work setting concerning confidential information, including passing information to colleagues. Information about other workers must also be handled in a confidential manner.

9) Working with other professionals

Advice and support should be sought from other professionals in the best interests of children and families, and information shared with them, subject to the principle of confidentiality. Respect should be shown for the roles of other professionals.

10) The reflective practitioner

Early years workers should use any opportunity they are offered, or which arises, to reflect on their practice and principles, and make use of the conclusions from such reflection in developing and extending their practice. Seeking advice and support to help resolve queries or problems should be seen as a form of strength and professionalism. Opportunities for in-service training / continuous professional development should be used to the maximum.

Care workers in the field of fostering and adoption will need to follow the code of practice for social care workers. While this code focuses on broader issues than the underlying principles, the standards may be of interest in defining good practice.

The General Social Care Council (GSCC) code of practice for social care workers

The GSCC has designed a list of statements that describe the standards of practice required of social care workers. This code is designed to apply to all care workers in the UK. A summary table of the principles in this code is set out below.

You must:

. . . **be accountable for the quality of your work and take responsibility for maintaining and improving your knowledge and skills.** (Meet standards, maintain appropriate records and inform employers of personal difficulties. Seek assistance and co-operate with colleagues, recognise responsibility for delegated work, respect the roles of others and undertake relevant training.)

. . . **uphold public trust and confidence in social care services.** (Not abuse, neglect or exploit children or colleagues or form inappropriate personal relationships. Not discriminate or condone discrimination, place self or others at unnecessary risk. Not behave in a way that raises suitability issues. Not abuse the trust of others in relation to confidentiality.)

. . . **establish and maintain the trust and confidence of children.** (Maintain confidentiality, use effective communication, honour commitments and agreements, declare conflicts of interest and adhere to policies about accepting gifts.)

. . . **protect the rights and promote the interests of children and carers.** (Respect individuality and support children in controlling their own lives. Respect and maintain equal opportunities, diversity, dignity and privacy.)

. . . **promote the independence of children while protecting them from danger or harm.** (Maintain rights, challenge and report dangerous, abusive, discriminatory or exploitative behaviour. Follow safe practice, report resource problems, report unsafe practice of colleagues, follow health and safety regulations, help children to make complaints and use power responsibly.)

. . . **respect the rights of children while seeking to ensure that their behaviour does not harm themselves or other people.** (Recognise the right to take risks, follow risk assessment policies, minimise risks, ensure others are informed about risk assessments.)

Figure 1.19 GSCC Standards of practice

If people's needs are not met by early years workers then people may be harmed; or deprived of the quality of life they might otherwise have had. All people have the right to be cared for in a way that improves their quality of life.

Young children are developing physically, intellectually, emotionally and socially all the time. In order to develop, children need to feel that they are physically and

emotionally safe. Children need contact with loving and caring adults. They need to be able to form relationships with adults who care for them. They need to feel that they belong within a group of caring people. Children need to find interesting and mentally stimulating activities to assist with their intellectual development.

If young children receive quality care, they are likely to grow up with a sense of being worth something – a sense of self-worth. If children grow up in a caring setting, they should growto like who they are, to be confident and to have self-esteem.

Figure 1.20 *Encouraging a child's social and emotional development*

When children do not receive good care, they may fail to develop a sense of belonging, they may feel very negative about themselves, and they may lack a sense of being worth anything. Children are vulnerable – their sense of who they are can be strongly influenced by the type of care they receive.

The early years worker is intimately involved with the child – giving the child a sense of belonging, of being loved and important.

THINK IT THROUGH

In Figure 1.20, how are the child's care needs being met?

The child's intellectual development can be helped by the exciting 'things to do' offered by the toy. The child's social and emotional development is encouraged by the carer who is using his relationship and communication skills with the child. Children who do not receive good care may not develop so positively.

Figure 1.21 *Ignoring a child's needs*

THINK IT THROUGH

What is wrong in Figure 1.21?

The carer's attention is focused on the TV – not on the child. The child is strapped into her chair, even though she is not tired. There is little activity to support physical or intellectual development. There is no sense of love or belonging for the child. If this child is often treated in this way, she may not develop fully. Children's development is influenced by the quality of care that they receive – children are vulnerable people.

Esteem, belonging and self-worth

During the first 18 months of life infants develop an emotional bond of love with their carer or carers. This bond represents the first relationship that a child forms with others and it may provide the foundation for emotional and social development throughout that person's life. Young children may not be able to explain their feelings and their emotions because their language abilities are not fully developed. However, research during the past 25 years suggests that young children have the ability to understand and respond to the feelings of others. Three-year-old children will sometimes try to comfort younger brothers or sisters who are upset. Children also need to feel that they are valuable to their friends and family. If a child enjoys good social relationships with carers then feelings of self-worth or self-esteem are likely to develop.

The psychologist Abraham Maslow developed a five-stage theory of human needs. This theory can be used to understand the needs of both children and adults. Early years workers have a duty to show respect not only to the children that they work with but also to their parents and relatives. The importance of respect is explained in the diagram below.

Development of full potential	Respect for individuality and support to help people take control of their own lives will often be necessary to help children develop their full potential
Self-esteem needs	Respect for diversity, dignity and privacy will be very important in helping people to develop or maintain a sense of self-esteem
Social needs	People need to be able to trust their carers and receive effective communication in order to meet their social needs
Feeling safe	People need to be free from discrimination, have a right to confidentiality and be free from risks if they are to feel safe
Physical needs	Freedom from abuse and neglect will be important, as well as food and shelter, in order to meet physical needs

Figure 1.22 *Human needs (based on Maslow's theory)*

Rights and responsibilities

Rights of individuality, freedom from discrimination, confidentiality, choice, dignity, independence, effective communication and safety all protect individual well-being and encourage self-development and self-esteem.

Rights usually carry responsibilities with them – they are balanced with responsibilities because membership of a community involves both. Children can expect respect, but they have a responsibility not to interfere with or damage other children's rights. They have a right to be free from discrimination, but also a responsibility not to discriminate against others.

Figure 1.23

One way to understand this idea of rights and responsibilities is to think about the issue of smoking. Adults have a right to choose to smoke even though smoking usually damages health and might shorten a person's life. Smokers have a responsibility to make sure other people do not have to breathe in their smoke. This means that in most places today, smoking is allowed only in specially set-aside areas.

Rights can be seen as protecting vulnerable clients.

Rights

Rights may work best when everyone shares the values on which they are based and when people's rights and responsibilities go together.

Rights and responsibilities

Figure 1.24 *Rights and responsibilities go together*

Usually, little is said about children's responsibilities because they have less power than staff and the managers of services. Children are generally vulnerable, while care workers usually have a degree of control over their own lives. Just because people are vulnerable, it doesn't mean care workers have a right to interfere with other people's rights, or for instance threaten people with racist or sexist behaviour.

It is an early years worker's responsibility to respect children's rights, but in turn care workers should expect to enjoy similar rights in their place of work. It is a manager's responsibility to check that children's rights are respected, but once again managers can expect to be treated with respect, not be discriminated against and to have a safe working environment.

Professional roles of an early years worker

Time management

Different people expect different things from you as an Early years worker. Children will often want you to spend time with them and give your attention to them. Many children feel special if you can spare time to listen and talk with them. Managers will expect that, as well as doing this, you will do all the tasks that are needed for all the other children. Other professionals will want you to understand how busy they are and perhaps hope that you have the time to do things that they can not – like spending time talking to children. Parents and carers will expect you to put their child, perhaps before other children.

People will all expect different things from you. Early years workers often have difficulty being able to please everyone!

1   Imagine that you work in a day centre and you promised to help a colleague tidy all the toy cupboards and to put up artwork at the end of the day before you go home. Most of the children have been collected and your colleague has started work. One of the parents stops you and asks how her daughter is getting on with the other children. Your colleague gives you a look as if to say 'why are you leaving me to do all the work'.

Who do you please – the parent or your colleague?

2   You are working with a small group of children, one of whom looks sad and wants to talk to you. Another child is busy climbing on a climbing frame and shouting 'look at me – look at what I can do'.

Which child do you give your attention to first?

Figure 1.25 *Professionalism involves the ability to balance different people's expectations.*

1   The underlying principles of good practice stress the importance of working in partnership with parents and families. If you did not stop and talk to the parent you would not show the respect that is expected. You might not make the necessary relationship with the parent needed to share information about the child's development. So you must stay and talk to the parent. But does your colleague understand what you are doing and why? As soon as you have finished talking to the parent you owe your colleague an explanation. It would have been unfair to leave your colleague to get on with the work if you had been discussing the latest soaps on TV! So you need to explain why you had to respond to the parent and put the parent first.

2   The underlying principles of good practice stress the importance of keeping children safe. Is the child on the climbing frame safe? The underlying principles stress the importance of the welfare of the child and that children need to be listened to. It will be very important to listen to the sad child, so if you believe the child on the frame is safe you might want to put the sad child first. You might want to say something like – I'll watch you in a minute. On the other hand, if you think there is a risk to children on the climbing frame you might need to attend to that first. Perhaps you could hold the hand of the sad child while talking to the child on the frame You would be showing that you cared, even if you had to quickly attend to something else.

Professionalism involves the ability to balance different people's expectations

It is important to manage your time so that you can work efficiently with a range of people. It is always possible to explain that you need to leave someone and be polite – perhaps offering to return at a later date.

Giving effective care means meeting people's needs. Effective care always develops a sense of belonging and self-esteem. Giving effective care takes time. If you worked with one child all day, you would get to know each other really well. If you had only one person to work with, you might understand their needs in detail. You might find it easy to encourage the development of their self-esteem.

Many early years jobs involve working with a large number of people. Working efficiently means providing a service for everyone to an equal standard. Early years workers often have to achieve a balance between the efficiency of their work (giving everyone a service) and their effectiveness at meeting individual, social and emotional needs.

As well as balancing the pressures of time with the need to give effective care, early years workers have to be clear about the boundaries of their role.

Boundaries

A boundary is like a fence – it marks where your role ends. You can think of a boundary as the line between your caring role and your ordinary relationships.

A boundary is a line you go up to – but should not cross over.

Boundaries of the early years worker role clarify what you should not be expected to do. Deciding on the boundaries of your role means that you need to decide the limits of what you can do and what you should refuse to do. If you are at work or on a placement, then understanding the boundaries of your role may be an important task. Setting boundaries may help you to feel safe and comfortable with the pressures that the caring role might place on you.

You need to decide:

- how much time it is right for you to give children

- how far you should become emotionally involved with children and their carers

- how far you should tell your parents or carers about your own life history, lifestyle and feelings.

Self-presentation

Early years workers need to behave appropriately in order to show respect for children and parents. Many people spend a great deal of time and money trying to look good – sometimes people want to attract attention, to shock others or to be different. It is important to celebrate differences in people and early years workers will want to dress in a way that acknowledges their cultural and lifestyle differences. However, there is an important issue to consider as a member of a care team. Team members are employed to care for others, not to be the centre of attention themselves.

Clothing which is designed to shock, to make the wearer look sexually attractive or frightening, may be OK at a club or party, but within an early years setting it can send the message: 'I'm the important person, I'm the one to look at – not you children.' The way early years workers present themselves to children, parents and other staff should convey respect for their rights. In turn, others have a responsibility to respect cultural diversity.

Self-presentation includes personal hygiene, which means clean hair, teeth, hands and nails. Many children or relatives may view body odour or a dirty appearance in an early years worker as a sign of not caring about others. Early years workers need to be sensitive to the messages that their appearance sends and need to consider health and safety.

- Flat shoes are necessary when lifting objects or physically supporting children. High-heeled shoes can increase the risk of falling or twisting an ankle.

- Long earrings could be dangerous – children could pull them or they could become caught in clothing.

- Necklaces and ties can get caught in children's clothing or dangle into food.

- Some rings, especially those with stones, may provide an opportunity for bacteria to collect or might tear protective gloves.

- Long hair can brush over children's faces and perhaps touch food – it may need to be tied back.

- Personal habits should include careful washing of hands to prevent the spread of infection. Lifestyle habits such as smoking need to be carefully thought through. Many parents may be concerned that their children may grow up to copy what they see adults around them doing. If you smoke in front of children, you may be sending a message that smoking is good. Parents may find this offensive.

■ It is important to use skilled listening techniques based on an understanding of the communication cycle. Non-verbal body language should show respect for children and colleagues.

As an early years worker you need to check policies on self-presentation with senior staff. There can be variations in policies between different settings.

Reviewing own performance

Why reviewing own performance is important

Working with vulnerable children and their parents is not a simple task. People have complex feelings and thoughts, and each person is unique. Because people can vary so much, and because people's needs are different, early years work involves constant learning.

If people were not complicated – if they were all the same – then it would be necessary to learn only a few simple rules and procedures in order to do a good job. Because each person has individual needs, it is important to get to know them individually. In order to care for a person you have to learn about their situation, their needs and their life. Both the early years underlying principles of good practice and the GSCC code of practice require workers to undertake relevant training or professional up-dating as part of the professional duty of a carer.

Figure 1.26 *Some ways of learning about children*

Good caring involves constant learning. How do you learn about people?

- Do you read about theories of needs and behaviour?

- Do you sit in a comfortable chair and think about early years work?

- Do you get into discussion groups and talk about early years work with others?

- Do you work with children – talk to them and listen to them?

All these ways of working could be useful. Many people would say that the best place to start would be to actually do the work – talk and listen to children. But the very best way of learning about people's needs is to use all the ideas listed above.

Working with people gives you experience, lets you learn naturally by watching other people and copying the way they do things. If you listen to the people you work with, you may get some feedback on how good your practice is. Gradually, you can change what you do – until things seem to work well.

Working with people gives you 'know-how' on care work.

Sitting and thinking is useful because it is only by thinking things over that people realise what is going on. Sometimes difficulties can be sorted out if you think things over, and thinking things through often helps you to feel confident about your ideas. If you picture things you have done, you can work out why certain things happened, and it can help you to see things from other people's point of view. Thinking things through can help us to have new ideas.

Thinking about your work with others can help make sense of things and help you plan for the future.

Discussing care work is a great way of learning – when people work on their own, they are likely to develop assumptions. We can all develop stereotypes, label others and even become prejudiced if we never check our ideas with other people. Other people are not always cleverer or better than we are; it is just that discussing things often helps us to understand things better. There is an old saying: 'I know what I think when I hear what I say.'

Discussion is useful because it can help to make things clearer – it can help to check assumptions in our thinking.

Reading and going on courses is useful because books and teachers may have new ideas, information or ways of looking at things, all of which can help in understanding the situations or needs that carers work with.

Reading is useful because it can help give new ideas and understanding of child care issues.

Emotions and working with people

The great thing about working with people is that they are all so different and each person provides a new learning situation, but having to find out about each child in a nursery, each adult in a day or residential centre, takes energy. It is always easier just to see people as being similar, and not to get too involved.

Not thinking about work, not discussing it, not reviewing your own performance saves emotional energy – but it can lead to a feeling that care work is boring. Once work seems boring, negative feelings about people and tasks take over. Emotions connected with boredom can make us want to give up and withdraw.

One reason for reviewing your own performance is so that you don't begin to see children as 'all the same' and feel the boredom that can go with this.

Working with people creates a lot of emotions and feelings – some of them nice and some not so nice. Some people we work with will be good to us – they may praise us, and tell us that they like us. Working with interesting, attractive or kind people may make us feel good. But some children will be worried or upset; these children may not always be rewarding to work with. Our first emotional reaction may be to want to avoid them. When we have to work with a child that is difficult it is only natural to feel 'I don't want to – I'd rather do something else'.

Figure 1.27 *Emotions and professional behaviour*

If we are to work in a professional way then we have to be sure that we don't follow the emotional urge to withdraw, but instead find ways of coping. Why does the child not want to do the activity? Is the child bored, frustrated? If we can think through some answers, we may be able to understand why the child is 'difficult'. If we can understand, we can cope with our emotions.

> *One reason for reviewing your own performance is to prevent negative emotions from blocking professional behaviour.*

Thinking a situation through can help us to solve problems. Why does a child throw his or her work on the floor? There could be many different reasons. Talking to other staff or to senior staff may help us to understand. Involving other people will probably help us to understand people we work with. Talking to the child may help us to understand. Observing what happens during the day may help. Thinking about our own behaviour – how good we are at talking or listening – may also help us to understand.

> *One reason for reviewing your own performance is to solve problems we face.*

You will have attitudes and beliefs and ways of understanding people based on your own life experience. It is possible that carers can make assumptions about other people – perhaps that they are bad or dangerous. Assumptions can turn into stereotypes and pre-judgements about other people. In the end there is a danger that children can be judged, labelled and discriminated against because they are different.

> *One reason for reviewing your own performance is to recognise assumptions in your thinking and to prevent these assumptions turning into discrimination and pre-judgements.*

It is very difficult to check our own thoughts alone. A good way to check our assumptions is to discuss practice with colleagues, tutors or workplace supervisors. Skilled supervisors may be able to help us question assumptions in our thinking.

How to review your own performance

It is often difficult to understand how we influence the people we work with. After we have been working with someone it is useful to stop and think about the work we have done. Sometimes discussing our work with supervisors, managers or other staff can be helpful to get new ideas. If we get new ideas they can be tried out in practice to see if they are right. When people have a problem to solve they sometimes go through a process like the one shown in Figure 1.28.

The important thing is to think about your experiences and learn from them. It is easy to forget our experiences and learn nothing from them if we don't think about them and discuss them. The main ways to review your own performance are to think about your work and discuss your work.

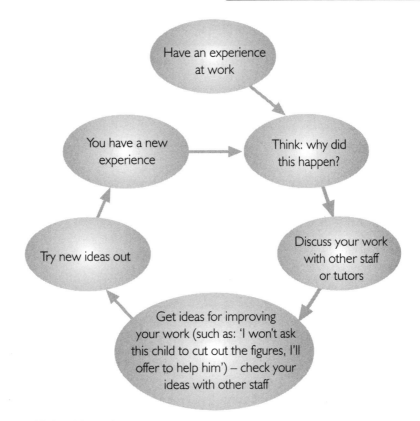

Figure 1.28 *A problem-solving process*

1 Think about the reactions you get from children – try to imagine how they see you. What does children's non-verbal behaviour towards you mean? What do children say to you? How effective is your work at meeting children's needs, including needs to belong and needs for self-esteem?

2 Review your work by discussing your views of children's needs and your work with them. You might discuss your practice with your work supervisor, a tutor or with colleagues.

When and where to review your work

Reflecting on and reviewing work is part of learning and developing care skills. Reviewing could take place at work, but you can think and discuss anywhere. College work should help you to review your practice, and the more you review practice, the more you may learn. Many work settings organise formal supervision or training sessions to help staff review their practice. Some work settings may use team meetings to discuss some practice issues. If months go by without any thinking about or any discussion of practice, then the risks of boredom, stress, negative behaviour towards children, prejudice, discrimination and unmet care needs all increase.

Supervisors, managers, colleagues and tutors should be able to help you review your practice.

ASSESSMENT ACTIVITY

Describe the basic values and principles for people working in care.

1 Use the description of the underlying principles of early years NVQs or, the GSCC Code of Practice and contents of this unit to make your own list of the values and principles that people working in care must follow. Share your list with other students in order to check that you have included all the important issues.

2 Think of a vulnerable child you have met on placement. Use your list of values and principles to think about the needs of this child. Were this child's social and emotional needs met by the way he or she was treated? What might have happened to this child if the staff had not behaved according to the values and principles on your list? Discuss your ideas with other students, and with tutors and placement supervisors if possible, so that you can check that you have not missed important ideas. Remember to keep details of the child confidential.

3 Visit several different early years settings and find out about their policies and procedures for providing quality care and education. Try to arrange to talk to staff about the values and principles of caring. You might ask about policies to prevent discrimination, policies on staff meetings, record keeping and staff training, supervision and feedback to staff on their performance. If appropriate, ask about the underlying principles and how these principles are being implemented and monitored. Some care services may have a booklet or a leaflet which can be given to parents which explains the entitlements that their children may expect. Compare the different information that you can get from different care settings.

Using the list you made for activity 1, write a report that describes the basic values and principles for people working in early years. Use the work you did for activity 2 so that your report can go on to explain how the values and underlying principles can affect children. Use the work you did for activity 3 to further develop your report, so that it compares ways in which different care settings promote the values and principles for people working in early years settings.

To achieve a **merit grade** you must identify the ways in which the values and principles of early years settings affect individuals.

To achieve a **distinction grade** you must compare ways in which different early years settings promote the values and principles of early years work.

Responsibilities of the individual early years worker

As well as forming professional relationships with children, it is important to form relationships with the team of people with whom you work.

Being in a team

Teams are important in early years work because it is hard to provide good-quality care on your own – support and help from others is needed to provide constant, effective care. Good teams share values and understandings about the purpose of care.

THINK IT THROUGH

Story one: Placement heaven

You arrive for your first day in a day care centre – you are greeted by your 'supervisor'. She is very friendly and has time to spare – gets you a drink and sits down with you. She tells you about the centre and explains who the children are and how the centre tries to provide good quality care. She talks about the importance of understanding the underlying principles such as celebrating diversity and working in partnership with parents. You are invited to sit in on a team discussion. The meeting includes some administrative issues but also a discussion of some of the children's developmental needs. Each member of staff looks interested. All the staff do not necessarily agree – but they all listen to each other. You can tell from the smiles and eye contact that the staff all care about each other's feelings. They also care about how you feel and are very concerned that you should feel included in their group – even though you do not know much about the centre. The manager seems to get on well with the staff and there is some humour in the group. The staff seem to get on with the manager. At the end of the meeting you feel welcome – you feel good about working with these people.

Story two: Placement hell

You arrive for your first day in a day centre – no one knows who you are or why you're supposed to be there. One staff member says 'You want to work in early years care – you must be mad, anyway you can come with me, I'll show you what to do – I could do with some help, we just haven't got enough staff you know – there is far too many kids for us to handle. It's all paperwork nowadays; the senior staff spend all their time in the office – got no time for the children – they have to get their reports done. You on one of them college courses then – I suppose you will end up with a sort of job. After a while it gets to you – all the paperwork, all the screaming kids I mean. I do not know how I ever had kids – it's enough to put you off having them you know. We do not have time for talking to each other usually, cause we pretend that we have meetings and go on courses and all that but we do not really have time for all that stuff.'

In story one there is a team.

- The team show respect for individuals.
- The team value equality.
- The team respect self-esteem needs of people.
- The team has good communication skills.

- The team believe that to give good quality care you have to receive a caring approach from others.

- The team believe that children have rights, staff have rights, managers have rights.

Because the staff in story one care for each other, they also work effectively with children. They share professional values about caring and early learning.

In story two the worker you meet no longer seems to enjoy working with children and there is no team.

- The staff don't spend time talking to each other.

- The staff might not really be concerned about the principles of good practice.

- The staff might not feel that they are doing a worthwhile job.

- The staff don't get a sense of self-esteem out of their work.

- In this situation the staff might not care about the self-esteem of a person doing a placement!

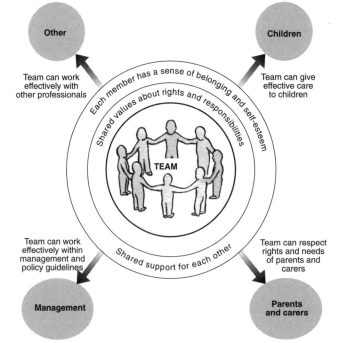

Figure 1.29 *Teams need to share values and support each other*

Team values and expectations

Teams in early years settings should value:

- the diversity and equality of people

- anti-discriminatory practice (being prepared to challenge discrimination)

- the rights of children – especially to self-esteem and independence

- confidentiality.

Together with these values, most teams will expect members to:

- present themselves in a way that shows respect for children, parents and other staff, and in a way that shows an understanding of safety issues

- maintain health and safety for all

- be reliable, punctual and show commitment to the team, including attending meetings

- maintain the security of children

- join in both the practical work and the administrative work that the team has to do

- understand their own role and be able to prioritise what is important in the job (time management) and show flexibility where necessary

- be able to review their own skills, recognise limitations and ask for help from others when necessary

- be willing to listen and communicate effectively with others, including being able to report and record events.

Being reliable and showing commitment

Most teams of staff have a heavy workload. If you turn up late or not at all, or if you don't let people know where you are, this leaves other people to do work that they were expecting you to do. Even if other people can cover for you, it sends a message: 'I don't care about the team – I don't want to be with you anyway.' It is not always possible to be punctual, and sometimes transport problems prevent people from getting to work or meetings on time. It is always important to apologise and offer a brief explanation for lateness – sending the message: 'I do care about colleagues.' If you are ill, you should always telephone to explain and let people know the situation, so that they can plan ahead. This also lets people know that you care about belonging with them. It is unprofessional not to let colleagues know when they expect you and you can not keep your appointment.

Joining in administrative work

Being a member of a team means sharing the practical and administrative work of the team. If early years work is right for you, you will enjoy building relationships with people and probably enjoy a lot of the practical work and activities. But not everyone enjoys the necessary report-writing and record-keeping.

Reports and records can be very important, however. Records of how children behave, and so on, help staff to know if their service is working effectively. Written records provide evidence that procedures were correctly followed. It is necessary to record details of all accidents and incidents in care that may need to be investigated.

Report-writing and record-keeping are skills. When you explain something in speech, other people can always ask you questions if they are not sure what you mean, and when you speak your non-verbal messages often give the listener a good idea of what you mean.

THINK IT THROUGH

Perhaps you are working with children and you say: 'Sam had a bad temper this afternoon – he hit me!' The listener could ask questions like: 'Did he hit you hard?' and your non-verbal behaviour would also help to explain how serious the incident was. If you were smiling while you spoke you would send a message saying: 'It's OK – it wasn't a real problem.'

When you have to write reports it is much harder to be sure other people will understand what you mean. Suppose you wrote a report including the comment 'Sam had a bad temper and hit me'. When someone else reads these words later, that person will not know exactly what happened – were you hurt, did he become violent and threaten the other children, or did he accidentally touch you when he was feeling angry or frustrated?

The problem with written language is that people have to imagine what words mean when they read them. People often form a mental picture in their heads, based on what they read. Somebody having a bad temper can mean different things. Writing that someone is misbehaving or angry, does not give a clear message, because words like 'misbehaving' can mean different things. A child could be violent or just not listening. Different people build different pictures in their minds.

When writing reports about people's behaviour, you should:

- say what you saw
- say what you heard
- be as clear as possible
- not put your own interpretation into your report.

Going back to the example above about Sam, the report writer should write a description like this: 'Sam threw his pencils on the floor and slapped my arm gently. When I asked him why he did this, he just looked at me and then looked away.'

Care plans

Workers employed by local authority social service departments are likely to be involved with the design and development of care plans. Early years workers in the field of day care, crèches, out of school care and childminding are likely to work with care plans such as Individual Education Plans (IEP), or will need to plan for any special needs a child may have.

Ofsted inspects day care and childminding services. Ofsted publishes guidance on meeting national standards for these services. Standard 14 of Ofsted guidelines requires that 'records, policies and procedures which are required for the efficient and safe management of provision and to promote the welfare, care and learning of children are maintained. Records about individual children are shared with the child's parent'. Staff working in day care or childminding services are likely to be involved with the maintenance of registers which record hours of attendance and detail of the children and the persons looking after them. Centres may also maintain records of achievement and other details of individual children's circumstances.

Health and safety

Under the Health and Safety at Work Act etc. of 1974, all employees must take reasonable care for their own safety and that of others. As a team member you will be expected to watch out for risks to your own and children's safety. This will include looking out for hazards such as wet floors, things you could trip over like boxes on the floor, loose rugs or carpets, trailing leads, overloaded electric points and so on. You must make sure you do not create any hazards, and report any problems that you are not sure about. As well as preventing or reporting hazards, you must understand and follow safety procedures while at work or on placement. Unless you have had formal training you should not lift people or heavy objects. You must follow safety procedures when using equipment or cleaning, and also when dealing with body fluids, like blood and urine.

Maintaining security

Early years workers have a responsibility to protect themselves and their children from safety and security risks. You will probably be aware of newspaper stories involving crimes in hospital or early years settings. It is important that you know who visitors to your setting are. You should ask if you can 'be of assistance' to any strangers who enter the building. Many early years settings ask visitors to sign in, explain why they are there and wear identification badges.

Maintaining security is a role that links with confidentiality. Before giving any information away about a child, you must check who is asking and that they have a need to know. If a telephone caller claims to be a social worker who needs to check on a child, you should ask to call back before giving any information and refer the call to a senior member of staff. By calling back you can check that the caller is of the address that he or she claims to be. Your work setting may have a policy about giving information on the telephone – you may be forbidden to give information to mobile phone users.

When contractors enter premises, they will usually carry identification, invoices or order forms proving that they are who they say they are.

THINK IT THROUGH

You enter a room to find a stranger unplugging the video recorder. The stranger says: 'It's OK, I'm just taking it for servicing.' You know nothing about this! Do you:

a   Stand in the way to prevent the stranger from leaving and call for help?

b   Shrug your shoulders and say: 'Nothing to do with me'?

c   Ask the stranger to leave the machine for a minute and come to the office to check details of the service contract with the manager?

Answer:

a   This could be hazardous if your assumption is correct that the person is stealing the video – the stranger may attack you in order to escape. You could be injured – you should not place yourself at risk in this way.

b   This is wrong – how do you know what the stranger says is true? You should try to protect the property, although your own personal safety is more important.

c   This is the best answer. If the stranger is a thief, perhaps he or she will run off without the video. If the stranger is servicing the machine he or she might congratulate you on your care – after all, you have been polite and have not jumped to conclusions.

ASSESSMENT ACTIVITY

Identify the qualities and skills needed to be a professional carer.

Use the diagram set out below to record some of your ideas about the skills and qualities that an early years worker needs. Check your ideas by looking at the statement of underlying principles or discuss your ideas with a colleague or a member of staff on placement. When you have collected enough ideas in note form, write a list of the skills and qualities that early years workers need and say why they are important.

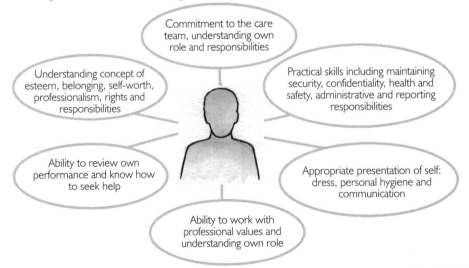

UNIT TWO

PHYSICAL, SOCIAL AND EMOTIONAL DEVELOPMENT

This unit provides an introduction to supporting children's physical needs and their social and emotional development. It looks at the milestones of development and introduces you to the basic principles of development. Later units look at aspects of development in greater detail, for example Unit 4 explores intellectual development. You will learn how important health is in promoting development and how you can encourage and support children in learning to behave appropriately.

In this unit you will learn about:

- physical, social and emotional development
- physical requirements for good health and development
- emotional development
- managing behaviour in young children.

Physical, social and emotional development

How does a tiny new-born baby grow from a helpless bundle into an active child, full of energy and intelligence? We will now examine that question. Although the subject of development is divided into topic areas it is important to remember that all aspects of development are linked together. For example, babies cannot learn to feed themselves until they can sit alone and have good control of their arms and hands.

Children's growth and development

Every new baby is a tiny helpless being at birth, yet by the age of seven or eight years, is a highly complex child who has all the basic skills for life, including talking, running, writing and the ability to think in increasingly abstract ways. Huge changes occur in a child in a very short space of time, especially from birth to eight years of age.

- Weight increases from 3–4 kg to about 25 kg.

- From being relatively immobile, the child becomes able to walk, run, skip and climb.

- From not being able to talk, the child becomes an able communicator.

- From being fully dependent, the child learns to dress, feed and think for him or herself.

- From wide arm movements and automatically grasping everything that is put into the hand, the child learns to pick up and use a pencil.

Growth and development are connected, but are very different. Growth is the very visible increase in size of a child. It can be seen in many ways, including weight gain, increase in height and increase in head circumference. Children grow very quickly; ask your own parents if they have a record of your weight and height gain.

Growth occurs in four phases,

- From birth to two years there is a rapid gain of up to 30 cm in height, and a tripling of body weight.

- From two years to puberty is a slower stage, with a gain each year of 6–8 cm in height and 3 kg in weight.

- Adolescence sees a rapid growth spurt, with gains of 8–16 cm per year.

- Slow growth continues until adult size is reached at about 18–20 years of age.

With growth, there is also a dramatic change in body proportions. Look at the size of a new-born baby's head in proportion to the rest of the body. Compare this with a child of seven or eight years.

Development is the gaining of skills in many aspects of the child's life. The stages of development are often split into five areas, the names of which can be remembered by recalling the word PILES:

- **p**hysical development; this refers to the body increasing in size, skill and performance and includes
  - gross motor development (using large muscles), e.g. legs and arms
  - fine motor development (precise use of muscles), e.g. hands and fingers

- **i**ntellectual development: this involves learning the skills of understanding, memory and concentration

- **l**anguage development: this refers to communication skills

- **e**motional development: this is about a child's identity and self-image, and the development of relationships and feelings about him or herself

- **s**ocial development: this is about learning the skills to live in society with other people.

You might see also the acronym SPICE used for the five areas of development. It stands for **s**ocial, **p**hysical, **i**ntellectual, **c**ommunication and **e**motional development.

THINK IT THROUGH

Write down the three headings 'Physical development', 'Social development' and 'Emotional development'.

List the following activities under the correct heading. Do some fit under more than one heading?

Crawling	*Tying shoelaces*	*Making friends*	*Distress when pet goldfish dies*
Riding a bike	*Using a fork*	*Sharing toys*	*Walking upstairs*
Starting school	*Recognising main carer*	*Threading beads*	*Using a pencil*

Basic principles of development

There are three basic principles of human development that apply to everyone from birth.

1 Development starts from the head and works down the body.

A new baby cannot hold up his or her head alone. Yet, within a few months, the baby will be able to sit alone. This is because control of the spine and central nervous system develops from the top of the head down to the base of the spine. You can see this control developing in a baby as he or she starts to hold the head without support. Similarly, a new-born baby waves his or her arms around vaguely, yet in nine months' time will find the tiniest crumb or piece of Lego easy to pick up with the thumb and finger. This is because the nervous system develops from the spinal cord out to the extremities (hands and feet).

2 All development happens in the same order, but can occur at different rates.

A baby has to hold his or her head up, learn to sit with support, and then without support, before he or she can stand by holding on to furniture and then eventually walk alone. No baby can learn to walk before sitting up. But it is perfectly normal for one baby to walk at ten months and another not to learn this skill until the age of 18 months.

3 All areas of development are linked together.

A baby cannot start to finger feed until he or she can sit up and is developing the ability to pick things up between the fingers and thumb. The speech development of a child is affected if the child has difficulties in hearing clearly or if no one talks directly to him or her. A child who does not receive love and attention may fail to grow and develop.

Finally, remember that to develop to their best potential, children need huge amounts of support and guidance from others in their lives. Failure to meet all of the needs of a baby or child will have devastating consequences on his or her development.

Milestones of development

Child development experts have carried out a lot of research on young children to study what children can do at different ages and the rate at which they grow. From this research, milestones of development have been identified. A 'milestone of development' refers to the age at which most children have reached a certain stage of development, for example, walking alone by 18 months.

Many children will have reached a stage of development much earlier, but what matters is whether a child has reached it by the milestone age. You will also read about average ages for developmental stages, and these will be different. An average age is in the middle of the range of ages when all children reach a certain stage, for example, for walking the range can be from 10 months to 18 months which makes the 'average' age for walking 14 months. All children develop at different rates and may be earlier in achieving some aspects of development and later in others, but the following table shows general milestones.

Some important milestones for development

Age	Physical	Social/Emotional
Birth to 4 weeks	Lies on back with head to one side Head lags when pulled up to sit	Imitates facial expressions Stares at bright shiny objects
1 month	Head control unsteady Hands in tight fists Head and eyes move together	Gazes intently at carers
6 weeks		Social smile at carers
4 months	Uses arms for support when lying on stomach Turns from back to side Holds on to and shakes small items	Smiles, engages and vocalises with carers
9 months	Sits alone without support Uses index and middle fingers with thumb in pincer grip to pick up small items Will take and hold a small brick in each hand	Very interested in all around Recognises familiar and unfamiliar people Shows stranger anxiety
1 year	Stands alone Enjoys self-feeding	Shows definite emotions and is aware of emotions of others Will play alone
18 months	Can walk alone Can walk upstairs with hand held Tries to kick a ball Squats to pick objects from floor Builds tower of 6 bricks Assists with dressing and undressing Can use spoon	Stranger shyness Dislikes changes in routine Starts toilet training Start of tantrums when upset Has separate sense of self Little idea of sharing and strong sense of 'mine'
3 years	Stands and walks on tiptoe Can kick a ball confidently Builds tower of 9 bricks and builds bridge with bricks Threads large beads Undoes buttons	Strong sense of gender identity Less anxious about separation Plays alongside others
4 years	Builds large tower Draws a person with head, body and legs, and a house if asked Can brush own teeth Cuts round an object with scissors and copies a square Can catch a large ball Walks backwards	Enjoys co-operative and dramatic play Understands co-operation and competition Responds to reasoning Can take turns Enjoys independence but still needs comfort and reassurance
7 years	Builds intricate models Controls pencil in small area Enjoys board games Enjoys hopping, bike riding, roller blading, skating	Becomes engrossed in activities Develops fears of ghosts, things under the bed Concerned about being disliked

The relationship between areas of development

At six weeks most babies will smile socially, not because they have wind or are practising using muscles, but because they have been talked to and smiled at by parents and other carers. Sadly, not all babies have loving carers, and for all sorts of reasons may not be smiled at and talked to. These babies may not smile at six weeks. A baby who has experienced lots of talking and communication will smile much earlier than six weeks, and will vocalise with the carer.

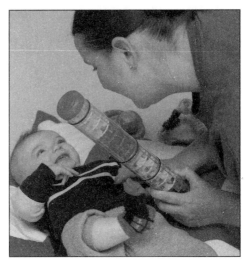

At nine months, a baby will sit without support, and can hold a small brick in his or her hand and pass it from hand to hand. As well as being able to play with bricks, babies can now sit up in a high chair and start to share family meals. Achieving progress in nearly all aspects of development is dependent on a child having opportunities to practise the skills. Although the human body is designed to move on to the next stage of development, without the opportunity to practise, the next stage may be delayed. If one aspect of development is not as expected for the age and stage of the child, for example sitting alone, then another aspect will be affected, such as the ability to finger feed.

Communication is an essential feature of social living. It is not difficult to see the benefits to a baby of learning to communicate with his or her family. While a young baby has only very basic needs, crying and smiling may be enough. As the child grows and has increasingly complex needs, talking becomes necessary. Imagine trying to make friends when you started school if you could not talk, or join in games with your peers. If you have ever been to school in a new country where people have spoken in different languages or dialects, you might have some idea of how that feels.

DID YOU KNOW?

Speech development can be seriously affected if a baby spends too much time in an environment with constant background noise, e.g. television or radio. We learn to talk by repeatedly hearing words directly from another person.

Adults and children communicate in a two-way process. Babies are skilled at influencing the way their family and carers behave with them. Watch a small child trying to attract attention from parents who are engrossed in conversation.

THINK IT THROUGH

Observe two children of different ages in your placement, or one in your placement and one in a family setting (if possible). Look at the skills and tactics they use to gain attention from adults. Note down the differences between the younger and older child. What does this tell you about their development?

ASSESSMENT ACTIVITY

Describe normal physical, social and emotional development.

1 Find a family with at least one and preferably two young children under eight. A family with a baby will be even better. Ideally you should know the family personally, but ask your tutor to help you to find a suitable family if necessary. Arrange to visit the family and ask if you can interview them and observe the children. Make sure that you go at a time that is convenient to the family.

2 Have a list of questions or an outline chart ready to record the ages at which each child started to smile, sit alone, walk, etc. in other words reached the various milestones of development. If possible, spend time observing the children and write down in detail what you see.

- Did the children all reach the milestones at the same ages?

- Record your findings in the form of a chart of the stages of development of the children.

3 Work with other students to compare your findings and ensure you have information on all ages from birth to eight years.

4 Present your chart on overall physical, social and emotional development, starting with an introduction on the basic principles of development.

No extension to merit or distinction is possible for this assessment.

Daily routines of care

Most people have various fixed tasks and practices that are part of their daily routine. These include washing, dressing, eating, travelling to work or school, relaxation time, watching TV, study, etc. Young children and babies also need a routine. Their routine will fulfil the basic needs for human existence. Look at the two routines shown overleaf for children of different ages. Both routines provide for the children's basic needs, but the baby spends far more time asleep, doing little more than sleeping, feeding and interacting with carers. The three-year-old has more time for the development of intellectual and social skills in her routine.

Baby aged 4 weeks		Girl aged 3 years	
6 am	Nappy change, morning feed	7 am	Wake, to parents' bed for cuddle
6.30–9 am	Sleeping	7.30	Breakfast with parents
9 am	Bath, play time	8 am	Shower and dressed
9.30	Feed	8.30	Travel to nursery
10–12	Sleep	9–12 noon	At nursery school – play in sand, paint, listen to story, take snacks at 10.30
12 noon	In baby chair close to carer	12.30	Lunch at Grandma's, watch TV
1 pm	Nappy change, feed	1.30–2.30	Afternoon sleep
1.30–3 pm	Asleep in pram during walk and shopping	2.30–5 pm	Shopping and baking with Grandma
3–4 pm	In baby chair playing with carer	5.30	Home with parents, playing with toys
4.30	Change and feed	6 pm	Supper
5–7 pm	Awake, grumbling, playing with carers	7 pm	Bath, story time, bed
7.30	Change, feed		
8 pm	Bed		
Midnight	Feed		

Routines are not developed for a child in isolation. Children belong to some type of family group, and part of social development is learning to fit our needs in with other people's needs. All families are different, and so their routines will be different. Look at the comparison of family routines given in the table below.

Activity	Family A	Family B
Getting up	All have shower in arranged rota.	First come, first served in bathroom.
Breakfast	All together in the kitchen, sitting at table.	Various times, Mum leaves first for work, Dad watches Breakfast TV.
Getting to school and nursery	Older children take younger ones, walk to school. Baby goes to childminder.	Dad takes children to school and nursery in car. Looks after baby at home.
Lunch	School/nursery meals.	Packed lunches at school and nursery, baby fed at home.
Tea time/home time	Children have snack, flop in front of TV.	Older children do homework in bedroom. Baby and nursery-age child have tea.
Early evening	Homework, more snacks.	Older children and parents sit down to meal together.
Bedtime	Whenever children are ready. Younger ones go with parents into family bed at parents' bedtime.	Strict bedtimes in order of age. All children in bed by 9 pm in their own rooms.

THINK IT THROUGH

Compare the daily routines of different families you know with children. If you have young children at home use your own family as an example. How do they vary? Think about time spent on child care, in bed, in the bathroom, eating, etc. Do the families have a casual approach to routines or a strict timetable? Why do you think there are these differences?

Rest, sleep and quiet periods

Why is rest so important? We all need to have rest and sleep as part of our everyday routines, not only because we get very tired, but because sleep and rest have several functions, not least allowing the body to recuperate. If we are deprived of sleep, we soon start suffering from memory loss, irritability and even hallucinations. Parents will often say a child is very irritable when tired. How do you feel after a very late night if you have to be up early for college the next day?

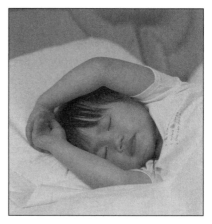

There is no fixed answer to the question of how much sleep children need. Some babies sleep 18 out of every 24 hours, others only 12. Some toddlers can cope on ten hours at night and a nap in the day, while others will sleep for 12 hours at night and then need two hours' sleep in the afternoon. Sleep patterns will change with changing routines and events in a child's life.

THINK IT THROUGH

Talk to parents of several young children, all about the same age. How much sleep does each one need? How has this changed since they were babies?

The body does not recuperate only by sleeping; rest will serve the same purpose. Very few children will spend all day running around, actively playing, as they would rapidly become overtired and unable to concentrate. They will sit down sometimes and watch the world go by, or ask to be read to, or watch TV for a short time. These are all resting or quiet periods. The body is regaining strength as it rests. Many people can take a very short nap of 10–20 minutes and wake up feeling ready for action. Children are no exception to this.

Rest periods built into the day are very important for a young child. Planning of activities is important to allow for short spells of quieter times during the day. Most nurseries and reception classes have a designated 'quiet' time in their daily routines to allow for children to recoup their energy. A skilled child care worker will build these times into the routine with children.

Case Study – Beechwood Nursery, Zak and Hassam

Beechwood Nursery has places for 24 children aged two to five years. Many of the children stay for the full day, from 8.30 am to 5.30 pm. At mid-morning the children have a quiet half-hour, sitting in small groups while a story is read to them, and then watching a short TV programme. After lunch the children lie down on mats with quilts for an hour to rest and recoup their energy.

Lizzie is a nanny for Zak, who is nine months old, and Hassam, who is three. Hassam attends playgroup each morning. Zak is awake all morning now and has a sleep from about 1–2 pm. By serving lunch for both children as soon as the three-year-old comes home from playgroup, Lizzie can enjoy a quiet hour with Hassam while Zak is asleep. This hour also gives Hassam a chance to rest, and occasionally he falls asleep on the sofa.

It is important to provide the right environment for the child to go to sleep. Children enjoy having familiar objects and routines when they are settling down to sleep, these could include:

- a bath before bed
- story time or songs
- a ritual of goodnights to the entire family, toys, etc.
- a warm drink.

It is essential to be sensitive to the changing needs of children. Sleep, rest and appetite needs may change in some situations, for example:

- during and after illness
- after the birth of a new sibling
- after changes in family circumstances
- before and after exciting events, e.g. a party or outing
- at the time of starting school.

You should be alert to the changing needs of children you care for. Sometimes these changes can be the first signal that something is happening in their lives.

THINK IT THROUGH

Imagine you are caring for a family of three young children, aged four months, two years and six years, for the weekend. The parents have had to go away and asked you to care for the children. Plan the weekend, paying particular attention to eating, sleeping and rest for all the children. How will you make sure you are not altering their routine too much?

When you are planning routines for children, it is important to remember that young children are all different, and will have slightly different needs. Carers need to pay attention to all areas of development when planning daily and weekly care for children, making sure that each child is treated individually. To meet their physical, social and emotional needs, children need a mix of exercise, rest and sleep, and they need toileting and washing, play time and story time.

The physical requirements for good health and development

Exercise, play and healthy development

You would be right to think that young children hardly need encouraging to play and exercise. Play is a constant feature of a child's life as children learn through play. However, recent studies have shown that many children do not have enough exercise, possibly as a result of parents transporting children everywhere by car, parents fearing to allow children to play far from their home, and increasing use of TV and computer games.

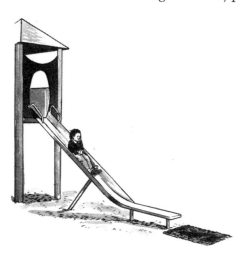

Figure 2.1 *Exercise helps to develop skills and confidence*

Children may need some direction to gain the opportunity to develop skills through play and exercise. Early years workers can help by suggesting and providing opportunities. Exercise is an excellent way to encourage the use of newly gained skills, or to help further development of skills a child may be struggling with. Here are some of the benefits of play and exercise.

- Children learn social skills such as turn-taking, and experience winning and losing, through energetic games and races. You can help less active children with example and encouragement.

- Adventure playgrounds with climbing frames, rope swings, etc. are ideal for children to learn from one another and are usually designed so that there are levels of climbing to suit different abilities.

- Energetic play can be an ideal way for children who are angry or upset to work off their aggression. Ask any teacher about the effect of bad weather resulting in enforced indoor play. A group of young children may react badly to not having the chance to work off their energy in the playground.

- Exercise uses the energy provided by the food a child eats. If exercise does not burn up enough energy, a child will gain excess weight.

- Exercise helps to develop muscles. You can see how important this is if you examine an arm or leg that has been in a plaster cast after a fracture for six weeks; it will be very much thinner and weaker than the other limb as a result of not having any exercise.

- The immune system is strengthened through exercise, so it can help a child to be less vulnerable to illness.

What type of exercise is best and at what age? The table below shows some examples of exercise and how they can help children to develop.

Type of exercise	Effect on health and development
Baby on changing mat without nappy – kicking freely, rolling for toys	Nappy area exposed to fresh air – healthy skin Physical stretching, building muscles in legs Development of mobility
Baby bouncing on knee of carer	Social interaction Developing strength in legs, practising standing
12–18-month-old child using push-and-ride toy	Practising walking with support Manoeuvring skills Independence Muscle movement
Two-year-old in the park, running, playing on the swings and slide Rough and tumble play in a safe environment – with foam mats, cushions, etc.	Developing gross motor control by physical activity Social interaction with other children Fresh air, sunshine – benefits for building the immune system
Swimming Gymnastics Dancing Football (any age)	Help to promote healthy development of bones, muscles and the immune system Social skills developed, team skills, self-esteem by achievement Co-ordination skills Learning about rules and turn taking
Music and movement (any age)	Co-ordination of body to music Creativity, imagination

Exercise may need only the child and his or her imagination, or some suitable space may be needed, or extra equipment and support. As a child care worker, you will need to consider indoor and outdoor exercise, and appropriate equipment for both settings. The requirements could include:

- space

- natural features, e.g. trees, streams with stepping stones

- swimming baths

- music

- skipping ropes

- balls of various sizes

- swings, slides, frames, benches

- tricycles, sit-and-ride toys

- tents, play houses.

The best resources to enable children to enjoy and benefit from exercise are their own imagination, space and someone to help them to use these resources and their bodies.

Adapting play for different children

When you are planning an activity of any sort, you should always consider *all* of the children who may be joining in. To a child who is timid about large groups, a boisterous game of chase or playing on the climbing frame may be very daunting and you should think of ways of helping the child to join in. You may need to think about providing two parallel activities, if staffing and numbers allow, in order to meet all the children's needs.

The climbing frame will not be suitable for a child who is a wheelchair user, without having a helper with the child at all times. Padded matting may be needed underneath the frame in case of falls. A child with reduced vision could enjoy using the frame if paired with another suitable child or assisted by you.

By using your imagination and thinking about the safety issues, you can help most children to enjoy most activities and equipment. They can usually be adapted to suit all children without losing the aim of the exercise. Careful thought must be given to making sure that no one is discriminated against in play and exercise.

There are many ways to include a child who is disabled. Many manufacturers make suitably adapted play equipment, for example tricycles with bucket seats. Equipment specifically designed for children with disabilities can usually be used by all children. The manufacturers of 'ball pools' and huge foam wedges in different shapes originally designed them for children with disabilities but they now feature in most adventure playgrounds for younger children. Careful use of foam mats can take much of the risk out of physical exercise for all children, so that falls do not have hard landings.

It goes without saying that, at all times when you are caring for a child, you have the responsibility for their safety. This applies especially when children are playing with or on equipment. Think about a child's stage of development and ability. Is the activity suitable for the child, without being too protective? Good play opportunities stretch a child's ability and help in his or her development.

THINK IT THROUGH

You are in charge of a group of eight energetic five-year-olds, five girls and three boys. Samir is slower than the others in walking, due to a condition affecting his muscles. Paul doesn't like rough games and is reluctant to join in groups. Lucy likes any game that is noisy and rough, but she broke her arm last week and has it in plaster. The weather was wet and windy all morning and now the sun has started to shine. The class teacher asks you to take this group outside and organise some exercise for them in the grounds of the school for half an hour.

How would you plan your half-hour to include all of the children? What play and exercise would you provide, and what would the benefits be for the children?

ASSESSMENT ACTIVITY

Identify play activities and routines appropriate to the age and stage of development of the individual child.

1 Over a period of a week, write down all types of play and exercise you see children taking part in. Try to observe a wide age range and a variety of activities. Remember that play and exercise do not have to be formally organised; children play and exercise spontaneously.

2 When you visit the family you are studying, ask if you can talk to them about their family routine. Ask about the daily routines including meals, bedtimes, going to work, nursery, school, etc. What type of exercise and play opportunities do the children have? Make a list of everything each child does/enjoys.

3 Compare your findings with those of other students. What differences have you found?

4 Present your findings in a simple format that clearly shows how the routines and activities are different for each age of child.

To achieve a **merit grade** you need to explain why the play activities and routines can promote all aspects of children's development. Use your comparisons with other students' findings and discussion with the family to help you write a short report on this.

To achieve a **distinction grade** you will need to use examples from your findings to analyse the effectiveness of activities in promoting children's development.

The importance of health, safety and hygienic practices

Children, especially very young children, cannot protect themselves. Young children cannot understand complicated messages about accidents and safety or recognise that food has been unhygienically prepared. It is the responsibility of all involved in their care to think about all the dangers lurking in everyday life that could harm a child.

Figure 2.2 *Germs and physical dangers are always lurking*

DID YOU KNOW?

- Four children are killed by accidents every day.
- Accidents are the most common cause of death among children aged six months or older.
- A toddler reaching for that interesting looking curly flex cannot see the boiling kettle up on the high work surface, or know the power of the electricity in those interesting holes in the wall.
- Every year one child in six goes to a hospital accident and emergency department.
- A child does not have the ability to learn road sense until at least six years.
- 150,000 injuries each year result from playground accidents.
- Dehydration resulting from gastro-enteritis can kill a baby or young child.

Think about all the possible causes of harm that could affect a child:

- accidents
- injury
- illnesses
- poisoning.

As a child care worker you have a vital role to play in protecting young children, but it is important not to be over-protective. If you protect a child from every single potential source of infection, for instance, he or she will never develop natural immunity or protection from illness.

To protect against dangers, you need to:

- keep dangerous substances out of reach, or locked away in cupboards
- keep the environment tidy – no trailing flexes or toys on the floor
- use safety equipment, for example socket covers for electric sockets, safety gates for stairs
- check equipment and toys regularly for loose parts, which could cause choking or injury
- closely follow hygienic practices when preparing and serving food
- keep toys and equipment clean
- supervise children closely at all times.

Good practice: health, safety and hygiene

1 You must always wash your hands to avoid cross infection:
   - before preparing or giving food
   - after changing a nappy or taking older children or yourself to the toilet
   - after playing with pets.

2 Strict hygiene is essential with food preparation and you must:
   - never re-use a partly finished bottle of feed
   - always keep bottle teats covered when not in use
   - never allow pets to use pots used for humans or to walk on food preparation surfaces
   - make sure that food is stored at the correct temperature
   - observe the correct order of storage of raw and cooked foods in a refrigerator
   - take an appropriate food hygiene qualification if you are involved in preparing or serving food for children in your care.

3 Always remember that young children, and babies in particular, have no sense of danger. They need protecting from:
   - animals, even family pets
   - dangers from heat, household objects, etc.
   - falls, dangerous objects, traffic, fires.

4 You should try not to expose babies or vulnerable children to known infections, although this is not always easy, as many conditions are infectious before symptoms appear.

5 Always put a baby to sleep on his or her back, with the feet at the bottom of the cot, and use blankets that can be tucked in and will not

---

billow over the face. This will help to prevent sudden infant death syndrome (cot death).

6 Never smoke in the presence of any child, especially babies. Smoking is a factor involved in sudden infant death syndrome.

7 Never be tempted to leave any child alone in a room or house.

Why is good hygiene so important? Every surface and nook and cranny has bacteria on it, including the human body. Bacteria are tiny organisms that cause disease if they are provided with the right setting. Bacteria are all around us and help to keep various parts of our body healthy. Problems occur when bacteria from faeces, that are transferred through failing to wash your hands after using the toilet, find their way into food. Equally, the bacteria that can live harmlessly in your nose and throat can cause food poisoning if you sneeze over food being prepared which then sits in a warm room for some time.

THINK IT THROUGH

Good practice in hygiene is your responsibility. Complete the chart below, putting in the solutions. The first has been done for you.

Topic	Hazard	Solution
Your own personal hygiene	Dirty hands, or hands contaminated from use of toilet Long hair dangling loose	Regular hand washing after 'dirty' activities
A child's personal hygiene	Poor toilet habits Not washing hands	
Hygiene in a child's surroundings	Sour milk in bottles Dog allowed to foul play areas	
Hygiene in a child's diet	Leftover food not thrown away Food spills on kitchen surfaces Food left in warm kitchen	

If you stayed at home every time you felt slightly ill, you would probably not be at work very often. Reliability is an essential part of child care work. It is important, though, not to go to work if you are a source of infection, for example if you have flu or gastro-enteritis. Likewise, children should not be going to nursery or school if they are infectious and could pass on an illness to the other children. Different child care settings have various policies about attendance. If there is an outbreak of an infectious disease, often a child is more likely to pass it on to others before the symptoms develop, so it could be argued that there is not much point in excluding a child from nursery when the infection has already been passed on.

ASSESSMENT ACTIVITY

You have been asked to produce a booklet for new parents at your placement that will explain why attention to health, safety and hygiene is so important.

1 Produce an easy to read illustrated booklet that will help to explain the importance of this aspect of child care.

2 Add a second section to the booklet that explains how your placement does everything possible to protect their children from the dangers associated with poor health, hygiene and safety practices.

No extension to merit or distinction is possible for this assessement.

Encouraging healthy eating

Food is a fuel; it helps children to grow and develop, and gives them the energy they need for the hard work involved in playing and learning. When they are small, children need help to ensure they have the right amount and balance of food. They are incapable of providing food for themselves, and to begin with they are unable to eat without help. Everyone needs to eat a balanced diet, to help to maintain health. The important parts of the diet are shown in the table below.

Nutrient	Function	Sources
Carbohydrates	Energy for growth and activity Aid digestion of other food	Potatoes, pasta, rice, pulses, sugar, fruit
Fats: Saturated form from animal sources Unsaturated from vegetable sources	Energy, body heat Contains vitamins (A, D, E and K)	Butter, cheese, meat, olives, vegetable and fish oils, nuts
Proteins	Growth and repair of the body	Meat, fish, soya, pulses, cheese, eggs, nuts, cereals
Vitamins: Fat soluble (A, D, E and K) Water soluble (C and all Bs)	A – promotes good vision and healthy skin B – aids blood formation, nerve and muscle function C – promotes healing D – encourages growth of bones and teeth E – protects cells from damage K – allows blood to clot	Fat soluble – oily fish, cheese, tomatoes, carrots, milk, liver, egg yolk, green vegetables Water soluble – fruits, juices, meat, leafy vegetables, beans, eggs

Nutrient	Function	Sources
Minerals: Calcium, sodium, potassium, magnesium, sulphur, flouride, trace elements	For healthy bones and teeth, balance of fluids, energy production, control of nerves and muscles	In nearly all foods in differing amounts. Sodium in salt, meat, fish and bread Fluoride in water supply
Fibre	Adds bulk to food to keep bowels functioning Thought to help in protection against heart disease and cancer	Oats, wholewheat bread, beans, leafy vegetables, prunes, apples
Water	Maintains fluid balance Helps in waste elimination	All foods and drinks in varying amounts

Certain proportions of each food group are required for a healthy diet. We need to be sure that food is eaten in balanced quantities, as shown in the following table.

Food groups		Nutrients	Portions per day
1.	Bread, potatoes, cereals, pasta and rice	Fibre, vitamins, minerals, carbohydrates	3 to 4 portions – one at each meal
2.	Fruit and vegetables	Fibre, vitamins, minerals, carbohydrates	5 portions
3.	Milk and milk products	Proteins, fats, vitamins and minerals	2 to 3 portions (a portion is 200 ml milk, 1 small yoghurt or 30 g cheese)
4.	High-protein foods – meat, eggs, fish, pulses, nuts	Proteins, vitamins, minerals, fats	2 to 3 portions
5.	Fats and oils	Essential fatty acids	Small amounts, infrequently

THINK IT THROUGH

Keep a record of your diet for two or three days, writing down everything you eat. How does your pattern of eating meet these requirements? Should you be making some changes?

How do children move from being totally dependent on milk to eating a balanced family diet, containing the correct levels of all the above foods? The process is called weaning. Foods other than milk are introduced usually between the ages of three and six months.

Eating can quickly become a battleground for parents and children if undue fuss is made about what a child will eat and what he or she needs both in terms of amounts and a balanced diet. Children will not starve themselves, and if they have the chance they will eat a variety of foods over a period of time that contain the nutrients they need. As a child care worker you have a big part to play in encouraging positive eating habits. One thing to remember is that there will be as many different eating routines as there are families. The many ways of encouraging good eating habits include:

- not fussing if a child isn't hungry

- keeping sweets and snacks for after meals

- offering small portions of attractive food

- avoiding over-filling a plate

- accepting a dislike for a food

- not using food as a bribe

- offering different eating experiences, e.g. with friends, in a café, picnics, etc.

- setting an example by eating healthy foods

- introducing changes to diets slowly, with one new food at a time

- involving children in choosing, cooking and serving their own food as much as possible.

'Junk' food is often dismissed as not providing a healthy diet, yet a burger, a pizza or fish and chips can provide a useful contribution to a child's diet. The secret is variety. Just as a constant diet of shepherd's pie or curry and rice would not meet all dietary needs, eating nothing but burgers is unlikely to give you a balanced diet.

Do you eat as much as all your friends and family? I am sure that the answer is 'no'. Some people eat a lot more than others, and their weight may show that. However, other people have very small appetites and are still healthy and active. This pattern starts in childhood and can also be affected by illness, stress or excitement. Often the first sign a child is ill, is that the appetite reduces. This can happen when a toddler starts to explore the world as well; after all there is much more excitement in playing than eating for some children.

A good rule to follow is that if a child is hungry, and the food on offer is palatable, he or she will eat. If the child is not hungry, he or she won't, and no amount of persuading will change that.

ASSESSMENT ACTIVITY

Identify the components of a healthy diet for young children

Plan a week's menus for a child of four or five years. Ideally, this could be a child you know, who attends nursery or school, and enjoys the occasional pizza or burger. You should clearly identify how the range of meals meets all the components of a healthy diet.

No extension to merit or distinction is available for this assessment.

Emotional development

Variations in children's social and emotional needs

Just as adults vary in their nature and temperament, so do children. A child may be sociable and outgoing, or shy and reserved. You will see many other variations of character among children in your care. These variations have several possible causes:

- genetic – inherited from one or both parents
- primary socialisation – learned behaviour
- position in the family
- experiences in early childhood; positive or negative.

Are you similar to one of your parents in character, and in the way you deal with feelings, or are you totally different from both of them? If you have brothers and sisters, does this apply to them? Social and emotional development starts at birth and continues throughout life. The general stages are described in the table below.

Age	Stage of social and emotional development
Birth	Responds positively to main carer.
6–9 months	Starts to show interest in other babies, smiling. Becomes more interested in social interaction, depending on amount of time spent with other children and their personality. Fear of strangers and distress at separation from carer. Interacts differently with various family members. Uses comfort object – blanket, etc. Seeks attention.
12–18 months	More demanding and assertive, emotionally volatile. Temper tantrums may start. Unhappy at changes in routines. Expresses rage at being told 'no'. Distinguishes between self and others, but still egocentric – only concerned with his or her own view of the world.
2–3 years	Enjoys other children's company but reluctant to share toys. May show concern when another child is upset. Engages in parallel play (alongside others). Remains egocentric. Becoming emotionally stable, but still prone to mood swings. Learning to separate from carer for short periods – e.g. while at nursery. Knows own identity.
3–4 years	Greater social awareness. Will play in twos or threes, sharing ideas. May have close friends. A lot of mixed play of the sexes. Stable and emotionally secure. Friendly to other children. Increasing independence, but still needs support from adults. Fears loss of carers.
5–8 years	Able to form firm friendships. Very supportive of each other, playing complex games. By the age of six or seven, playing in separate sex groups. Fairly independent and confident. Increasing sense of morality – right and wrong.

The above table outlines only the 'normal' expectations of social and emotional development. These are the aspects of development that are most dependent on a child's experiences and family life. Many children do not achieve these stages of social and emotional development as quickly as expected. There are many possible reasons for this.

- Children may have delayed language development, affecting their communication with others.

- Children may not speak the same language as the setting where they spend time.

- Children who are physically unattractive may be shunned by their peers.

- Children may be immature, unfriendly or aggressive.

- There may be prejudice and discrimination from other children against those who are of a different racial group or have a disability.

- There may be poor primary socialisation.

- Serious illness may have occurred in the first years.

- The death of a parent, or a traumatic separation may have occurred.

THINK IT THROUGH

Have you observed children who are very different from each other, for example one who is exceptionally shy, or too rough and boisterous, or perhaps slow to speak? Can you think of any reason for these differences? Have you seen any difference in the way they are treated by other children or adults?

Strategies to help children cope with their feelings

Young children live very much in the present, and an explosive outburst will often pass very quickly, with the child returning to his or her previous activity, possibly leaving other children and adults feeling exhausted. Dealing with outbursts can be challenging. A two-year-old child who is frustrated by something or someone can be like a whirlwind of anger, and it can be very difficult not to react to this with anger yourself.

Hugh Jolly, a child care expert writing in the 1970s, felt that if you ignored temper tantrums and walked away, while providing the child with easy access to you, the outburst would soon burn out and the child would approach you for a cuddle. Recent guidelines suggest that you gently hold children to prevent them from hurting themselves or others, and be ready to cuddle when the fury is over. In these circumstances a child will not start to feel ashamed of the outburst and will not find it difficult to approach the carer. You might see this practice referred to as 'holding therapy'. It developed from being used for children with special educational needs when they had bouts of temper tantrums. Remember to always ask your placement to give you guidance – placements will have differing views on the use of techniques that involve restraint.

As a child grows, tantrums become more unacceptable. Through the socialising effect of home, nursery and school, children learn that tantrums are unlikely to achieve the desired result, and other children may shun them. Children should be encouraged to express their feelings in ways that are acceptable to society. As a society, we find it easier to accept expressions of happiness, rather than of sorrow. Part of your role in working with children is to encourage the expression of all feelings, including the following:

- happy

- pleased to see a friend

- proud of work well done

- sorry about something done wrong

- sad that a friend has been hurt

- unhappy that the pet rabbit has died

- angry if property is spoiled.

Most children are spontaneous and wholehearted in their expressions of emotion. This means that children who are not so open will be obvious in a group. A child who is inhibited in expressing emotions at home may stand back and not join in open laughter with a group of children. It is usual for a child below the age of five or six years to express anger spontaneously. For instance, if one child takes a toy from another, the wronged child may hit out or start to cry. A child who just accepts the theft and turns away or fails to express feelings should give cause for concern.

Studies of children in hospital or residential care whose parents were not regularly present found that the children soon stopped all outward displays of distress. At first this was regarded as the child accepting his or her situation. In fact the child was giving up in the face of feelings about being abandoned, and had realised that crying was not going to bring the parents back. When the parents returned, such a child often rejected them. Serious emotional damage occurred to children who were separated from their familiar carers for long periods. As a result of this research, parents have been actively encouraged to stay with their children in hospital.

It is easy for a child to pick up the message that expressing emotion is not acceptable. But if children are unable to express their emotions directly, all that happens is that they are expressed in another way, through unwanted behaviours, regressing to wetting, ill health, etc. How can you help children to cope with their feelings? Look at the example in the case study below.

Case Study – Lois

Lois is aged three and a half and has been at nursery for five months. Staff have been worried as she is very slow to join in with other children, despite all their best efforts. Her mother appears to be concerned as well, and reports that Lois is reluctant to go to bed at night, and often wakes with nightmares.

Last week Lois bit another little girl for no reason, and has started to burst into tears very easily. Her mother came into the nursery for a discussion with the supervisor, and it emerged that Lois's father left home 18 months ago. As Lois was only two at the time, her Mum didn't think it had bothered her; she saw her Daddy every week. However, Lois's father has a new partner and she met a new stepsister last month. Visits have been reduced to once every two weeks, and Lois does not like her stepsister.

Lois is clearly a little girl in distress. She has had to deal with many changes in her short life, but has not been able to express her feelings. It is doubtful that Lois would be able to speak about these intense emotions, and they have been emerging in other ways. Lois and her mother obviously need a lot of understanding and support. Her mother could be very upset about the situation with her ex-husband, and transfer some of her emotions to Lois. Support for the mother is not within your scope, but a supervisor should talk to her about counselling or seeing a health visitor or doctor.

As a worker with Lois, you have a vital role to play. Lois needs acceptance. She already feels she has been 'rejected' by her Daddy and replaced with a new daughter. If you are cross with her for biting and leave her alone when she doesn't want to join in, all her feelings of rejection will be magnified.

Taking time to discover what Lois likes to do, playing on a one-to-one basis with her, and gradually introducing her to other children will help. Paying full attention to Lois, trying to prevent battles occurring and offering distractions when necessary should avoid biting incidents in future. Rather than punishment, Lois needs a lot of praise and attention for her self-esteem, and activities to encourage her to express her anger and distress. Home corner activities can help, allowing her to vent her anger on dolls, teddies, etc. and use them as vehicles of expression. Outdoor play using a lot of energy can also help to relieve anger.

How would you try to work with Lois to cope with the changes that are affecting her life? Write down a list of positive actions that could help to support her.

THINK IT THROUGH

When you are working with children, it is important to be aware of the feelings a child or group of children may produce in you. A child expressing extreme anger may bring out feelings in you related to how your own parents reacted to you as a child. If you were shouted at for showing anger, or even smacked, or if you witnessed anger in others, it may be uncomfortable for you to deal with this type of situation. Sometimes a response may come to mind that is a reflection of your own experiences, and it may not be appropriate in the situation. It is important to recognise this, and accept that recognising your responses is an excellent step on the path to being a professional worker. You may be able to work it out for yourself, or you may have a supervisor or colleague with whom you can share your feelings.

Promoting self-esteem, self-reliance and self-confidence

Adults involved in caring for children sometimes forget that children need to make mistakes in their drive for independence. All children are working towards the ultimate goal of full independence in all areas of life and having a clear view of the answer to 'who am I?'. As early years workers our role is to support them in reaching this, to a level appropriate to their age and stage of development.

Self-esteem is when a child or adult feels good about him or herself. If a person feels that he or she are not worth spending time with, this shows that the person has 'low self-esteem'. The opposite is 'high self-esteem' when a child or adult feels that he or she is worth spending time with. Self-esteem is important for children in middle childhood, from about the age of seven or eight, but the foundations are laid from birth from the responses of other people to them. How do you think constantly being told you are useless will affect a child's self-esteem?

Self-confidence is linked to self-esteem. How can we be confident about ourselves and happy to engage with others, if we have a low self-esteem. It is easier for a child with high self-esteem to try new things out, make friends and find out about the world. Promoting self-confidence is part of your role in caring for young children. How can you create opportunities for children to feel good? Think about games you plan for them. Do you make it possible for everyone to win sometimes? How does a child react if he or she doesn't win? Turn taking is important in promoting self-confidence. A shy child may need a gentle helping hand to go first for once, and not be overwhelmed by a more assertive child.

By encouraging independence, we automatically encourage self-reliance, self-esteem and self-confidence. I am sure you can think of people you know who claim not to be able to look after themselves in basic tasks such as preparing a meal or washing clothes. Such people might have a reduced amount of work to do, but is this good for their self-esteem?

Feeding a child is much faster than encouraging self-feeding, but this tactic will not be appreciated when the child starts school and still needs help. Self-reliance is needed in a child when he or she starts school; a child has enough to deal with in adapting to all the new demands of school without the worry of not being able to use the toilet alone, or not being able to cope with changing his or her clothes when it is time for PE.

Attachment, bonding and socialisation

The development of the deep feelings between parents or carers and their children comes about through a process of bonding and attachment. This attachment is helped in the early months by:

- skin contact
- smell
- talking, and listening to parents' voices
- feeding
- bathing
- changing nappies
- play
- eye-to-eye contact.

The researcher John Bowlby described 'bonding' and 'attachment', and confirmed the idea that all children need consistent carers to allow them to develop attachments and start to form loving relationships with their carers. If the period following birth is interrupted by illness in mother or baby, or is characterised by many different carers, a child may have difficulty in forming close relationships in later life. Other children can have difficulties in this process due to visual or hearing problems, or because of severe learning difficulties. Parents of children who have problems affecting the bonding process need extra support and encouragement.

It used to be thought that a baby could form a close attachment only to the mother, but this has been shown to not be the case. Children can and obviously do form strong bonds with a wide range of people, e.g. grandparents, siblings, friends and others. It is regular and frequent contact that is important, and even where a child has a normal attachment to parents and family, it is important that in a nursery setting he or she is allowed to develop attachment to at least one regular carer.

A child who has formed close bonds with several important people will be far more secure than a child who has not done so. Where there is a strong sense of security in a child, there is likely to be less emotional trauma caused by future separations from the main carers. Often a very clingy child will have had some difficulty in the early years in forming a close bond with carers.

Helping a child who has moved into a new child care setting provides a very good opportunity to observe the effects of self-esteem and self-confidence. A confident child with a high self-esteem is more likely to settle into a new setting. Knowing that your main carer will be waiting at the end of the session to ask you all about your first day at school and will want to see your painting is a much better scenario than being made to feel a burden that you are bringing home yet another piece of rubbish.

Research shows that children who have a close bond with their family are more confident about trying new experiences.

THINK IT THROUGH

Look at some of the new children in a nursery or school. Why do you think some have settled in more easily than others?

If you are working in a nursery, look at the procedure for moving a child into another grouping or on to school. A good placement will make sure that time is taken to introduce the new place, with the child accompanied by a familiar face. A favourite toy might be taken, and time spent with the familiar face in the new setting. A gradual introduction like this, phased in over time, has a far better result than an abrupt separation from a familiar place.

Very often a child may seem to 'regress', for example, start to want a bottle again, or wet him or herself when they are highly distressed. Accept this as normal and recognise it as a call for help in making a transition or adapting to a new brother or sister. Sometimes a regression in behaviour may be the first sign you have at nursery about some disruption at home.

Socialisation is all about learning to cope in the family and society we live in. The socialisation process will by its definition vary from family to family, and in different societies. **Primary socialisation** is the socialisation that takes place within the family, in the first years of a child's life. **Secondary socialisation** starts when children come into regular contact with people and settings outside their home. This includes playgroup, nursery and school, and continues throughout life.

Secondary socialisation teaches children about:

- society's views of gender roles
- how to interact with other adults
- how to interact with peers
- the views of peers
- the 'rules' of society, what is acceptable and what is not.

Your role as a child care worker is part of the process of secondary socialisation; children will learn a great deal from your behaviour, both obvious and hidden behaviour.

Supporting behaviour in young children

Good and inappropriate behaviour in children

All children need attention, and all children thrive on praise from their carers. These two statements may seem very obvious to you, and are sentiments that you can empathise with. The definition of good behaviour is relative; relative to time, place, the age of the child and the relevant culture. What is perfectly acceptable behaviour in one family may be condemned as unacceptable in another. You may have experienced this in your parents' attitudes to staying out late, friendships, helping at home, etc. as compared to the attitudes of other parents. All child care establishments have an accepted code of behaviour, which is explained to children and parents, but within each establishment there will be individual differences of interpretation among staff.

It is important to remember a few basic rules when considering and dealing with children's behaviour.

You should **always**:

- be specific when describing a child's behaviour, e.g. Shanaz bit Poala on the arm, rather than Shanaz was cruel to Poala
- consider causes behind unwanted or inappropriate behaviour
- beware of listening only to one side of a dispute between children, and be sure you have all the facts before intervening
- remember that children will repeat behaviours they have experienced
- make sure that a child knows that it is the behaviour you do not like, not the child.

You should **never**:

- use physical force or violence towards a child
- belittle a child who has behaved inappropriately
- make threats or promises that you will not keep.

Factors contributing to behaviour

Behaviour is a vague term. Do you remember being told as a child on a special occasion to 'be on your best behaviour' and wondering what it meant? Children are often described as being very good or naughty, with no definition of these terms. As we have already seen, behaviour is relative, and it is particularly relative to the age of the child.

THINK IT THROUGH

Imran sat on the floor turning the pages of a book for two minutes. Then he noticed some big fat crayons his sister had been using, and went over to pick up the red one. He looked around for a second, and then started to scribble on the wall. At that moment Imran's mother came into the room.

Was Imran being 'naughty'? That depends on how old he is. If you knew he was 18 months old, would your opinion be the same as if he was five years old? At 18 months, we would not expect a child to concentrate on an activity for much more than two minutes. The incident with the crayons would be annoying to Imran's parents, but an 18-month-old would have no conception that he was not using the crayons in an appropriate way. At five years of age it would be reasonable to expect him to crayon on paper, and to understand that the wall is not a suitable place.

This is an example of age and stage of development being an important factor in judging appropriate behaviour.

Whenever you consider whether a child's behaviour is appropriate, it is important to look at the child's age. Parents often have unrealistic expectations of a child, not recognising that very young children will not have a sense of good and bad. If a toddler is told not to touch something, within minutes he or she will have forgotten this instruction if the desired article is very attractive.

It is important to be specific in describing appropriate and inappropriate behaviour. Look at these two statements.

A Joel was annoying his friend; he kept distracting him and stopping him working. Then he started to draw attention to himself.

B Joel repeatedly jabbed his pencil into his friend's side, and snatched his book from him. Then he started to rock on his chair and scrape the legs on the floor.

Statement B is much more precise than A. We have a very clear picture of Joel's behaviour. As a student in Joel's class, you would be giving the teacher a much better description if you wrote down B.

THINK IT THROUGH

In pairs, write down specific examples of what the following descriptions mean to you, in

a) a child of two years and b) a child of six years:

■ *naughty*
■ *bad tempered*
■ *sulking*
■ *being a nuisance*
■ *being disruptive.*

Compare your ideas with those of another pair. How many different ideas do you have for each word or phrase?

Inappropriate behaviour

Inappropriate behaviour can be a symptom of problems and issues in a child's world. Think about the times when you felt out of sorts because of an argument with a friend or parent before leaving home in the morning. For a while afterwards you feel snappy and grumpy with everyone, and may slam a few doors. Young children are no different. There are all sorts of factors, some minor, some major, that can affect a child's behaviour.

Case Study – Elizabeth

Elizabeth had seemed very quiet at nursery, and did not join in easily with the other children on Monday. The staff were surprised as this was unusual for her. When they were playing in the sand, Elizabeth pushed Tracy hard when she tried to take the funnel. Tracy fell over and started to cry. Elizabeth ran into the home corner and burst into tears. When her mother came to collect her, the staff mentioned the incident. Elizabeth's mother told them that the family dog had died at the weekend.

The case study above is a typical example of upsetting incidents affecting behaviour. Other potentially upsetting incidents include a new baby in the family, moving house, parents separating or rowing, access visits by absent parents, a poor night's sleep, minor illness, a parent losing a job, a new teacher or class, moving schools and so on. Any change in routine can upset a child, and it is your responsibility to be alert for changes in a child's behaviour and report these to a senior person.

Behaviour policies and procedures

Children need security to thrive and develop. Going for the first time to playgroup, nursery or school are momentous events in any child's life. They should not have to cope with inappropriate behaviour in the form of abuse, racism or sexism. Being on the receiving end of abuse or racism has damaging effects on a child, and can affect self-esteem and confidence, especially if the behaviour is not challenged by carers. It is the responsibility of every child care worker to make sure this does not happen. Child care settings therefore need to have clear policies and procedures relating to many things, but in particular to behaviour. This does not mean to say that a long list of rules should be drawn up in nursery that children have to learn. Children as young as four or five will understand simple rules related to caring for others, not being unkind, and not taking items belonging to others.

A **policy** is a statement of what is expected or is provided in a setting, e.g. 'All children will be treated with respect'. The related **procedure** would state something such as: 'Cases of children taking items not belonging to themselves must be reported to the member of staff in charge of that group. Parents must be informed.'

The related **rule** might be: 'All children are expected to look after their own and other people's property. Children should not bring their own toys into nursery.'

All child care settings have stated policies and procedures dealing with issues such as bullying, stealing, deliberate damage, etc. and these are known and understood by staff. Children and parents should be aware of the associated rules where appropriate; in some cases this will be only the parents if the children are very young. Clearly, policies will depend on the age of the children who attend the setting.

A very important point is that policies and rules must be fair, consistently applied, and all consequences followed through. Children should understand as soon as possible what the result of breaking a rule will be, and why the rule exists.

THINK IT THROUGH

In your placement, ask if you can see the policies, procedures and rules relating to behaviour. If possible, copy them down. How are they related to the ages of the children at your placement? Do you think they are reasonable? Are any rules missing? Imagine you had to amend them for children either two years older or younger. What changes would be needed?

Strategies for dealing with common behaviour problems

Inappropriate behaviour does not happen without reason. Think about teachers you may have had yourself, or seen in placement. Have you ever been in a classroom with a teacher who shouts all the time? Have you ever seen a parent who seems to shout and tell the children off all the time? In comparison, think of a quietly spoken parent or teacher who seems to have well-behaved children. A carer's behaviour can greatly influence the behaviour of the children.

The way staff deal with issues that arise in the classroom or nursery can have a huge impact on the response of the children. Ignoring bullying, racism or disruption passes all the wrong messages to children, and encourages equally bad behaviour. In

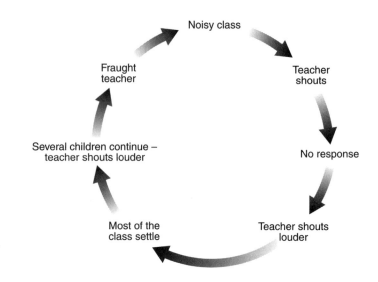

Figure 2.3 *Inappropriate behaviour can set up a 'vicious circle'*

contrast a fair adult, who deals with issues promptly and fairly and shows respect for all the children, will encourage a calmer, happier setting.

When a child expresses inappropriate behaviour, this requires a lot of co-operation and teamwork, with both parents and staff involved. Observations are needed to decide on the exact nature of the problem behaviour, and targets must be set to improve it through positive behaviours. Through a series of rewards for good behaviour, targets are gradually raised. This method is called 'behaviour modification'. Even as a student, you can use some of the skills developed from this method. Imagine never being the object of positive attention, but only of negative, in other words being shouted at, told off or punished. This is not an ideal attention, but it is attention, and for some children it is better than none. For many children with behaviour problems, this is the cycle they have got into. From their first entry into nursery some children, become known as the 'naughty one', and their reputation sticks. I am sure this sounds familiar to you.

The next time you are working with children, try to listen to other staff and yourself to see if you and they spend more time praising children or telling them off. It is important to try to look for something to praise, even if it is only that a child has sat still for a few moments, done a good painting or shared something. Most schools have a merit or reward system, with children being given small rewards such as stickers. An example of a merit chart is shown in Figure 2.4.

Merit chart for Zoe One smiley face for each time span of sitting still. 5 stickers to choose the book for story time.						Stickers
Monday 2 mins	☺☺	☺☺	☺☺	☺☺	☺☺	✓✓
Tuesday 3 mins	☺☺	☺☺	☺☺			
Wednesday 3 mins	☺☺	☺☺	☺☺	☺☺		
Thursday 3 mins	☺☺	☺☺	☺☺	☺☺	☺☺	✓✓
Friday 5 mins	☺☺	☺☺	☺☺	☺☺	☺☺	✓✓

Figure 2.4 *A merit chart may be used to help children earn small rewards such as stickers for consistently good behaviour*

THINK IT THROUGH

In a group of four or five students, thought share the different ways of managing children's behaviour you have seen in different settings. Try to decide if they were effective or not.

Child protection laws

The main legislation aimed at ensuring children's rights is the **Children Act 1989**. Until 1989, laws protecting children were numerous, unco-ordinated and confusing, even to people working with them. There were many loopholes in all the different laws. Often, children and families were visited by a host of different professionals, operating to different guidelines and sometimes working against each other.

The Children Act co-ordinated all these and introduced the legal concept of 'parental responsibilities'. Previously, parents had had rights, but now they had responsibilities to meet the rights of children in their care.

■ People who are not natural parents can have parental responsibility; this may be aunts or uncles, grandparents or even non-relatives.

■ Parenthood is for life; parents are encouraged to share parenting even if it is not in the same household.

■ Parental responsibility can be shared, e.g. between divorced parents, or foster and natural parents.

In order to make sure that children's rights are given priority, statutory services are based on five principles:

■ Services must be provided for all 'children in need'. The needs of these children must be co-ordinated and known by the local authority.

■ There should be partnership with parents.

■ Services must take a child's race, culture, religion and language into account.

■ Services should be co-ordinated to support the family.

■ The individual needs of an individual family must be recognised.

The Children Act has led to a new approach in protecting children from abuse, based on the belief that in most cases children are best brought up with their natural family. Child protection is based on:

■ Prevention, by identifying and supporting families under stress.

■ Formal intervention only where a child is at risk of 'significant harm' from sexual, physical or emotional abuse. The tools available for this include:
  – a child assessment order
  – an emergency protection order
  – a recovery order
  – a police order.

The key feature is that all professional bodies, e.g. health visitors, social workers, police, teachers, etc., work together to help support the family and protect the child.

Underlying the Children Act are several basic beliefs.

■ Children should be listened to.

■ Children's wishes should be identified and taken seriously.

■ Children should be treated with respect.

■ Children should play a part in decisions taken about them.

■ Children should be protected from harm.

■ Children should be loved and cared for..

The laws relating to children are very complex in their full form. It is important that you understand the basic principles behind them, however, and are aware of how these laws are applied in child care settings. Every child care setting has to have an equal opportunities policy, and has to have policies relating to child protection. There will certainly be rules about how you deal with incidents relating to these policies. As you progress in your child care career, there will probably be additions to the Children Act 1989. You must make sure you are aware of them.

ASSESSMENT ACTIVITY

Describe the role of an adult in managing behaviour and promoting self-esteem, self-reliance and self-confidence in a child:

1 In a small group consider each of the following examples and make notes reflecting

   a) how you think the named child will feel in each situation

   b) what effect the adult in each case has had on the child's self-esteem and confidence.

   ▪ Sarah, aged three, spends an hour finishing a model of a castle from cereal packets. When her mother collects her from nursery, she throws Sarah's model in the nearest waste bin.

   ▪ Leila, aged seven, has recently come to live in England with her grandparents. On her first day at her new school all the children sit on the floor in a circle and start to talk about what they did at the weekend with their families. Leila does not understand what is happening or much of what the children are saying. At break time she hides in the cloakroom away from the other children.

   ▪ Instead of putting on her coat to play outside, Shuli, aged five, goes and sits on the mat for story time as she has not heard the instructions. Mr Jones tells all the other children to look at Shuli being silly and not listening properly.

   ▪ Every time Miss Glory chooses the order for children to go for snacks, Sam is last, because he is always the slowest finishing his work.

   ▪ Imran's behaviour chart of reward stars only has two stars. When he looks at the chart he can see that most of the other children have far more stars than him.

2 Summarise your discussions in a short report.

3 Describe how the adults concerned in each case should have responded in order to encourage and develop each child.

4 Consider the factors and issues relating to behaviour management that we have discussed in this unit. Describe how your placement creates an appropriate atmosphere for encouraging good behaviour. List examples of practice you may have seen in all your different experiences that have encouraged inappropriate behaviour.

To achieve a **merit grade** you need to discuss ways in which an adult can promote self-esteem, self-reliance and self-confidence in a child (at different ages), and explain, using examples, a range of methods of managing children's behaviour.

To achieve a **distinction grade** you must compare methods of promoting self-esteem, self-reliance and self-confidence in children at different life stages.

UNIT THREE

GOOD PRACTICE IN CHILD CARE SETTINGS

This unit looks at issues you should always be aware of in your work with children, including equal opportunities, health and safety, and meeting specific needs.

In this unit you will learn about:

- equal opportunity issues in child care settings
- specific needs in child care settings
- health and safety in the child care setting.

Equal opportunity issues in child care settings

Legislation to ensure equal opportunities

All children have a right to be treated fairly and with due attention to their particular needs. The United Nations Convention on the Rights of the Child recognises this. The UK became a signatory to this agreement in December 1991, agreeing to recognise that:

- the views of children should be listened to and carry weight
- all children have a right to parental care and family life
- parents have the right to appropriate help in child rearing
- children have the right to protection
- children have the right to be treated as individuals who have feelings and ideas, and who need to be listened to and respected
- children need to be with people who show them love and affection, usually their family
- children's development needs should be met and protected.

THINK IT THROUGH

Sure Start's Birth to Three Matters *framework has ten clear principles that you should see in practice in child care settings.*

- *Parents and families are central to the well-being of a child.*
- *Relationships with other people are of great importance in a child's life.*
- *A relationship with a key person at home and in a care setting is essential to young children's well-being.*
- *Babies and children are social beings, they are competent learners from birth.*
- *Learning is a shared process and children learn most effectively when, with the help of a knowledgeable and trusted adult, they are actively involved and interested.*
- *Caring adults count more than resources and equipment.*
- *Schedules and routines must flow with the child's needs.*
- *Children learn when they are given appropriate responsibility, allowed to make errors, decisions and choices, and are respected as competent learners.*
- *Children learn by doing rather than by being told.*
- *Young children are vulnerable. They learn to be independent by having someone they can depend on.*

Consider the key principles listed above. Can you think of examples you have seen or heard about when a child has not had this type of support? What effect did it have on the child?

We cannot take it for granted that all children live in an environment that meets all these needs, so laws are necessary to protect and support these basic rights. The relevant legislation follows two main strands:

- general legislation that applies to everyone
- specific legislation that applies to children.

General legislation involves everything you have considered in relation to equal opportunities. The most important laws affecting equal opportunities are outlined below.

The Sex Discrimination Act 1975 and 1986

It is illegal to discriminate against anyone because of his or her sex in the following circumstances:

- in employment
- in selling or renting property
- in education
- when providing goods or services.

The part that applies to child care workers in particular is the education section. You already know how important it is to treat all children as individuals, and not deny them something because of individual characteristics. The Equal Opportunities Commission was set up as a result of the 1975 Act and investigates alleged discrimination. The 1986 update applies the law to small businesses.

The Race Relations Act 1976 and 2000 amendment

This Act makes it illegal to discriminate on racial grounds in employment, housing or services. Racial grounds include colour, race, nationality and ethnic or national origins. Discrimination is often thought to be targeted at ethnic minority groups with a visible difference, e.g. skin colour. Often unrecognised targets are people with white skin who are refugees from European countries. The Act makes it an offence to incite or encourage racial hatred. Both direct and indirect discrimination are unlawful.

Race relations law was strengthened and widened by an amendment in 2000 in order to prevent discrimination in any public situation. The Commission for Racial Equality (CRE) was set up in 1976 to make sure that the law against racial discrimination works. It can investigate cases of discrimination and give advice to people who wish to take up related action. Discrimination can be:

- **direct,** such as refusing to carry out services for or sell something to someone because of race

- **indirect,** when rules are made that are impossible for someone of a different race to follow.

The Commission for Racial Equality performs a watchdog function for this Act, and like the Equal Opportunities Commission it can prosecute offenders.

The Disability Discrimination Act 1995

This Act is designed to prevent discrimination against people with disabilities. The Act covers access and provision for disabled people in the following areas:

- employment

- access to goods, facilities and services

- letting or selling land or property

- education

- public transport vehicles.

The Act's implications for education are particularly relevant, and it is important that you are familiar with the intentions of the law in this area. Essentially, all children with special educational needs have the right to be educated in mainstream schools. Schools must publish their policy and procedures related to this provision.

The Disability Rights Commission was set up by the Disability Rights Commission Act 1999. The commission has the power to conduct formal investigations and to serve non-discrimination notices and take other actions to prevent discrimination against people with a disability.

It is important that you are aware of the legislation that forms the basis of equal opportunities practice, but legislation is not enough. What is important is how you work with children to ensure that those from all backgrounds are recognised and their cultural needs met. You are a role model for the children you work with, so you have a responsibility to act in a non-discriminatory way and to promote equal opportunities. Sometimes this is not easy; you may observe practices and actions that are discriminatory, but never feel that it is acceptable to do so yourself. You should have the courage to challenge or at the very least report to a supervisor any such action.

DID YOU KNOW?

David Milner identified that children between the ages of three and five learn to attach value to different skin colour, and think that it is better to be white than black. There have been incidents where black children who may perceive that it is better to be white have washed in milk or bleach in an attempt to have white skin.

THINK IT THROUGH

What would you do in these situations?

1 You are asked to line up the children ready for outdoor play with the girls in one line, the boys in another.

2 Mrs Smith complains because her daughter has been playing with a little girl with cerebral palsy.

3 A boy in the reception class uses abusive racist language.

4 The owner of the nursery insists that all children wear shorts in nursery, although there are many children who are Muslim.

These are all incidents that have occurred in child care settings, and all are discriminatory. Think about how you would feel if you witnessed these incidents, and what you should do about them.

In all aspects of your contact with children you need to ensure that you are working in a non-discriminatory way, with the needs and rights of all children in your care uppermost in your thoughts. You can use the following checklist to help you do this.

Good practice: equal opportunities

- Always be a good role model; mix girls and boys evenly in a group; ask a child who may be slow in moving to help you set out an activity.

- Always challenge racist behaviour, especially from other children. You can do this by making it clear there are words and actions that will not be tolerated.

- Put yourself in the shoes of someone who has been the subject of offensive remarks.

- Be ready to question your own attitudes and beliefs, challenging them if necessary.

- Use any opportunity to extend your own knowledge about cultures and groups other than your own.

- Be clear and consistent about what is acceptable and unacceptable behaviour.

- Double-check plans to ensure you are not inadvertently excluding or offending anyone.

- Be prepared to report incidents to your supervisor.

- Celebrate the diversity of the children you work with.

- Always consider every child as an individual with his or her own needs.

The last two points are vital. It is too easy to group children together based on a particular characteristic; this is stereotyping children. Remember that if you treat each child as the individual he or she is, and consider the child's individual needs, then you will always treat a child fairly and should never risk behaving in a discriminatory manner.

When you are planning any activity with a child or group of children, or helping with personal care or meal times, consider the needs of each child. Routinely setting the table for children who can all sit at the table to eat with a knife and fork is inappropriate if one of the group uses an electric wheelchair that does not fit under the table, or another child cannot manipulate a knife and fork. Think about the type of food you offer to children; routinely preparing vegetarian dishes for all the children encourages new eating tastes, and does not single out a child who is vegetarian as someone different. Think about how a game can be made easier for a child with a particular need; if the child can win fairly and use the particular need to his or her advantage, encourage this.

ASSESSMENT ACTIVITY

Outline legislation and guidelines relevant to equality of opportunity and health and safety

Look again at the United Nations Rights of the Child and the equal opportunities legislation. Produce a section for the brochure of a local nursery school, or a poster for the entrance, to show how the nursery ensures that it respects these rights. Under each heading give an example of activities or policies in the nursery that show its commitment to equal opportunities.

To achieve a **merit grade** you need to explain the ways in which the legislation affects a chosen child care setting.

To achieve a **distinction grade** you need to suggest ways in which a child care setting can check that the culture, values and beliefs of all children are being valued.

Activities to encourage diversity

Learning about, and participating in, different cultural activities helps to prepare children to live in a multicultural society. You should investigate the customs and practices of the different cultural groups to which the children you work with belong. It is important to remember also that not everyone who feels that they belong to a particular religion, for instance, follows exactly the same practices. To assume they do is to stereotype a person, and stereotyping leads to discrimination.

There are many cultural differences that distinguish different groups of society. These differences can be based on culture, race or social class, but it is important to remember that not everyone from each group will strictly follow a certain code of behaviour. However, you will find it useful to be aware of some of the major cultural differences, as shown in the table overleaf.

Examples of respecting cultural differences

Food and diet	Muslim people do not eat pork, and all meat should be halal. Hindu people do not eat beef. Buddhists are vegetarian. Jehovah's Witnesses will not eat blood products like black pudding.
Religious observances	All adult Muslims must pray at five specific times each day. Jewish people observe Saturday as their holy day.
Religious festivals	Nearly all religions celebrate special festivals. These may vary in date according to the lunar calendar. Examples of festivals include the Hindu festival of lights (Diwali), Muslim Eid, Christian Easter and Jewish passover. Some religions, such as Jehovah's Witnesses, do not celebrate festivals at all.
Family traditions and values	Muslim families have strict views about separation of the sexes after puberty.

Children should be made to feel that their way of life is valued, no matter how different it may be from the rest of the group. Children are usually very curious about other people's lives and this can be used to their advantage by encouraging them to learn.

Ways of raising awareness

The home corner is an ideal setting in which to raise awareness of different cultures. If a child care setting has many different cultures represented in its group, parents can be encouraged to help in the home corner on a rota system, representing their own culture. Cultures that are not represented among the children in a group should be included; you will have to do some research for these. It should not take too much imagination to think of all the aspects that can be covered.

Games from different cultures can be included; if there is a mix of cultural groups among the staff this will be easy, otherwise you could ask some of the parents or do some research. Displays could focus on a different country or culture at different times. One idea is to link these into specific festivals, e.g. Diwali, or to a country in the news. You can do a lot to show

Figure 3.1 *Home corners can display items that help children learn about other cultures*

children the positive side of other cultures. For instance, a country that is in the news because it has suffered from some natural disaster like a flood or famine could be the subject of a project to show the children how life usually is in that country. Use a 'news' or 'carpet time' slot for children to bring in objects from their culture, or others they have read about or travelled to. Different items and techniques you can use to show children about other cultures and ways of life include:

- pictures and posters
- artefacts such as statues, chopsticks, pots, items of clothing, small pieces of furniture
- asking parents to come into school or nursery to talk to the children
- videos, slides or photographs
- visits to areas nearby if possible, e.g. a Chinatown district.

Considering children's needs

Equal opportunities is not about treating everyone exactly the same. It is about making sure that all children are treated with respect and according to their own specific needs. Some children need more help with some activities than others if they are to gain the most from them. Planning activities for a group of children means thinking very carefully about the needs of the group. Look at the example in the following case study.

Case Study – Zarha

Zarha planned an activity around the book *The Very Hungry Caterpillar*. She planned to read the story, discuss it with the children and then help them to make a wall display based on the story. The children are aged from three-and-a-half to five years. Three of the children are from families who originate from Bangladesh, and speak very little English. One girl, Jane, has difficulty with activities requiring fine motor skills. One boy has a severe hearing impairment.

Zarha's choice of book is a good one as it is a very visual book, so it can help with language and hearing difficulties. By making sure that the children with little understanding of English and the child with a hearing impairment were sitting at the front, Zarha helped them to see the pictures. An interpreter helped with the discussion. Asking the children to draw pictures of the story also helped. While the children were drawing, Zarha talked to Jane about her ideas for the wall display, and both of them then put these ideas to the rest of the class. As the display took shape, Jane and Zarha directed the tasks.

If you are organising a game that relies on recognising colours and you have a child in your group who has a visual impairment, talk to him or her about the colours, or perhaps you could attach a noise or texture to each colour. A game using a ball and involving running around will need to be adapted for a child in a wheelchair; you may need to push the child in the chair, or change the game to avoid the running around.

THINK IT THROUGH

Prepare an activity which takes into consideration the diversity of individual children within a group.

You have been asked to plan a display with the children with the theme of 'celebration'. This could be a wall display, a table display, or even a small play performed by the children which you could video. Develop your plan, including at least six different types of celebrations that reflect different cultural groups.

Positive images of gender and race

One of the ways that children learn is through identifying with pictures and images that are familiar to them. All children have the right to see (in stories and on posters) adults and children who are like themselves and their carers, as this gives value to that child and his or her family. Material showing stereotypes should have no place in society, least of all in child care settings. Examples of stereotyped images include:

- mother always caring for the children

- people with disabilities being looked after

- men and women in 'typical' jobs, e.g. male car mechanics, female shop assistants

- female nurses, male doctors

- policemen always with white skin

- father doing home repairs

- black people as bus conductors or shopkeepers.

As an effective child care worker you should aim to provide positive examples to children. Many posters and books are available that show adults of various cultural backgrounds and people with and without disabilities in a range of jobs and situations.

THINK IT THROUGH

Does your placement have posters, books and pictures that provide positive images of different people? If not, what could you do to redress the balance?

Toys and books supporting equal opportunities

Stories that you read to the children should have girls as heroes as well as boys, and children with disabilities as central, active figures. Books in dual languages are essential to children for whom English is a second language.

Learning to read involves the parents at home. Having a story i
example, will encourage a child to start reading in his or her la
as English, and possibly help adults at home.

Books and posters reflecting the range of diversity in society h
become aware of people and settings outside their immediate family
experience, as well as ensuring that all children have the opportunity to
identify with familiar images and settings. All good bookshops have these
types of books in stock, and your placement should certainly have them.

THINK IT THROUGH

*Choose five books from the story-reading stock in your placement. Devise a
chart briefly describing each story, its 'hero', the racial mix of the characters,
and whether there are any images of people with disabilities.*

*Of the five, choose one that has a limited range of types of characters and
produce an outline showing how you could reflect a more balanced view of
racial, gender or disability issues.*

As child care workers, we need to ensure that the whole range of racial and
cultural groups are used in the planning of activities, even if people at the

particular nursery or school come
from only one or two cultural groups.
Sometimes you might find people
expressing surprise that this is
necessary, but it is important to take
this responsibility seriously. If a
nursery puts up just one poster with
positive images of diversity but does
nothing else, this is **tokenism.**

If you look and listen in the street, at
work, on the bus, at school, in college,
and watch television, you will see
evidence of the rich variety of cultures
that exist in every community.
Valuing diversity in society and
learning about it will enrich everyone's life. Unfortunately, this diversity can
be viewed in a less positive light, resulting in stereotyping and prejudice,
where there is a lack of knowledge and understanding. By helping children to
develop an awareness of different cultures you can help to prevent such
misunderstandings. Ways of widening the experience of the children include:

- cookery sessions from different cultures

- songs and dances from other cultures, perhaps on video

storytellers from a range of ethnic groups, perhaps telling stories in their own languages

- displays of items from other cultures, such as eating implements, arts and crafts

- celebrating different festivals, appropriate to children in the setting and to others

- a theme week based on a particular culture.

ASSESSMENT ACTIVITY

Plan an activity that will reflect the diversity of belief and culture in a group of children.

This activity may need the involvement of the parents of younger children. Think about a range of daily activities/features of life; these might include extended or nuclear families (who lives with whom and where), celebrations (birth of a new baby, Christmas, Diwali, Eid, birthdays). Choose one of them that offers the most potential for diversity. Ask all the children to bring in/talk about what their family does for these occasions. Produce a display or poster including the children's contributions to reflect the diversity within the group.

To achieve a **merit grade** explain the importance of ensuring that different religions and cultures are reflected in all pre-school activities.

To achieve a **distinction grade** suggest ways in which a child care setting can check that the culture, values and beliefs of all children are being valued.

Specific needs in child care settings

Most people have a special need of some kind. If you are short-sighted and use spectacles, you have a minor disability that can easily be dealt with. Special needs range from a mild disability to a profound physical disability and/or learning difficulties. It is important that you approach the task of meeting specific needs in the right way, that is to look at every child's individual needs and celebrate the diversity. It is society's responsibility to provide an environment and facilities that everyone can access, and to ensure that no one is excluded because of some physical or intellectual feature. All children have the right to access a broad and balanced curriculum.

DID YOU KNOW?

In the United Kingdom in 2002/2003 1.4 million pupils were identified as having special educational needs.

The Special Educational Needs Code of Practice states that children with special educational needs should normally have their needs met within mainstream schools or early years settings.

There are many different causes of physical and learning disabilities, and society has different ways of viewing the effect of them. Which of the following two models reflects your view?

- A **social model** recognises that any problems of disability are created by society and its institutions. If someone is a wheelchair user, problems are caused not by the wheelchair but by the fact that some buildings do not have ramps and that buses are difficult to access. The solutions to problems of disability are therefore in society's hands, and involve changing the attitudes of the able-bodied.

- A **medical model** views the disability as the problem. Disability is seen as a tragic, incurable fact leaving the sufferer with little chance of a normal life. It focuses on the disability the person has, rather than his or her abilities. Under this model, people with severe disabilities are cared for in institutions with little hope of independence.

THINK IT THROUGH

Look at these two examples of children with a disability.

Sam, aged seven, was born prematurely after a pregnancy of 30 weeks. As a result of problems during his delivery, Sam has cerebral palsy. He uses a wheelchair to move around and a voice synthesiser to communicate. Although he cannot play sports, Sam loves watching football, and enjoys playing games related to football. Sam and his friends spend a lot of time together playing games at weekends. School swimming sessions are his favourite time. With the support of a personal assistant, Sam attends a mainstream primary school and is looking forward to moving to senior school with his friends.

Lorna, aged six, was also born with severe cerebral palsy and relies on her wheelchair to move around. Her parents were never encouraged to hope that Lorna could attend a mainstream school. She attends a special school with children who all live a long way from Lorna. Lorna's parents are not happy to let her visit the one friend she has nearby, as they worry she will not cope without them. Although Lorna loves shopping, her parents do not take her very often as it is hard work, and they find it difficult to cope with people staring at her. They think that Lorna will eventually live in a residential unit with care assistants looking after her.

Compare these two children, both with similar physical difficulties, and think about why they have different lifestyles. Which would you prefer?

Causes of physical or learning difficulties

Special needs can be grouped into several categories, as shown below:

- **Physical impairments** cause problems with co-ordination and/or mobility. An example is cerebral palsy.

- **Chronic (long-term) diseases** and **terminal illnesses** include conditions such as cystic fibrosis or serious heart defects.

- **Learning difficulties** (both learning disabilities and specific learning difficulties) may be moderate to severe, or specific (e.g. dyslexia).

- **Communication difficulties** are caused by speech or language problems.

- **Loss of sensory abilities** includes the impairment of vision or hearing.

- **Emotional difficulties** include mental illnesses or severe family disruption.

- **Behavioural difficulties** include hyperactivity and attention deficit disorder.

Some children may have needs that fall into two or more categories. A child who has cerebral palsy may have a physical impairment, communication difficulties and also be a gifted child. A child who has a long-term illness may also be affected by dyslexia. Within all these categories there are several possible causes for the presence of special needs, as indicated in the table below.

Cause	Example	Effects
Genetic – chromosome abnormality	Down's syndrome	Heart problems, low intelligence
	Haemophilia	Bleeding easily into joints, soft tissues
	Brittle bone disease	Bones break easily, causing deformities to limbs
	Cystic fibrosis	Lack of vital enzymes in digestive and respiratory system, causing problems with breathing and digestion
	Achondroplasia	Very short arms and legs, resulting in small stature
Drugs taken during pregnancy	Thalidomide	Missing and shortened limbs, facial deformity
	Alcohol	Foetal alcohol syndrome
	Heroin	Addicted baby, small for its age
	Nicotine	Small for dates, chest problems e.g. chest infection
Environmental, e.g. radiation, pollution (often difficult to specify cause)	Spina bifida	Lower limb paralysis, hydrocephalus
	Early childhood cancers	Variable
	Toxocaris (from dog and cat faeces)	Blindness
Illness of mother in pregnancy	Rubella	Heart malformations, blindness and deafness
Birth injury	Lack of oxygen to brain, trauma to limbs or head from forceps	Cerebral palsy – gross motor skill and sensory delay, poor fine motor skills
		Learning difficulties/disabilities
		Weakness of arm or leg
Illness of child	Meningitis	Learning difficulties/disabilities
	Polio	Paralysis
	Otitis media	Deafness or hearing impairment
Accidents and injuries	Home or motor accidents, or abuse	Brain injury, paralysis
		Delayed development, physical injury or disability
		Emotional and behavioural difficulties

The cause of the disability does matter to the child and his or her family. As a child care worker, you should be more concerned with how a child's development is affected by a disability, and how you can support the child so he or she can lead a full and active life.

Meeting particular requirements of children with special needs

The Disability Discrimination Act makes it illegal not to provide access for all children to educational facilities, indeed to all facilities for all in society. The Act requires 'reasonable' adjustments to be made to allow access. Clearly a very old building with narrow stairs to the main services could be very difficult to change to give access for a wheelchair user. Buildings and services like this are in the minority, and changes such as wider doors, lifts, ramps, suitable toilet facilities, etc. must be provided in public places. Society has moved a long way from the dark ages when a child with a disability would be kept out of sight and often placed in institutional care. However, it is still very difficult for disabled people to access some facilities, and to avoid the pointing and staring of some people.

You have a responsibility to promote the rights of all children, especially those who may find themselves discriminated against in some way. It is important for child care workers to ensure that a child is not discriminated against in terms of the opportunity to reach his or her full potential. Look at these three examples.

- Jodi has hearing difficulties and as a result her speech has been delayed. She experiences communication difficulties unless alternative methods of communication are considered. When her group at nursery has story time, the nursery nurse always makes sure that Jodi sits at the front and that the story has a lot of visual appeal, using puppets, pictures and miming.

- Samir has cerebral palsy, which means he has difficulty in controlling his movements without shaking. Playing in the home corner was difficult because it was a small area, and Samir tended to knock things over. His teacher has relocated the home corner so that it is in a bigger area and Samir can now play safely in it.

- Wheelchair users may have difficulties in playing outside with other children, unless ways are found to overcome obstacles. Rajeet has difficulty getting into the playground as access is up two small steps. However, he can move very quickly once in the playground in his lightweight wheelchair. With the help of one of the staff, Rajeet's friends have invented a new form of football that allows him to use his arms instead of his feet.

There are many other ways to overcome difficulties. It is essential to structure activities and opportunities for the entire group of children in your care, taking needs into account. All children can benefit when activities are adapted, such as making story time a wider experience, and learning new ways of playing traditional games.

Adapting equipment for children with special needs

Sometimes special equipment may be needed to allow children with special needs to practise and develop all their skills.

- A child who has poor fine motor skills and difficulty with fine hand and eye co-ordination may benefit from the use of thicker pencils and other tools.

- Children with delays in developing gross motor skills (large body movements such as walking or running), or sensory problems (vision, hearing, etc.) may enjoy large-scale toys such as ball pools and soft foam cushions.

- A child with a visual impairment may be able to read large-print books, books written in Braille or Moon and will enjoy listening to stories recorded on tape.

Some centres are equipped with multi-sensory rooms that provide opportunities for children with a wide range of specific needs. These rooms feature a range of lights, sounds, smells and touch sensations that stimulate (or in some cases soothe) the senses. Any activity, game or toy designed to develop an aspect of a child's skill should aim to allow the child to use the skills that already exist, and encourage him or her to extend them. For example, when a child reaches the stage of being able to turn the pages of a book, make sure the child has books with thick pages, showing pictures of interesting objects.

Sometimes there is no need to adapt equipment, but you may need to change your methods of promoting an activity. A child who has difficulty sitting still for long will struggle to take part in a modelling activity lasting 15 minutes. Think about how you can adapt; you could sit with the child and keep up the encouragement, or ask to look at progress at frequent intervals. You could give the child some responsibility for drawing all the children's efforts together, say for a display. This may help to prevent the child's behaviour becoming unacceptable.

Maintaining self-esteem

You must never forget the importance of maintaining a child's self-esteem. Offering a child an activity usually aimed at much younger children could make the child feel inadequate and frustrated. The best person to consult is very often the child involved. For example, a child who has some delay in development of fine motor skills may have difficulty with small Lego bricks. Using larger bricks may be easier, but ask the child first and let him or her make the choice. This will help to maintain the child's self-esteem. Children sometimes act in a cruel manner by mocking others who are struggling to keep up in games or activities. Your role is to stop such mockery and steer conversations or activities so that the emphasis is placed on children displaying their skills.

> **THINK IT THROUGH**
>
> *Create an activity/toy that is designed to meet the particular requirements of a child with a specific need.*
>
> *Choose a popular game or activity that you have used with children.*
>
> *If you had a child with visual impairment and another child with difficulties in gross motor skills, how would you adapt the activity to meet the needs of both? If you feel the game or activity cannot be adapted, design a toy or game that would be suitable to allow both children to gain full benefit from it.*

Children with restricted mobility

Children may find that their mobility is restricted for a variety of reasons, including:

- physical disability causing full or partial loss of function of the legs
- visual impairment
- hearing impairment that also affects balance
- cerebral palsy
- brittle bone disease; the child is at risk of fractures
- frequent seizures or fits.

> **THINK IT THROUGH**
>
> *Look at these three examples.*
>
> *1 Millie has cerebral palsy. She may see and recognise an obstacle and know that she needs to avoid it, but the message from the brain to her legs is not effective, so she tends to appear unco-ordinated in her movements.*
>
> *2 Jawed has a visual impairment; he cannot see outside a narrow tunnel of forward vision. He often falls over objects that are outside this limited visual field. Crossing the road safely is difficult, as he cannot see all the vehicles around him.*
>
> *3 Danny is a wheelchair user and becomes very frustrated when he cannot move around the classroom because of thoughtlessly placed furniture. Sometimes he finds it difficult to get close enough to work he is doing if tables do not allow his wheelchair underneath.*
>
> *How could you help Millie, Jawed and Danny to take part in normal class or nursery activities?*

A number of mobility aids can be used to assist children with restricted mobility, such as:

- wheelchairs, which can be self-propelled or electric
- walking frames, tripods or quadruped
- trolleys
- walking sticks or elbow crutches
- calliper splints.

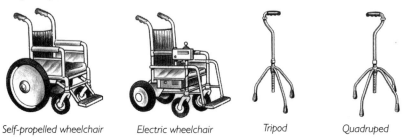

Self-propelled wheelchair   Electric wheelchair   Tripod   Quadruped

An able-bodied child can see obstacles and has the body control necessary to avoid them. A child with restricted mobility may not be able to do so. How can the environment be adapted to suit children with restricted mobility?

- Sometimes it is simply a question of avoiding leaving items lying around on the floor, and making sure equipment is kept in its proper place.

- Adaptation may be as simple as placing large foam pads and cushions around a slide, or providing a play area made up of shaped foam blocks to allow a child to roll, jump and fall in safety.

- Equipment such as slides, climbing frames and bicycles may need to be adapted to suit the needs of a particular child. Usually when a child has a special need of some type he or she will have had an assessment by an occupational therapist (a professional who specialises in adapting everyday equipment and recommending specialist equipment). If you have worked with a child who has cerebral palsy, for instance, you may have experience of electric wheelchairs, possibly with a special extension to support the head.

- Children who tend to fall over and injure themselves may need to wear some form of protection to allow them free access to indoor and outdoor play space, such as helmets, knee and elbow pads.

Although the safety of all children in your care is of paramount importance, you also need to strike a balance so that children are allowed the freedom to enjoy their activities. Occasionally it may be necessary to support a child in play if he or she cannot play alone. In this situation you should respond to the child's wishes as far as is practical, not stop the child exploring and developing his or her skills.

ASSESSMENT ACTIVITY

Describe why children may have particular needs and outline the ways in which an early years setting must adapt to their needs:

1 List as many reasons as possible for physical or learning difficulties. Group the possible causes under the following headings:

   ▪ hereditary and congenital
   ▪ developmental in the uterus
   ▪ caused through accident or illness.

2 Describe in general how a nursery or school must consider the needs of particular children.

3 Create a checklist of the adaptations necessary within a play area so that a child with a mobility aid can safely take part in the activities.

4 Louise, who is aged four and has limited mobility, is starting at your placement.

Louise has difficulty walking far, and occasionally uses a wheelchair. Her parents want her to experience everything available at your nursery, both indoors and outdoors. What adaptations will be needed to allow her to participate fully in all activities? Draw a plan of the area and write a checklist of the changes you would make.

To achieve a **merit grade** you need to explain the adaptations which can be made to buildings and equipment to meet the specific needs of children.

To achieve a **distinction grade** you need to explain the need to discuss some issues faced by children with particular needs with their parents when starting in a new early years setting.

Health and safety in the child care setting

Ofsted registration

Ofsted is responsible for the registration of anyone who wishes to provide care for children under eight years old. They carry out a rigorous process to satisfy themselves that anyone from a childminder, day nursery or crèche to out of school club meets the requirements of the 14 National Standards. By doing this they can offer some reassurance to the children's parents and encourage care providers to maintain high standards of safety, care and education. All registered child care providers are inspected regularly, and extra visits will be made if Ofsted feels there is a need. Inspectors have a legal right to enter any registered premises, or premises that should be registered, at any time. The Children Act 1989 requires inspectors to carry out checks before the person in charge, the owner or the setting can be registered, and again at least at yearly intervals.

There are slightly different requirements under the 14 National Standards for different kinds of child care settings. Ofsted are responsible for registering nurseries, playgroups, childminders, crèches, after-school clubs and play schemes. Requirements for ratios of staff to children vary; a good rule of thumb is that the younger the children, the more staff are required.

The 14 National Standards cover a range of important issues in relation to safe and effective child care. There are slightly different interpretations for childminders and larger day care providers, but the underlying principles remain the same. Many of the implications of the standards are covered throughout this book, putting your role as a child care assistant into perspective.

- **Standard 1 Suitable person:** Adults providing day care, looking after children or having unsupervised access to them are suitable to do so.

- **Standard 2 Organisation:** The registered person meets required adult:child ratios, ensures that training and qualifications requirements are met and organises space and resources to meet the children's needs effectively.

- **Standard 3 Care, learning and play:** The registered person meets children's individual needs and promotes their welfare. They plan and provide activities and play opportunities to develop children's emotional, physical, social and intellectual capabilities.

- **Standard 4 Physical environment:** The premises are safe, secure and suitable for their purpose. They provide adequate space in an appropriate location, are welcoming to children and offer access to the necessary facilities for a range of activities which promote their development.

- **Standard 5 Equipment:** Furniture, equipment and toys are provided which are appropriate for their purpose and help to create an accessible and stimulating environment. They are of suitable design and condition, well maintained and conform to safety standards.

- **Standard 6 Safety:** The registered person takes positive steps to promote safety within the setting and on outings and ensures proper precautions are taken to prevent accidents.

- **Standard 7 Health:** The registered person promotes the good health of children and takes positive steps to prevent the spread of infection and appropriate measures when they are ill.

- **Standard 8 Food and drink:** Children are provided with regular drinks and food in adequate quantities for their needs. Food and drink are properly prepared, nutritious and comply with dietary and religious requirements.

- **Standard 9 Equal opportunities:** The registered person and staff actively promote equality of opportunity and anti-discriminatory practice for all children.

- **Standard 10 Special needs (including special educational needs and disabilities):** The registered person is aware that some children may have special needs and is proactive in ensuring that appropriate action can be taken when such a child is identified or admitted to the provision. Steps are taken to promote the welfare and development of the child within the setting in partnership with the parents and other relevant parties.

- **Standard 11 Behaviour:** Adults caring for children in the provision are able to manage a wide range of children's behaviour in a way which promotes their welfare and development.

- **Standard 12 Working in partnership with parents and carers:** The registered person and staff work in partnership with parents to meet the needs of the children, both individually and as a group. Information is shared.

- **Standard 13 Child protection:** The registered person complies with local child protection procedures approved by the Area Child Protection Committee and ensures that all adults working and looking after children in the provision are able to put the procedures into practice.

- **Standard 14 Documentation:** Records, policies and procedures which are required for the efficient and safe management of the provision, and to promote the welfare, care and learning of children are maintained. Records about individual children are shared with the child's parent.

THINK IT THROUGH

You and your friend are planning to open a nursery for 20 children between the ages of two and five years. You have planned the nursery and had advice from all the appropriate authorities.

In a group use flipcharts to show how you intend to meet the 14 National Standards.

Health and safety

The Health and Safety at Work etc. Act (1974) lays down basic ideas and principles to ensure health and safety at work, imposing duties on both employers and employees. This means that when you are working in a child care setting (or anywhere else for that matter) you have the right to expect that you will not be exposed to any dangers to your health and safety; it is your employer or placement's duty to protect you and everyone using the building, its surroundings and equipment. The legislation covers all of the following:

- buildings and services; design and maintenance
- cleanliness of the environment and of food preparation areas
- safe storage and use of equipment
- working practices that promote health and safety
- provision of a safety policy.

As an employee, even if you are in an unpaid placement, you have a duty to make sure that you do not expose anyone to any danger to health and safety. This obviously includes yourself as well as the children in your care. If you notice anything that could be a source of danger you must report it immediately and/or take steps to protect other people. You must also co-operate with your employer on health and safety issues, for example not using unsafe equipment or ignoring warning notices. Blocking fire exits with toys or uncovering electric sockets, for example, are very serious offences because they go against safety regulations and can cause death or serious injury.

While the general principles of health and safety legislation apply to everyone, there are also codes of practice and standards that give guidance for specific places of employment. There are special standards for child care settings; children often do not have the ability to protect themselves, and as in all other aspects of child care we have a duty to protect them. The following standards apply to different areas in a child care setting.

Buildings and maintenance
- Doors opening into entrances and exits from the building must not be capable of being opened by young children.
- Floors should not have any loose rugs or pieces of carpet.

Cleanliness of the general environment
- There should be a high standard of cleanliness throughout the buildings.
- Spillages should be immediately cleaned.
- Toilet areas should be regularly cleaned and checked.

Food preparation areas
- All staff dealing with food should have a food hygiene certificate.
- All regulations relating to food storage should be followed.

Safe storage and use of equipment
- Cupboards at 'child level' should not contain cleaning items, knives, tools or any other potentially dangerous items.
- Toys with very small parts should be kept well away from children under three years of age.
- Children should not be able to touch heaters and radiators.
- Outdoor slides, swings, etc. should have safe, impact absorbing matting provided.

Working practices that promote health and safety
- Adults must not leave bags or coats containing medicines within reach of children.

- Adults must not bring hot drinks into the same room as children.

- All stairs should have fixed guards at the top and bottom.

- Children using babywalkers, bicycles, etc. should be supervised at all times, wearing helmets where appropriate.

If you talk to a nurse or doctor who has worked in an accident and emergency department, you will hear a catalogue of examples of incidents where children have been seriously injured, scarred for life or even killed as a result of adults not being fully aware of possible dangers to the children in their care.

DID YOU KNOW?

Between 2000 and 2001 there were 2,000 hospital admissions for accidental poisoning from painkillers. In addition there were 541 admissions due to suspected iron overdoses in children aged one to four.

THINK IT THROUGH

In a small group, work through the lists of possible hazards given above, and write down your ideas of the sort of accidents that could happen if good practice was not followed in each case. Think about babies and toddlers, as well as older children aged three to five.

Creating a safe environment

It would be impossible to think about every possible danger and avoid it; children are notoriously good at finding things that could injure them, but it is possible to eliminate the majority of risks and protect the children in your care. The skill of protecting children from injury involves a thorough knowledge of child development. Children can move on to a new stage of development before carers realise it, and can be at risk of injury.

So far we have looked at dangers in 'official' child care settings, from childminders' homes to playgroups, nurseries and schools. Do you think the same considerations apply to private homes where children are cared for? Obviously, childminders are subject to the requirements, but what about a child's own home? You may in the future be employed as a nanny in a private home, or even just to babysit.

THINK IT THROUGH

Look at the picture opposite. How would you make the room safer for a young child?

Figure 3.2 *How many dangers can you spot in this picture?*

Being aware of potential dangers to a child's health and safety is not enough; you must plan procedures and routines that ensure safety. Every person working with children is responsible for monitoring their safety. Some of the necessary procedures are listed below.

- Equipment should be regularly checked for broken parts and sharp edges.

- Arrangement of large equipment and toys should allow safe use by all children.

- Outside play areas should be checked daily for broken glass, syringes and other dangerous litter.

- Toilet and washing facilities should be regularly checked, and you should ensure that children use them at all appropriate times.

- Locks, catches, etc. that stop children leaving the building alone should be operating.

- Cupboards and shelves that are accessible to children should not contain dangerous items, e.g. knives or bleach.

- Outings from the placement should be carefully planned, with all possible dangers being considered and strategies introduced to deal with them.

- Written parental permission must be given for outings.

- There must be strict use of procedures to deal with spillages of urine, faeces, blood and vomit.

- Procedures must be in place to deal with visitors to the setting – reporting, signing in, etc.

- Food must be prepared and served in safe, hygienic conditions.

THINK IT THROUGH

Create a checklist of routine procedures that must be followed to ensure the health, safety and hygiene of children in a range of early years settings.

You have been given the responsibility for the daily safety checks in the toddler room at the nursery where you are working. Your supervisor has asked you to write down your checklist of points for safety in the room. Make your list showing the checks you would carry out to ensure the safety of all the children in your care.

Childhood illnesses

All children pick up infections, and become ill from time to time, as they are developing their immunity. Immunity is the ability of the body to resist infections. All of us are in constant contact with bacteria and viruses, but we do not develop an illness from each one because of our immunity. There are several ways that children become immune to germs. In the uterus (womb) and during breast feeding, the child develops immunity to all diseases to which the mother has immunity, with protection passing from the mother through the placenta and later through breast milk. In the first year of life and later, immunity is built up as a result of experiencing illness such as colds and stomach upsets. Immunity can also be gained from immunisations, e.g. for polio, diphtheria, mumps and whooping cough.

Timing of the vaccinations is important. If they are given too early the natural antibodies inherited from the mother can stop the vaccines working. These natural antibodies have gone by two months of age and so it is important to stick to the schedule to avoid a baby being unprotected. You should be familiar with the immunisation pattern for children. Ask at your doctor's surgery or health centre for a leaflet. You will see a chart similar to the one shown overleaf.

DID YOU KNOW?

It is common for children to have a cold up to eight times in a year. Most colds get better naturally in five to seven days. Cough and cold medicines are not always an effective treatment and may produce side effects in young children. Fevers can be treated with an age appropriate pain and fever relief medicine. As children grow they gradually build up immunity to some of the different viruses that cause the common cold.

Age	Immunisation	Age	Immunisation
8 weeks	Diphtheria Tetanus Pertussis (whooping cough) Hib (viral meningitis) Polio Meningitis C	12–18 months	MMR (mumps, measles, rubella) as one injection
		3–5 years (pre-school)	Polio, diptheria, tetanus and pertussis
12 weeks	As for 8 weeks	10–14 years	MMR BCG (tuberculosis)
16 weeks	As for 8 and 12 weeks	13–18 years	Diphtheria and tetanus Polio

Child care workers should be sure that they are protected against diseases, and should talk to their doctor about the need for boosters of immunisations, particularly rubella or polio. If workers are ill, they should not go to work in case they spread their illness to colleagues and the children.

You should be familiar with the signs and symptoms of childhood illnesses in order to care for a sick child and to protect other children. The following chart shows some of the common signs and symptoms, the treatment needed, whether an immunisation is available, and the incubation period (the time before the child shows signs of the illness after catching it).

Illness	Signs and symptoms	Treatment or action needed	Immunisation available?	Incubation period
Common cold	Sneezing, sore throat, runny nose, headache, temperature.	Treat symptoms with rest, plenty of fluids. Encourage child to blow nose.	No	1–3 days
Gastro-enteritis	Vomiting, diarrhoea, dehydration.	Replace fluids (encourage child to drink water), seek medical help.	No	1–36 hours
Tonsillitis	Very sore throat, fever, headache, aches and pains.	Rest, fluids, medical attention as antibiotics may be needed.	No	Varies
Scarlet fever	Fever, loss of appetite, sore throat, pale around the mouth, 'strawberry tongue', bright pinpoint rash over face and body.	Rest, fluids and observe for complications.	No	2–4 days
Dysentery	Vomiting, diarrhoea with blood and mucus, abdominal pain, fever and headache.	Medical attention, rest, fluids. Strict hygiene measures e.g. careful hand washing.	No	1–7 days
Chicken-pox	Fever, very itchy rash with blister-type appearance.	Tepid bath with soda bicarbonate, and calamine applied to skin to stop itching. Try to stop child scratching to avoid scarring.	No	10-14 days

Illness	Signs and symptoms	Treatment or action needed	Immunisation available?	Incubation period
Measles	High fever, runny nose and eyes, later cough, white spots in mouth, blotchy red rash on body and face.	Rest, fluids, tepid sponging. Medical attention to check for complications.	Yes	7–15 days
Mumps	Pain and swelling of jaw, painful swallowing, fever. May be swollen testes in boys.	Fluids, may need a straw to drink, warmth to swelling, pain relief.	Yes	14–21 days
Rubella (German measles)	Slight cold, sore throat, swollen glands behind ears, slight pink rash.	Rest, treat symptoms. Avoid contact with pregnant women.	Yes	7–21 days
Pertussis (whooping cough)	Snuffly cold, spasmodic cough with whooping sound and vomiting.	Medical attention. Rest, fluids, feed after a coughing attack.	Yes	7–21 days
Meningitis	Fever, headache, drowsiness, confusion, dislike of light, very stiff neck. May be small red spots.	Immediate urgent medical attention. Take child to hospital.	Yes for some strains	2–10 days

In nearly all cases a child is most infectious to others before the symptoms appear. Many illnesses have a cold or fever as their first signs; it would not be possible to exclude all children with these symptoms from nursery, nor would it have much effect on the spread of a disease. Different settings have different rules about excluding children with common illnesses, ranging from excluding all children with symptoms, to excluding only while the child feels unwell.

Your role includes encouraging parents to have their children immunised wherever possible, and to make sure that routines in the nursery, school, etc. help to protect children from illness. For example, good practice involves careful hand washing, blowing of noses, covering up coughs, and cleanliness of toilet areas. You should also be sensitive to the needs of a child who has been ill. Even when fully recovered from an acute illness, a child may need activities that are usually more suited to a slightly younger child, or more reassurance and attention.

Parents may ask you for advice about their children when they are ill or appear unwell. Always suggest they take their child to the doctor if they are uncertain what to do. Family doctors prefer to see a child, even if for a minor illness, rather than miss a serious illness such as meningitis. When a child is taken ill in your care, the parents or guardians must be informed. As a student or junior worker you should always check with your supervisor. You can provide support to a child who is ill while his or her parents are coming by sitting quietly with the child, perhaps reading a story.

Often after a visit to the doctor a child may need to take medicine while at nursery or school. Most settings have a policy that parents must give written consent for their child to have medicines administered by the nursery nurse or teacher. Child care workers are not allowed to give medicines to children without this written permission under any circumstances.

Accidents and emergencies

Young children are prone to having accidents and injuring themselves. Even a simple banging of heads when two children run into each other could be serious if the carer failed to notice symptoms that something was wrong. All child care settings must have at least one person qualified in first aid. As a child care worker it is your responsibility to take a first aid course if your tutors do not provide it. You should keep your first aid knowledge up to date. Everyone working with children should be able to deal calmly with an accident and decide when it is necessary to call for additional help. The following information gives a simple basis for dealing with common emergencies involving children, but to be effective in an emergency you must take a recognised first aid course.

DID YOU KNOW?

Over 1 million children under the age of 15 are taken to accident and emergency departments following accidents in the home. Children under four years are the most at risk from accidents in the home. Most accidents happen between late afternoon and early evening, in the summer, school holidays and at weekends. Most accidents are preventable by increased awareness and improving the environment. For more information visit the ROSPA website.

What is an emergency?

An emergency is whenever someone is injured or seriously ill, or in danger of being so. Examples include:

- choking
- severe bleeding
- convulsion
- broken bones
- swallowed poisons
- allergic reactions
- head injuries
- unconsciousness.

Before you do anything, you must follow the AABC code:

A: Assess the situation. It is no use trying to deal with an incident if there is danger to yourself or any other person. Other children should be moved away from the scene as quickly as possible, and someone should be asked to look after them. Assess the scene for dangers, e.g. electricity, broken glass or spillages. Then you must give attention to the casualty's:

A: Airway

B: Breathing

C: Circulation

The simple aims of first aid are to:

- preserve life

- stop the condition getting worse

- promote recovery.

The following table shows examples of common emergencies that may affect children in your care, and how to deal with them (this is not a substitute for attending a first aid course).

Emergency	Treatment
Severe bleeding	Apply firm pressure to the site, preferably with a clean pad, but with just your hand if needed. If there is a foreign object in the cut, e.g. a piece of glass, do not try to remove it, apply pressure at the sides of the wound. Lay the casualty down and raise the bleeding part above the level of the heart if possible. Ring 999 for an ambulance.
Cuts and grazes	Inspect the wound and if severe bleeding, treat as above. For minor cuts and grazes, wash with clean water if dirty and cover with appropriate dressing.
Head injury	Control any bleeding by applying pressure with a pad. Lay casualty down. Take or send to hospital. Monitor level of consciousness, vomiting, etc.
Convulsions – often the result of a high temperature in a child	If hot, cool child by removing clothing (except underwear). Protect from injury; clear surrounding objects. Sponge with tepid water. Place in recovery position. Dial 999 for an ambulance.
Back injury – always suspect after a fall from swing, slide, tree, etc.	Do not move or attempt to move. Steady and support neck and head. Dial 999 for an ambulance.
Allergic reaction to stings, medicines or irritants – red, blotchy skin, swelling of face and neck, problems with breathing	Dial 999 for an ambulance. Put into comfortable position. Monitor condition.
Choking in young children	Give five back slaps between shoulders (lean an older child forward, put a baby over your knee face downwards). Remove any obvious obstruction from mouth. If this fails, give five chest thrusts (stand behind the child, make a fist against lower breast bone, grasp with other hand, and press sharply into chest. For a baby, press two fingertips on lower half of breast bone). Check ABC. Dial 999 for an ambulance.

Treatment	
Asthma attack	Make child comfortable, seated in position most comfortable for the child. Let child use inhaler; usually a blue reliever. Encourage to breathe slowly. If attack does not subside, call for medical help.
Loss of consciousness – could happen for many reasons, e.g. from a faint or after a head injury or due to a serious illness	Send for help; dial 999. Check the child is breathing and has a clear airway. Maintain the airway by tilting the head backwards. Place in the recovery position. Do not leave the child alone.
Suspected broken bones or sprains	Support the affected limb, if an arm with a sling or padding. Take to hospital or call an ambulance.
Burns and scalds	Cool the burn with water for at least ten minutes or until the skin feels cool. Remove any clothing that is not stuck to the burn. Cover with a sterile or clean dressing or even a clean plastic bag. Call an ambulance or take to hospital for any burn or scald on a young child.
Poisoning – drugs, plants, etc.	Dial 999 for an ambulance. Try to find out what has been taken and keep the evidence. If unconscious, check airway and put in the recovery position.

In the case of an accident, in addition to taking action to help the casualty, you must:

■ send for a qualified first aider if you are not qualified yourself

■ call for your supervisor

■ calm the other children

■ inform the child's parents

■ record the incident in the accident book.

Consideration and thought for the children in your care can help to prevent potentially serious emergencies. For example, very young children learn a lot from putting things in their mouths and exploring taste and texture. Unfortunately this can lead to accidents, so always be careful

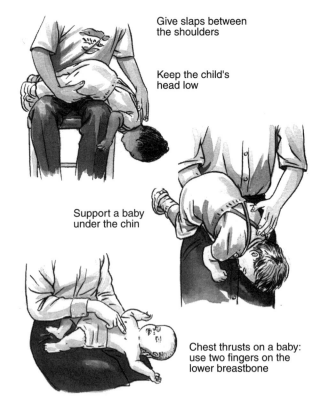

Give slaps between the shoulders

Keep the child's head low

Support a baby under the chin

Chest thrusts on a baby: use two fingers on the lower breastbone

Figure 3.3 *Treating a child or baby who is choking*

about giving a child a drink or food while playing, because innocent items can be lethal when combined.

When dialling 999, always have ready the details of the accident and injury, the age of the child and of course where the injured child is. In serious incidents involving breathing difficulties or severe bleeding, an ambulance should be summoned as soon as possible, preferably while first aid is being given.

Always make sure you know where the first aid box is kept, and what is in it.

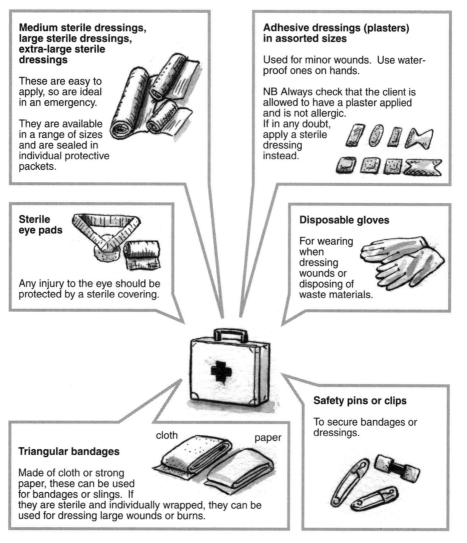

Medium sterile dressings, large sterile dressings, extra-large sterile dressings

These are easy to apply, so are ideal in an emergency.

They are available in a range of sizes and are sealed in individual protective packets.

Adhesive dressings (plasters) in assorted sizes

Used for minor wounds. Use water-proof ones on hands.

NB Always check that the client is allowed to have a plaster applied and is not allergic. If in any doubt, apply a sterile dressing instead.

Sterile eye pads

Any injury to the eye should be protected by a sterile covering.

Disposable gloves

For wearing when dressing wounds or disposing of waste materials.

Safety pins or clips

To secure bandages or dressings.

cloth   paper

Triangular bandages

Made of cloth or strong paper, these can be used for bandages or slings. If they are sterile and individually wrapped, they can be used for dressing large wounds or burns.

Figure 3.4 *What you would expect to find in a first aid box*

A good first aid box should have the following items in it:

- a range of plasters in different sizes
- triangular bandages (slings)
- disposable gloves
- scissors
- cotton wool
- medium and large sterile dressings
- sterile eye pads
- safety pins
- crepe bandages
- tweezers
- non-alcoholic cleansing wipes.

Many of these items are illustrated in Figure 3.4.

THINK IT THROUGH

The next time you are in your placement, find out where your first aid kit is and have a look inside. Do the contents match the list above? Is anything missing? Are there any extra items, and if so what are they for?

Procedures after an accident or emergency

Dealing with the immediate situation in an accident is only part of the procedure for the nursery or school. The next important action is to inform the child's parents or carers. The child will have a record card in the office giving emergency contact numbers. This may not be the child's parents, because work commitments may make it difficult for a parent to be contacted. The number may be the child's grandparents or aunt, for example. It should be someone who is usually easy to contact, and who in turn can contact the parents. The person in charge must get in touch with the emergency contact as soon as possible and inform the relevant person of the incident, and where the child is being taken. Obviously someone the child knows well should go to the hospital with the child until the parents or other carers arrive. This will help to reassure the child, and be a point of contact for the parents when they arrive.

Even with a minor accident that does not need hospital treatment, an entry should be made in the accident book. Under certain circumstances the accident may need to be reported to the Health and Safety Executive, particularly if the child is seriously injured. A full report is needed, and in any incident the person in charge should examine the circumstances to see what could be done to prevent a similar emergency occurring in future. Preventive measures may be as simple as having more adults to supervise the children at outdoor play, or there may be the need to change equipment or put more safety protection in place, such as more matting under swings. A review of the policy on accidents may be needed, but at the very least some type of preventive action is likely to be taken. Accidents are less likely to happen when:

■ potential dangers are seen, e.g. kettle flexes are kept well away from worktop edges, ponds are properly covered or filled in

■ children are not over-protected and are allowed to develop skills to keep themselves safe

■ adults are good role models and set a safe example

■ children are never left alone

■ wherever possible toys and equipment purchased have the kitemark or safety mark on them to show they are of a good standard. The British Standards Institution gives kitemarks and safety numbers to approved products. The Lion mark is put on British-made toys that meet British safety standards, and the CE symbol means products have met both British and European standards.

Kitemark of the British Standards Institution (BSI)

BSI safety mark

Lion mark

CE mark

Figure 3.5 *Look out for these safety marks on toys and equipment*

ASSESSMENT ACTIVITY

Identify common childhood illnesses and explain basic first aid and safety procedures:

1 Design and make a booklet for parents at your placement describing the features of the common childhood illnesses.

2 You are in charge of two small children, aged two and five years, at their home. Their parents have gone shopping for the afternoon. At 2 pm, during a game with a ball, Iqbal (the five-year-old) trips and falls heavily on his left leg. You see that his leg is swollen and it looks a strange shape.

a) Describe what you would do, in the appropriate order. You should include contacting his parents, and remember his little sister.

b) Now imagine this incident had happened at school; describe anything else that you think would have to be done.

No extension to merit or distinction is possible for this assessment.

UNIT FOUR

INTELLECTUAL AND COMMUNICATION SKILLS

This unit considers how children develop the skills of learning and communication. Communication and the development of skills are central to a child's progress. As an early years worker you have a vital role to play in supporting a child in this development. Early years workers do not work alone in this task; the unit also explores how you can develop your own skills of working with other adults in promoting a child's development. The emphasis is on activities that promote a particular aspect of a child's development. However, it is extremely unusual for an activity to only help with one aspect of development. All play promotes development to some degree, and all activities count as play. Play is work to children; it is what they do on the path to growing up.

In this unit you will learn about:
- children's sensory and intellectual development
- children's language and communication skills development
- activities that promote sensory, intellectual and communication development
- the role of the early years worker.

Children's sensory and intellectual development

The patterns of sensory and intellectual development are the same as for other areas of development.

- Development is a process that happens in stages.
- Skill development has a predictable order.
- Children need to practise their skills to develop competence in them.

The table below shows the milestones of fine motor skill and intellectual development.

Age	Milestone
Birth	Grasps objects when they touch the palm of the hand Blinks in reaction to bright light Turns to soft light Stares at carer Cries when basic needs require attention
1 month	Stares at soft light Gaze caught by and follows dangling ball
3 months	Follows movements of large and smaller objects Watches movements of own hands, plays with own hands Holds rattle for a few seconds if placed in hand
6 months	Very curious, easily distracted by movements Immediately fixes sight on small objects close by and reaches out to grasp them Uses whole hand in palmar grasp, passes toy from one hand to another Puts everything in mouth Watches toys fall from hand within range of vision
9 months	Can hold a toy in one hand and take a second in the other Lifts block but can only release by dropping Pokes at small item with index finger Will pick up small item between finger and thumb – this is called the inferior pincer grasp Looks in correct direction for falling toys
12 months	Neat pincer grip – picks up anything tiny from the floor Drops toys deliberately and watches them fall – this is called 'casting' Looks in correct place for toys that have rolled out of sight Starting to show hand preference Clicks two cubes together Puts cubes in box when shown Recognises familiar people at 6 metres

Age	Milestone
18 months	Uses delicate pincer grasp for tiny objects Holds pencil in primitive tripod grasp and scribbles Builds tower of 3 cubes when shown Turns pages of books, several at a time, enjoys picture books Points to interesting objects outside
2 years	Builds tower of 6 cubes Holds pencil in normal grip and will copy lines and V shape Turns single pages in book
3 years	Threads large beads, builds bridges with blocks when shown Copies circle and cross, draws man with head Matches 2 or 3 primary colours Paints with large brush, cuts with scissors
5 years	Threads large needle Copies square, and range of letters – some spontaneously Draws man with head, body, arms, legs and features, and will draw house Colours pictures neatly Names 4 primary colours and matches 10 or more colours
6 years	Ability to write developing – able to write some words and copy others Reads simple books Increasing sophistication in drawing and painting Fine motor skills allow finer manipulation of building bricks, jigsaws, etc.
7–8 years	Able to understand concept of conservation – e.g. the amount of playdough remains the same if you make a ball of dough into a long, thin snake Developing the ability to think about several things at once Enjoys games and rules Understands the use of symbols in maths, writing, etc. Great curiosity in relation to workings of his/her environment

Encouraging fine motor skills and sensory development

Many skills depend very much on how much practice and experience children get in using them. Sensory development and the development of the fine motor skills involves all of the senses linked together.

The gathering of sensory knowledge starts from birth. Even a very young baby will enjoy watching the branches of a tree

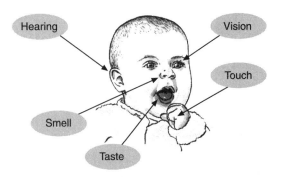

Figure 4.1 *All of the senses work together*

blowing in the wind, or a bright mobile suspended over the cot. Different sounds will soon be recognised, with some noises being enjoyed more than others.

Hand–eye co-ordination is closely linked; from watching his or her own fingers at close quarters, by three months a baby will be putting those fingers in the mouth to explore what he or she has been watching. Until around 18 months, a child explores as much as possible of the world through the mouth. With a little imagination, you should be able to think of endless ways of encouraging sensory and hand–eye development. Encouraging curiosity in babies and very young children brings great rewards as they grow older; they should be full of curiosity about the sensory world. The table below gives some ideas.

Sense or skill	Possible activities
Sight	Mobiles and cot/pram toys
	Posters with different images/colours, frequent changes of some
	Rolling balls/toy in view
	Setting a mirror by the baby's chair, cot, etc.
	Bright picture books
	Selective use of TV
	Pointing out moving objects inside and outside
	Using photographs of familiar people
Touch	Using different textured fabrics in clothes, covers, etc.
	Offering safe objects of different textures
	Putting the child's hands on different textured surfaces
	Using the language of texture when talking to children – rough, smooth, soft, spiky, etc.
	Encouraging massage and stroking by appropriate adults
	Encouraging messy play – with playdough, finger painting, 'slime', etc.
	Making a feely box or bag – several different textures and objects
	Using the outdoors as much as possible – crunchy leaves, splashy puddles, wet rain, soft and hard snow
Smell	Offering different smells – soap, flowers, food as appropriate
	Using the language of smells whenever possible – mealtimes, cooking, outdoors
	Games with different smelling objects – smelled 'blind'
Taste	Offering different tastes – using foods
	Encouraging experiences of different tastes, but introducing them gradually
Hearing	Lots of talking to a child from birth
	Limited use of TV and radio
	Using different noises at varying levels close to, further away from, at the sides and behind a child
	Alerting to noises outside and inside
	Using recordings of different sounds
	Using different kinds of music and encouraging singing and dancing

Sense or skill	Possible activities
Hand–eye co-ordination	Over-the-cot toys encouraging reaching out
	Use of play centres with range of activities
	Using squeakers, rattles, etc.
	Encouraging reaching for objects after baby is 3 months of age
	Encouraging self finger-feeding with bread, apple, etc.
	Offering smaller items to hold as pincer grasp develops
	Using range of activities to encourage development of skills, bricks, Lego, pencils
	Playing finger games and rhymes – e.g. Incy Wincy Spider
	Use of games such as yoyos, cats cradle, hand and finger puppets
Memory and concentration	From age 3–4 years keeping a diary of events
	Discussions in circle time
	Taking a simple message to a colleague
	Copying a short sequence of sounds on a musical instrument
	Posting a sequence of small items into a box after watching you
	Simple version of remembering items on a tray
	Verbal games of 'I went to the shops and bought ...' in a round of adding items and repeating
	Jigsaw puzzles, games with simple rules
	Involving children in simple searches
	Spotting games, e.g. 'I spy', looking out for a specific item

THINK IT THROUGH

Can you think of other activities you have seen or used that help to develop understanding, memory and curiosity?

Encouraging creative and intellectual development

Young children are naturally very curious and need little encouragement to explore their environment. However, with support and encouragement this natural curiosity can be of maximum benefit to the development of the child. We need to provide children with a stimulating environment to encourage them to try out their own ideas. Even before they are mobile, babies visually explore their surroundings, and they test out objects through their senses as much as possible. Once they are mobile they can test even more by going to all the interesting objects on display.

In early childhood, the imagination soars as children play and explore. Children do not have preconceptions of adulthood; what to you might appear to be a simple cardboard box could represent a house, car, cave, spaceship or whatever the child's imagination wants it to be. Given a range and variety of play materials (which can be everyday household objects) a child will try out ideas and develop creativity and imagination. It is important to offer a child the opportunity to work with as many materials as possible. The only barriers to a child's imagination are those put there by carers. Good quality play with children can extend their imagination even more. When a child explains to you that he or she is in a boat, sailing on the sea, going to a land where trees grow everyone's favourite sweets, ask how long it will take, or what teddy (who is also in the boat) will find on the trees.

Try leaving a selection of empty cardboard boxes of varying sizes with a group of children and observe their play. Painting is also an excellent medium for a child's imagination. Depending on the paint and paper available, a group of children will each produce a totally different picture. Asked about the painting, children will give you a wide range of explanations. A golden rule to remember when asking a child about his or her work, of any creative nature, is never to ask a closed question, e.g. 'Is that a painting of your brother?' It is far better to ask an open question, e.g. 'Tell me about your picture'.

As a child develops language skills he or she will be bursting to find out the names of objects or activities. The 'what is it?' stage can be very tiring for parents, but is a child's natural response to the surroundings. It is no coincidence that speech and full mobility develop in parallel. To a two-year-old who can run around, climb and explore, the obvious question to ask is 'what is it?' Once sense has been made of the surroundings, and names given to everything, the next question is 'why?' At around three-and-a-half, a child wants to find out what something does, or why there are trees or why it is windy or why we have to go to bed. Simple, clear answers are needed to encourage and stimulate intellectual development. Ignoring, brushing off or giving incorrect answers to questions is not helpful, and will discourage questions in future. If you can extend our answers, so much the better. You are giving more fuel for the fire of intelligence.

THINK IT THROUGH

A Lewis, aged three, is busily playing with some bricks when he notices a big box being brought into nursery. He rushes over and asks what is in the box. 'Nothing for you', says the nursery nurse, and carries on pushing it into the storeroom. Lewis stands and looks uncertainly at the box and then wanders back to his bricks.

B Lewis's nursery nurse tells him that the box he has noticed being brought into the nursery contains some new books that have been brought in a van. If Lewis goes to the window quickly, she says, he will see the big red van which is going back to Manchester. 'Where's Manchester?' asks Lewis. The nursery nurse says they will find a book with a map in it to show Lewis, and she also looks at all the new books with him, making a mental note of the ones in which he shows particular interest.

Which scenario do you think stimulated Lewis' imagination?

Books, painting, clay, playdough, walks in the woods or fields, storytelling, pictures of unfamiliar scenes and settings, the list of activities that can be used to encourage intellectual and creative development is long. An excellent way to encourage children's development is to pick up on a subject they are already interested in. Look at the example in the case study below.

Case Study – Jennifer

Jennifer noticed that the children at her placement were fascinated by the wind, running around in the playground laughing at their hair blowing around, and watching the washing blowing on the line. She asked her supervisor if she could plan some activities with the children later in the week. By using windmills, a hairdryer, kites, stories about the wind, pictures of waves and tornadoes, and games using air movement, the children's natural interest was expanded to enlarge their understanding.

Simple, everyday activities such as baking can be used to encourage intellectual development. How many eggs and how much flour etc. is needed to make a cake? How do eggs, flour, butter and sugar change to make a cake mix? What happens in the oven to make it rise and turn brown?

Types of play

Children use play to make sense of their lives. Through play they can:

- learn about how things work
- improve their skills
- work through emotional upsets
- practise relationships
- enjoy themselves.
- copy adults
- make friends
- express their feelings
- learn about rules and turn taking

Play uses a lot of energy and can be hard work; it needs a lot of time. Asking a child to play for ten minutes is not very helpful; all activities are play to children, so a child can be confused if given this instruction. Meaningful play can take a considerable amount of time to develop. Play is now actively encouraged where children are in unfamiliar settings, for example hospitals and social services units, and increasingly in doctors' and dentists' surgeries. Quality play can help a child to express fears about procedures in hospital, or be used to explain what is going to happen.

In order to help children play effectively, you need to have experienced using the materials yourself. Ask your tutor if you could have a practice play area, or ask in placement if you can try dough, plasticine, painting, Lego, anything you have not used before. Adults have an important role in encouraging play. They should facilitate play, not organise it. This means that the adult provides resources if necessary, ensures a safe environment, allows time for play and does not interfere or direct the play. Of course, for some play, the adult might be needed or wanted by the children, but as a participant, not an organiser.

Play can take many forms, and it can be helpful to use a system of categories to describe different activities. Very often, a play activity will fall into several categories, so do remember that there are no clear-cut divisions between the types.

Type of play	Examples	Some benefits
Physical play	Running, skipping, cycling, rough and tumble	Encourages and promotes physical and social development. Understanding of concepts such as area, energy, etc.
Creative play	Painting, modelling, cooking, puzzles, junk modelling	Hand–eye co-ordination, creativity, self-expression, emotional release, learning about colour, shapes
Pretend play	Role play, domestic play, dressing up, puppets	Coming to terms with their world, release of stress, communication, countering gender-role stereotyping
Exploratory play	Exploring new ideas and objects, e.g. magnets, old telephones	Intellectual development and creativity
Constructive play	Using Lego bricks, Meccano, K'nex	Fine motor skills, imagination, sense of achievement, early numeracy skills
Messy play	Cornflour and water, sand, water, playdough	Exploring textures, colours. Release of stress and inhibitions

Children of all ages and stages of development can experience play of all types, appropriate to their level of skills.

Stages of play development

Learning to play with other children happens gradually. Until the age of two, children usually prefer to play alone, but with the support and reassurance of adults nearby. Eventually, by the age of seven, most children can play well with others and follow complex rules of games. To reach this sophisticated stage of social interaction children's play goes through several stages.

- Solitary Play: This is the first type of play seen in a child and is predominant until approximately the age of two years.

- Parallel Play: A toddler will often play alongside another child, showing some awareness of them but without sharing the activity.

■ Associative play: This develops from about the age of three years and is characterised by watching others and copying. Younger children may observe older children playing.

■ Co-operative play: This is the final stage when children actively play together; they talk about their play and make decisions together. You may hear remarks like 'let's play dressing up' or 'shall we make a tower'.

Play can be a group activity, often called **social** or **group play,** or children can play by themselves.

THINK IT THROUGH

Try to observe at least three children playing throughout a session at nursery or school. Try to watch them on at least three separate occasions. Write down what they are doing on each occasion. Make a chart showing the play you witnessed, resources used, which type of play you think it was, and the benefits to the children.

Did you see any difference between the three children in their approach to play?

Resources for play

Toys do not have to be expensive, complex items with only a short lifespan in terms of interest and durability. Media advertising bombards children with images of the latest inventions of toy manufacturers, many centred on the latest craze or pop group. At Christmas you will hear parents giving accounts of the time they have spent looking, often in vain, for the latest desired toy. All this is not a necessary part of providing toys and play experiences for children.

You have already explored the idea of using seemingly ordinary items, such as empty cardboard boxes, for play. A look around your home will reveal many resources for a child to play with: kitchen pots and pans, packets of food for playing shops, furniture for making dens, dressing up clothes, water in sinks with plastic utensils, the list is endless. Many of these items can be used in the nursery or classroom. Most children have a selection of toys available for play, ranging from the most simple to highly technical, e.g. paper and crayons, dolls, bicycles, construction toys and technical computer equipment and games. There are a few basic rules for choosing a successful toy. It should be:

Figure 4.2 *Many items found at home can be used as a resource for play*

- right for the stage of the child

- strong enough to be used

- safe to play with

- suitable for a range of play.

Children should be encouraged to try all sorts of toys without gender or culture bias. Boys can enjoy the home corner, cooking or doll play, and girls can enjoy construction, climbing or car play. As an early years worker you have an essential role in encouraging equal opportunities in all areas including play. Many useful books have been written about play, and some toy manufacturers produce catalogues that are worth studying.

THINK IT THROUGH

Choose one of these everyday activities or events: the wind, going shopping, a trip to the park, spring time.

What activities could you plan to help a child explore your idea? Think about songs, rhymes and stories. Collect samples of materials that would be appropriate.

ASSESSMENT ACTIVITY

Describe the factors which influence the ways in which children play.

1   Take some time to watch children playing in different settings: at your placement, in the park, on television, videos at college, your family.

2   List the different ways they play; think about type and stages of play development.

What has influenced the different ways of playing you have observed? Write your findings up as a brief report.

No extension to merit or distinction is possible for this assesment.

Children's language and communication skills development

The table overleaf summarises the milestones achieved by most children in developing their language and communication skills.

Children communicate even before they are born. A baby in the uterus will respond to loud noises or distress by moving. A new-born baby communicates through crying and quietening with increasing sophistication. It does not take

Age	Milestone
Birth	Cries when basic needs require attention
1 month	'Freezes' when a bell is rung gently close to the ear, moves head towards the sound Stops crying at sound of human voice (unless very upset) Coos in response to carer's talk
3 months	Becomes quiet and turns head towards sound of rattle near head Vocalises when spoken to and when alone
6 months	Makes singsong vowel sounds, e.g. aah-aah, goo Laughs and chuckles and squeals aloud in play Responds differently to different tones of voice Starting to respond to noises out of sight with correct visual response
9 months	Vocalises for communication, shouts for attention Babbles loudly and tunefully – dual syllables in long strings, e.g. dad-dad, baba, mam-mam Imitates adult vocal sounds, e.g. coughs, smacking lips Understands 'no' and 'bye-bye' Instant response to hearing test conducted 1m behind child, out of sight
12 months	Knows own name Jargons loudly in 'conversations', includes most vowels sounds Understands words in context, e.g. cup, dog, dinner, and understands simple messages, e.g. 'clap hands', 'where are your shoes?'
18 months	Growing number of words – uses 6 to 20 recognisable words, understands many more Echoes prominent or last word in sentences Tries to join in with nursery rhymes Responds to simple instructions – 'fetch your shoes', 'shut the door'
2 years	Uses more than 50 words, makes simple 2-word sentences Refers to own name, talks to self during play
3 years	Large vocabulary, can give full name, sex and age, holds simple conversations Asks many questions of the type: what? why? and how? Enjoys repetition of favourite stories Counts to 10
5 years	Speech is fluent and correct, using descriptive language Gives full name, age, birthday and address Enjoys jokes, singing, rhymes, etc.
6 years onwards	Rapidly expanding vocabulary Recognises new words and asks the meaning of them Will accurately copy accents heard Can be bilingual Produces most sounds, with some residual difficulty with some letter groups

Figure 4.3 *Children probably use non-verbal communication more than adults*

long for a carer to recognise the meanings of different cries: hungry, tired, cold, fed up, needing a cuddle, etc.

Non-verbal communication is as important to children as it is to adults. Indeed, children probably use it more than adults do. Observe a group of young children playing and try to work out what is happening without listening to their speech.

Speech is an aspect of development that can vary widely without any relationship to other developmental aspects or to the child's intelligence. Parents often become very concerned that a child is late in talking compared with an elder sibling. This can be simply because the older child is anticipating all the younger one's needs, removing any urgent need for the child to talk.

ASSESSMENT ACTIVITY

Describe the milestones in development of social, intellectual, language and communication skills.

I Tom is aged three months. His parents are keen to give him a head start in his development. Describe the stages and milestones of social, intellectual, language and emotional skills through which they will see progress up to 18 months of age.

To achieve a **merit grade** you will need to explain the reasons for variations in milestones of development of social, intellectual, language and communication skills.

To achieve a **distinction grade** you will need to analyse the implications for child care settings of working with children at a range of different stages of development.

Encouraging language and communication skills development

Communication is the area of development that most dramatically shows the effects of input by carers. A baby as young as two or three months who is regularly talked to, sung to and experiences general communication will vocalise far more than a baby who has little one-to-one communication. From birth, babies learn patterns of speech and are absorbing them ready for when they start to reproduce all the sounds. The vocalisations of babies and toddlers are part of the pre-language skills that prepare a child for speaking fluently.

Some element of repetition is involved in learning a language. This is clearly demonstrated in children with 'glue ear' (a blockage of the tubes in the inner ear which stops sounds travelling to the auditory nerve). They cannot hear consonants at the beginning of words, so they hear 'bus' as 'us', 'car' as 'ar', and they repeat them as they hear them. Some children have 'grommets' inserted between the outer and middle ear which allows air into the middle ear. The main activities that help a child learn to talk are for a child to:

- listen to voices
- hear other people talking to him or her
- practise making sounds
- copy sounds made by others
- learn the meaning of sounds and words.

Activities to encourage language development

One of the easiest ways to encourage the development of communication skills in a child is simply to listen to the child and explore different sounds and experiences. Show that you enjoy listening to the child's view of the world and ask questions about things. Use open questions that need more than a simple 'yes' or 'no' response. You can engage a child in a wealth of activities to encourage language development. Some examples include:

- singing songs, especially with clear, easy-to-follow words
- talking about events in the child's life, e.g. what happened at the weekend
- relating nursery rhymes with accompanying actions
- reading stories, especially those with interesting pictures that can stimulate conversation
- gentle repetition of words that have been mispronounced, and encouraging the child to repeat them.

As a carer, you should always try to:

- ask open-ended questions, for example, 'could you tell me about your painting?'
- listen to a child and respond with a fair and true answer
- give a child time and attention, getting down to the child's level and looking at him or her
- check for hearing difficulties
- encourage exercises given by speech therapists, etc.

■ allow time for the child to express feelings and reactions; try to avoid rushing a child's attempts at communication

■ show that you value a child's communication.

These 'rules' apply to any child, but are particularly important for children who find communication challenging, for example children who may have hearing impairments, speech difficulties, a second language or emotional problems. Very often a child who seems delayed in language development will make rapid progress after starting nursery or playgroup, because the constant contact with other children and adults helps to stimulate speech. A child may, of course, require professional intervention to help him or her to make progress, and this is explored further below.

THINK IT THROUGH

You are asked to keep an eye on a new child at nursery, Jay, who is four years old and seems very shy. He has never been to any pre-school group before, and his health visitor and family are concerned about his lack of speech. How will you help Jay to develop his communication skills?

Songs, music, rhymes and stories

From birth, many children hear a carer singing lullabies and rocking songs. As children grow they delight in songs and rhymes; the constant repetition makes it possible for them to join in these familiar, sing-song types of communication. New songs and rhymes introduce new words and phrases, which are quickly learned. Once a child is attending any sort of group, from toddlers to school, songs are an important activity. Used with actions or puppets, group songs allow a child to try joining in without being singled out. Songs and rhymes can fit very easily into themes and topics in the nursery or school.

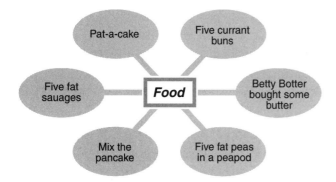

Figure 4.4 *Some songs and rhymes on the theme of food*

Music

Music is a medium to which most children respond. A piece of music can serve many functions including soothing children, allowing them to express themselves in movement, promoting dance and providing inspiration for a painting. All these are forms of communication, and are especially important when a child has difficulties in verbal communication. Apart from listening to music, children love to make music, and again this can be used for communicating. Clapping hands is the simplest form of music making. Have a look at the range of musical instruments in your placement. Do they include any of those shown below? Try them out to see what type of noise they make.

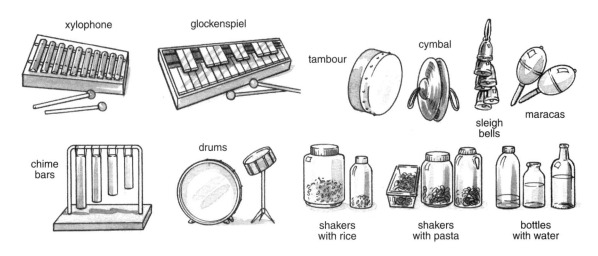

Figure 4.5   *A range of musical instruments for children*

You should develop your own library of songs, music, rhymes and stories that encourage communication and language development. Every time you hear or see a new example in a book, in your placement, etc. write down or copy the details. Create a resource file with various headings. Choose a theme, for example autumn or animals; an ideal theme would be one that is in current use at your placement. Collect as many relevant songs, rhymes and examples of music as possible and file them in your resource file. Choose one of each and try them out with a few children in your placement, making notes on the success of the activities.

Books

As with music, you should look at the range of books available to seek out ones suitable for helping language and development. Reading stories to children is an important part of communicating; very few children, if any, do not enjoy hearing a story, either as part of a group or on a one-to-one basis. Reading promotes all of the aspects of intellectual and language development.

Choosing the right book is important. The choice of book has to be related to the child's:

- age
- ability to understand the story
- stage of development
- interests and cultural background.

a link with a child's own experiences

new experiences

Books provide...

something to smile or laugh at

an escape from unpleasant happenings

something to think carefully about

familiar scenes

a calm ending to the day

an opportunity for close contact with a loved adult

stimulation for discussion

Figure 4.6 *Books help in many ways to promote intellectual and language development*

The same book can serve different age groups. A storybook with bright, attractive pictures will provide stimulation to a toddler who enjoys the pictures, and an older child who enjoys the story. Books that open up discussion are an excellent medium for promoting language development. Examples include books that show familiar scenes, e.g. a shopping street. The book will help you encourage children to talk about their local shops and the goods inside, or about lorries or vans.

Books can be central to developing a theme for further activities. *The Very Hungry Caterpillar* is an excellent example. This book describes the growth of a caterpillar into a butterfly, showing what the caterpillar ate on its way to forming a chrysalis. Work on food, growth, change, insects, numbers and colours can all develop from reading this one book. It is a book with a story that is easy to remember, so it can help in memory development with children.

Having heard a story from a book, children can be stimulated to produce paintings, models and collages. Older children might develop their own related story. Children will enjoy verbally extending the story they have heard, or 'writing' their own story in pictures. These activities all help in the development of communication.

> ### THINK IT THROUGH
>
> *Choose at least two different books and briefly describe them. Make a list of all the extra activities that can be linked to the books, and how the book and the activities will help to promote language and intellectual development.*

Overcoming barriers to language development and self-expression

Those who can communicate well, and are communicating with people who speak the same language, do not give much thought to the skills they use. They wish to say something, open their mouths and say it. For some children this is not always easy. For a range of reasons, they may have problems in communicating or there may be barriers preventing them from making themselves understood.

THINK IT THROUGH

An ideal way of realising just how difficult it can be to make sense of the world when you cannot understand what is being said is to put yourself in that situation. Exercises have been carried out by inviting someone into a classroom and asking them to give some information and instructions in a language that is not known by anyone in the group. Imagine being confronted on your first day at college by a Russian speaking tutor who gets very frustrated when you are not filling in your college enrolment forms, also in Russian. How do you think you would feel? Now transfer those feelings to a child who understands very little English, or who is deaf. What can you do to help them?

Having English as a second language, having a hearing impairment or being deaf, has no relation at all to the child's intellectual abilities, or any other ability. What it does do is to make the child's need for support in developing appropriate communication skills for his or her education a high priority. If we cannot hear and communicate effectively we may find it difficult to learn. It is important not to underestimate the skills a child has who has learned a second language. Think about the complexity of learning one language, now double that, and think of how rarely multilingual speakers mix their languages up. Effective communication with the parents of a child for whom English is a second language will require thought and consideration. Letters home may not be effective and it is essential that such families are not excluded from information.

Reasons for delays in speech development

A child may be delayed in speech development in relation to his or her peers, but will eventually catch up. There are several possible causes for the delay of speech development:

■ genetic: there may be a history of a late start in speech

■ deafness or hearing impairment: a child has to hear before he or she can speak

- lack of opportunities to be spoken to: some children rarely have the pleasure of one-to-one communication

- lack of encouragement: a baby must be responded to when he or she is making attempts at communication

- a child may be concentrating on other aspects of development, such as walking, and will start to talk when other skills have been mastered.

Some barriers to communication are shown below:

- physical barriers: there may be damage to the parts of the body involved in speech production, e.g. the ears, vocal cords or parts of the brain

- emotional barriers: shyness, fear or lack of confidence may be preventing communication skills from developing

- cultural barriers: different languages, accents or backgrounds, or being the child of deaf parents can cause problems

- communication problems: stammering may be hampering the development of speech.

In order to overcome communication barriers, it is important to find the reasons for the barriers, and if possible take steps to remove them. This is not always easy, but some possible approaches are shown in the following table.

Barrier	Intervention needed
Deafness or hearing impairment	Hearing test and investigation as to cause Possible surgery to drain glue ear Hearing appliances for nerve deafness Use of alternative communication modes, e.g. Makaton
Cultural – different language	Use of adult who speaks the appropriate language Input to help the child learn the new language – bilingual assistants Use of games, activities that allow a child to learn the new language
Physical causes	Referral to speech therapist to help the child to develop speech mechanisms Use of Makaton, electronic speech synthesisers
Stammering	Referral to speech therapist to develop strategies to overcome stutter Giving a child time to speak, not interrupting or attempting to finish off the sentence
Emotional cause	Investigate underlying cause of speech difficulties and try to address Try to gain the child's confidence – use of books, communication by other means such as non-verbal, through painting, etc. Referral to speech therapist
Lack of individual attention	Lots of one-to-one attention, mixing with other children and adults

As a child care worker you can be of great help to a child with communication problems by:

- giving a lot of one-to-one attention

- reading stories

- talking clearly to the child

- encouraging communication by asking open-ended questions about things the child understands

- encouraging social and emotional development

- responding to the child as an individual

- working with other professionals who are involved with the child, e.g. checking with the speech therapist how you can help, reporting on progress or otherwise, and above all liaising with parents and carers

- learning how to use alternative methods of communication, e.g. Makaton, electronic speech synthesisers.

There are several methods of alternative communication that can be used effectively if a child has hearing or speech difficulties. If you work on a regular basis with children using one of them you should ensure that you can use the 'language' to some effect, preferably learning it yourself. Makaton uses a series of hand symbols and gestures to represent words and phrases. British Sign Language (BSL) uses the hands to represent letters, words and phrases in a more complex way than Makaton.

DID YOU KNOW?

You may meet different attitudes to using sign languages; some view this as excluding a child who may be deaf from the rest of society and that lip reading is a better alternative. Other people feel that signing can help a child to participate.

Case Study – Liam and Zak

Liam, aged four, is a very shy child who lives in an isolated village with his single mother. His contact with other children has been limited, and he seems to have a serious degree of speech delay. He often seems to have difficulty in hearing what you say to him.

Zak is also four and is the eldest of three children. His parents came to England from Pakistan just before he was born. Although his parents do speak some English, they speak in their mother tongue of Urdu at home.

Consider these two cases. Which other professionals do you think might be involved with the children? How could you help these two boys to overcome their barriers to communication?

Activities that promote sensory, intellectual and communication development

Safe practice in the delivery of activities

Unit 3 explains the checks that are necessary to ensure the health, safety and well-being of children in early years settings. Every time you plan to do something with children, you must think through the safety aspects first. A checklist should include the following questions.

- Is there a suitable space for this activity? Is there enough room? Is the surface safe (e.g. for water or sand play)?

- Is all the appropriate safety equipment in position (e.g. mats under large play equipment, guards on the cooker)?

- Are all materials used safe, especially for very young children, e.g. paint, dough?

- Will I need to control the numbers of children? There may need to be maximum numbers in force for using the sand tray or running around outside.

- Is another activity going on that will clash with it? There may be another class in the playground at the same time.

- Are there enough adults to ensure adequate supervision? If scissors or some other potentially dangerous equipment or tools are being used, numbers of adults may need to be increased.

- Can I make sure that the children will not be harmed by equipment being used, e.g. a cooker when baking?

- Is help available if a child is harmed by the activity? A child may get paint in his or her eyes, or fall off outdoor equipment.

It is your responsibility to think through every activity you provide for children, and every outing you make with them. Almost all accidents that occur could have been prevented. Prevention is far better then cure. You should automatically think through every stage of everything you do, in advance, and think of what might happen. Some events you cannot predict, and others you cannot do anything about, e.g. the weather, or outside events, but you do need to carry out what is called a 'risk analysis'. This means asking yourself whether you have done everything reasonable to ensure that the children in your care will not be at risk from injury.

The early years curriculum

Until 1996 there were no national standards suggesting what children should be learning in their pre-school years. For older children, the National Curriculum for compulsory education (that is from the age of five onwards) has been in operation since the 1988 Education Reform Act. It states the minimum requirements for a curriculum in schools. The core subjects are English, mathematics and science. Foundation subjects include design and technology, history, geography, art, music, languages and physical education.

There is now a clear pathway to support and encourage the potential development of a child from birth right through to formal education at school. In the early years there is involvement of health care, education and social services practitioners from across the spectrum, all with the well-being of the child as the focus of their efforts. The Sure Start programme best demonstrates this in their aims to make sure that all children, particularly from disadvantaged backgrounds, have the best start in life. Sure Start is a programme where all public service sectors work together for the benefit of a child and the child's family.

In November 2002 the minister for Sure Start launched *Birth to Three Matters: A Framework to support children in their earliest years*. This lays down guidelines to support early years workers in their work with children from birth to three years. The underlying principles reflect the importance of parents and families to a child's development. Unit 3 opened with the key principles of the framework. The four aspects of *Birth to Three Matters* look at the skills that a child needs in order to reach the early learning goals of the foundation stage. These are:

- a strong child
- a skilful communicator
- a competent learner
- a healthy child.

In 1996 the Desirable Outcomes Curriculum was introduced for the under-fives, laying down six areas of learning. In 2000 these six areas were replaced with the foundation stage with six similar areas of learning which form the basis of the foundation stage curriculum. Each area of learning has a set of early learning goals as targets for achievement by a child:

- personal, social and emotional development

- communication, language and literacy

- mathematical development

- knowledge and understanding of the world

- physical development

- creative development.

The foundation stage covers children from the age of three to five years, until the end of the reception year at school, and as the name suggests, aims to build the foundation for successful learning in children. The six areas help early years practitioners plan the learning environment, activities and experiences and provide a framework for the early years curriculum. This does not mean that all of young children's learning is divided up into areas. As we have seen in this and other units, one experience may provide a child with opportunities to develop a number of competencies, skills and concepts across several areas of learning.

'Stepping stones' identify progress towards the early learning goals and so help practitioners to understand what the goals mean for young children throughout the foundation stage. These stepping stones identify developing knowledge, skills, understanding and attitudes that children need if they are to achieve these early learning goals by the end of the foundation stage.

THINK IT THROUGH

Look at the plans at your placement; you should be able to see how the staff have planned to meet all of the early learning goals. Talk about some of your activities with your supervisor, and ask for feedback and suggestions for developing them further.

Below are some examples to show how activities can be linked to the foundation stage.

- **Music, song and dance**: Listening and moving to music, and physically using the body, covers physical development, language, maths (if there are numbers in a song or the counting of steps in a dance) and creativity in movement, sounds and interpretation.

- **Mealtimes**: Personal and social development is involved in talking about food, passing things, saying please and thank you, and sitting down for a length of time.

- **Painting and model making**: Activities may be solitary or in a group, and use different materials such as paper, card, dough, paints, glue and glitter. The needs for creativity, maths, language, and personal and social development may be met.

- **Water play**: Using a range of containers, funnels, sieves, coloured water, and learning about temperatures all helps in an understanding of the world, maths and creativity.

- **Story time**: Using a range of different books and relating them to other activities could cover all the development areas.

- **Baking**: From simple non-cook or 'cold-cook' items to quite complex baking, cooking is an activity that most children enjoy. The transformation of flour, eggs, sugar, etc. into edible buns will encourage their language, practical maths, understanding of the world, creative development, and physical development.

- **Outdoor play**: Ranging from the use of large equipment, climbing, and running around, to games such as hopscotch and hide and seek, outdoor play offers potential for all the areas of development.

Early years settings usually plan their activities a number of weeks ahead to allow time for preparation. The planning often starts with a theme or idea, such as movement, spring time or the colour red. From this central theme, all aspects of the early years curriculum are considered in order to provide suitable activities and opportunities for the children.

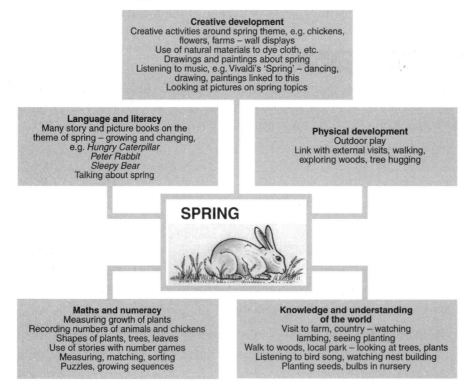

Creative development
Creative activities around spring theme, e.g. chickens, flowers, farms – wall displays
Use of natural materials to dye cloth, etc.
Drawings and paintings about spring
Listening to music, e.g. Vivaldi's 'Spring' – dancing, drawing, paintings linked to this
Looking at pictures on spring topics

Language and literacy
Many story and picture books on the theme of spring – growing and changing, e.g. *Hungry Caterpillar*
Peter Rabbit
Sleepy Bear
Talking about spring

Physical development
Outdoor play
Link with external visits, walking, exploring woods, tree hugging

SPRING

Maths and numeracy
Measuring growth of plants
Recording numbers of animals and chickens
Shapes of plants, trees, leaves
Use of stories with number games
Measuring, matching, sorting
Puzzles, growing sequences

Knowledge and understanding of the world
Visit to farm, country – watching lambing, seeing planting
Walk to woods, local park – looking at trees, plants
Listening to bird song, watching nest building
Planting seeds, bulbs in nursery

Games and activities that help develop new skills

In a group child care setting, most activities are planned with the early years curriculum in mind, and by their very nature these activities will develop new skills. If you are working in a child's own home, or with one child in a group setting, you may need to plan your activities to develop particular skills.

In order to develop new skills, a child must have reached the stage in development where he or she is ready to do so. This may sound obvious, but a child will not be able to read, for instance, until he or she has mastered letter and word recognition. One theory is that all the major skills will develop at an optimum point in a child's development, that there is a right time to learn a skill. If this time is missed, then the skill will prove much harder to learn later. In practice, when a child is asking questions such as 'why is the sky blue?' or 'where does rain come from?', it is an ideal time to start some work on those topics.

THINK IT THROUGH

Describe games and activities that help develop new skills in children of a range of ages.

The theme in your placement is 'creativity', and it has been decided to aim to help children develop interest in a new creative skill. Choose one of the areas of development (physical, intellectual, emotional or social) and think of as many ways as possible to assist development of relevant skills in children aged between three and five years. Describe two of the activities in detail.

Activities for children with specific needs

Whenever you are planning an activity you should consider the needs of all the children in the group you are working with. Unit 3 includes a section about supporting children with special needs, and you should refer to this for more information. You may wish to help a child to improve skills in an area that is giving him or her some difficulty. When you are thinking of an activity to help skill development, break it down into the steps involved in the relevant skill. Then look at activities that use two or three of these steps together. For example, taking off trousers involves:

- unfastening the button
- unzipping the zip
- pulling down the trousers
- stepping out of the trousers.

If the child's problem is with fine motor co-ordination, try devising something that will help with that. Using a task toy that has different sizes of buttons or fastening a toy scarecrow coat will be a fun way to practise button fastening. A zip could be incorporated into the same task toy.

Children who have a specific problem, such as a visual impairment, will miss opportunities for learning in particular ways. Think what you learn visually: colours, shapes, what things look like, and how things fit together. Hearing-impaired children miss out on sound recognition and different inflections of speech. Children who are unable to walk cannot enjoy the sense of running around freely, or of dancing to music in the same way as another child can. It is your role with children who have some form of disability to help them to discover the missing aspects.

Case Study – Ahmed, Susie and Lucy

Ahmed is three years old and has a visual impairment. To make toys more useable they should be big, bright and colourful to help him make the most of any sight he may have. A bigger area of a bright colour, hung in a window area, illuminated with a lamp, is one example. Home-made jigsaws, with shiny colours in very big pieces, will help in the development of fine motor skills. Touch can replace vision; jigsaws with different textures can be used to learn matching. A different texture can represent a different colour for playing picture dominoes. Raised surfaces will help in number or picture recognition.

Susie, aged five, is profoundly deaf, yet she loves music. One reason is that she has had a lot of percussion music played to her, e.g. drums and piano, so she has picked up the vibrations of music. Story time is as enjoyable for her as any other child as lots of pictures are used. Her carers have all learned Makaton, and they always make sure that the story is accompanied by gestures and mime.

Lucy, aged four, spends most of her time in a wheelchair. She is quite limited in her physical skills, but has developed her sense of space and the outside world through time at the swimming baths, through big movement activities on soft foam on the floor, by going out in her wheelchair and experiencing new sights, and by getting out of her chair to lie and roll in snow and fallen autumn leaves.

THINK IT THROUGH

Identify activities that may be used for children with specific needs.

You are told at a staff meeting that a new child will join the nursery in a few weeks' time. Amira, aged three, has a severe hearing impairment and, because of loss of function in her leg muscles, she has some difficulty walking. The Christmas holidays are approaching and all the children are starting to practise for the end-of-term concert. How would you involve Amira in the activities?

Plan and carry out play activities that promote social, intellectual, language and communication skills.

I   Choose two children of different ages, either at your placement or other children you have contact with.

2   Plan and carry out two activities with each child to promote the above skills. In your plan, list the resources you will need. Write down which skills each of the activities will develop. You could do this by creating a

chart with three headings: Activity, Resources and Reasons for choosing.

To achieve a **merit grade** you will need to justify your choice of play activities and explain the expected outcomes.

To achieve a **distinction grade** you will need to evaluate the extent to which your chosen activities achieved the expected outcomes.

The role of the early years worker

Ensuring the success of activities

Children need support and help to encourage their development in all the areas we have been looking at. The role of the carer is to support the children without interfering in play. To do this the carer needs to:

- allow plenty of time for play

- avoid over-organising and allow children to lead their own play

- provide a wide range of materials and show ideas of how to use them

- test out new ideas first before introducing them to children

- make sure that activities and equipment are safe to use

- ensure that all equipment is in working order and suitable for the activity

- make sure there is enough of all materials for all the children involved

- use as many opportunities as possible for children to meet people and see examples of creativity

- avoid the use of templates, pre-drawn outlines, colouring books and tracing

- be a helper in play or activity, not a leader.

The layout of a room is important for ensuring the success of an activity. There must be enough space for all the activities that are going on, or the children and adults may both become frustrated, little may be achieved and accidents may occur. Even a small room can support a number of children and allow a range of varied activities. Well-designed and well-planned storage is the first priority. Storage boxes should be clearly labelled, and easily accessible so that children can help in the setting out and clearing away. In a small room it may only be possible to have one or two activities going on at the same time.

A larger room needs just as much organising as a small one. Lack of planning and organisation will result in disorganisation and lack of progress. Again, storage and clear labelling are essential. In any setting a clear plan for the day, of which all staff are aware, is a necessity. Staff who know the routine and the position of all equipment will ensure the smooth running of a nursery or classroom. A well-organised nursery or class never appears to be *too* organised. Careful organisation and structure can give the impression that the children have control over their own activities.

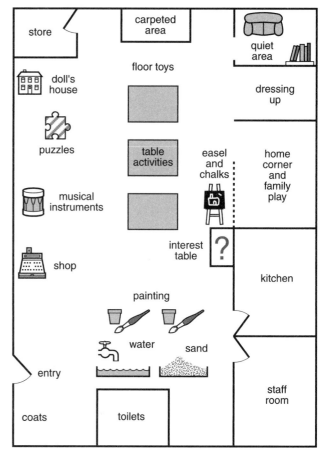

Figure 4.7 *One layout used in a well-organised nursery*

THINK IT THROUGH

Observe a well-structured and well-organised nursery or classroom for part of a session. At the end, ask the person in charge how the session was planned and organised. Make notes and write down an example of how to improve the running of a session with children. Think about aspects of the adult's roles or the use of materials that particularly impressed you, say if anything surprised you, and indicate if you feel there were areas for improvements.

Evaluating activities

Evaluating activities is discussed in Unit 5. In this section we shall cover the main points. Every action you carry out in your work with children has an important effect on them. You have a duty to ensure that at all times you are working as effectively as possible in your role as a child care worker. The only way of checking this is to evaluate your actions. It should become second nature to you with experience, but in your early years as a care worker you should be asking yourself the following questions.

- Was that an enjoyable experience for the children? If so, what features made it enjoyable? If not, what made it less enjoyable, and what could I have done to overcome this?

- Did I meet the needs of all the children involved?

- What changes are needed to make sure all children get full benefit?

- If I were doing this again, what would I do differently?

- What sort of feedback have I had from the children and from other staff?

Everything can be improved, even something that has worked really well and has met all your aims. Never be complacent and think that you have already done your best; there is always potential to make something even better.

THINK IT THROUGH

Look at one of the activities you have recently carried out with a group of children. Using the checklist above, carry out a written evaluation of your activity.

Cultural variations

In your child care career you will encounter carers from many different backgrounds. You would not expect everyone to have the same ideas or preferences about food, leisure activities or religion, so you should not expect all adults to have the same expectations about children's behaviour and development. Examples of different cultural backgrounds include:

- religion
- race
- gender
- education
- age
- social class.

THINK IT THROUGH

In a small group discuss how you feel about the two different ways of child rearing described below.

- *Child A, aged four, appears to be a 'model' child. At home he is expected to play in his own room. At mealtimes he eats everything that is put in front of him, and is allowed a dessert only if he has eaten all his main course. Bedtime is 7 pm sharp, after a bath and a story read by his father. He already understands that he has to fit in with the routine of his parents.*

- *Child B is also four, and would be regarded as a very unruly child by A's parents. Her play takes place wherever she feels is best at the time. She is always asked what she would like to eat, and meals may be eaten while she is playing on the floor or occasionally at the table. There is no pressure to eat more than she wants to of any particular food. She usually goes to bed when her parents go, and often shares their bed.*

Do you think one is preferable to the other? Which fits most closely with your own experiences? How do you think the cultural backgrounds of the children affect people's expectations of them?

In the 1950s, child care experts would have been horrified by Child B, but very approving of A. Today's 'experts' tend to be more relaxed, and recognise that within certain boundaries it is more important that patterns of care and behaviour fit comfortably with the family. Those boundaries are matters that affect a child's health, safety and well-being. Within these limits, parents should feel free to develop a pattern of routines and behaviour that they are comfortable with. Children are not pre-programmed into acting in one particular way. A child whose parents work at night could easily develop a routine of sleeping all day and being awake at night. Problems might arise, however, when that child starts to go to nursery or school.

Expectations of intellectual development, too, can reflect wide cultural variations. In certain communities, four- and five-year-olds are expected to be making rapid progress towards fluent literacy. In other communities, they would be expected to be developing skills through free expression. Different theories of nursery and primary education, such as the Steiner or Montessori system, reflect different cultural expectations. As a child care worker it is your responsibility to recognise cultural differences in expectations, and to respect these. In addition to respecting them you should ensure that these differences are reflected in activities in the care setting.

THINK IT THROUGH

After discussion with your supervisor, choose three or four children who you feel reflect cultural variations in expectations about their behaviour and intellectual development. Try to identify six areas of behaviour and intellectual development, and compare the children in the light of these. If possible, talk to some of the parents to ask about bedtimes, mealtimes, etc.

Duties and responsibilities of early years workers

When you are caring for children, you carry a great responsibility. When you are caring for someone else's child, you have been entrusted with that child's safety and well-being. Never underestimate this responsibility, because failing to meet it could have tragic results. In practising your child care skills, you must meet the responsibilities outlined below.

Commitment to the needs and rights of all children

The needs and rights of all children, regardless of any personal preference or prejudices you may have, must be respected. Working within equal opportunities guidelines is a vital part of your responsibility, and it includes challenging others who do not operate within them. You should treat all the children in your care as individuals, meeting their specific needs, rather than working to group needs alone. In protecting children's rights, you have a responsibility to report any bad practice that you may see; this is called 'whistleblowing'. It is not tale-telling, but is vital in protecting the rights of children in your care.

Case Study – Jane

Jane was a student in a private day nursery. While she was working in the toddler room with the owner's daughter, she was horrified to see the young woman smack some of the toddlers on the legs on several occasions. At first, Jane did not know what to do. She knew that it is against the law for a care worker to smack a child. She spoke to her tutor at college, who then went to see the owner. As a result, the owner sacked her daughter for the offence.

If you were Jane, how would you have dealt with this situation?

Witnessing bad practice puts you in a difficult situation. While you are a student, your tutors in college and placement supervisors are always a good source of help. They will have a knowledge of the local situation and will know how to handle the problem. Once you are qualified, you should speak to your line manager or his or her manager if necessary. Ultimately, you may have to report a problem to the social services department or the education authority. Never ignore bad practice; you have a responsibility to the children not to do so. A responsibility for the safety of children also means that you should always challenge any stranger who appears in the child care setting. If a person has a right to be there, he or she will not mind providing proof of identity. If a person should not be there, a challenge may make him or her leave quickly.

Respecting confidentiality and trust

In any area of care, you will hear and see a lot of confidential information about children and their parents. Remember that confidential information is not to be discussed with your friend on the bus, or told to your family at home. It could be that the person sitting behind you on the bus is linked to the family concerned.

Sometimes, however, you have to share information with colleagues. As a student or a junior worker remember: 'If in doubt, shout!' but rather than shouting, have a quiet discussion with your supervisor. This is called 'professional confidentiality', sharing information for the good of the children in your care.

THINK IT THROUGH

■ *Jolene, aged seven, tells you that she and her mummy are going on holiday to Spain next summer, but that it has to be kept a secret in the meantime from her little brother, aged four.*

■ *Javeed, aged six, tells you that his uncle has been showing him his penis, but it is a secret and no one has to know.*

Do you think you should keep both of these secrets to yourself, or should you share either of them with your supervisor? You do not need to share Jolene's secret with anyone, but clearly Javeed could be in need of protection, and it is your responsibility to share that secret. You should always tell a child that you cannot promise to keep everything he or she tells you a secret; if you do not say so, you may lose a child's trust.

Respecting parents and other adults

You will come across many differing types of child care practice and opinions on good practice. Life would be very dull if everyone had the same views. Provided that these diverse ways are all safe practice, that is fine. Different practices develop for all kinds of reasons, e.g. cultural, religious, geographical or social class. Your role as a carer is to respect other people's views, especially the views of parents whose children you care for, and to support them.

Good communication skills are your best working tools. You need to communicate with many different people.

Teamwork is all about communicating. Planning an activity with a group of children, and not telling other members of the team, could lead to conflict as someone else may have planned a similar or conflicting activity. You should always communicate the results of your observations. If you see a child being sick or sitting very quietly when he or she is usually very active, this information must be passed on.

Figure 4.8 *Child care workers need good, two-way communication with many different people*

Parents may need to be contacted, the child will certainly need some attention, and other children may be at risk. In order to communicate effectively in a team, it is important to know the procedures for doing so. There are usually lines of communication, or reporting must be done through line managers, in a large organisation. In a small organisation it may be appropriate to speak directly to the owner, manager or class teacher. Make sure you know who you should report to.

Other duties

Apart from these rather heavy responsibilities, there are several duties that you have towards children in your care. If you are a committed child care worker, the well-being of the children will be foremost in your thoughts. The following list shows some of your duties towards children you are caring for.

- Care for the children by showing you are pleased to see them, and expressing concern if they hurt themselves.

- Respect children as individuals and enjoy the fact that some children will want to play rough and tumble outdoor games with you, while others will prefer time in the story corner with you.

- Try to view the world through the eyes of a child. Suspend your own adult view of why the world is as it is, and you will get a lot of enjoyment from listening to a child's view.

- Try to enjoy yourself when working with children. If you are miserable at work, then the children in your care will be miserable as well.

- Aim to provide stimulating, enjoyable activities for children, but also to recognise when they need gentle, relaxing times.

- Help and promote children's activities, without taking over and running their lives for them.

- Remember that the children have parents and families who want to know about events in their child's day.

Parental consultation and involvement

Always remember that children have parents or guardians/carers. Stop and think why children attend their playgroup, nursery or school. Some of the reasons are:

- parents or carers are working

- a child needs playmates

- a need for intellectual and social stimulation

- to encourage delayed speech development

- the legal requirement to attend school

- parents need some space apart from their child

- the chance to play with toys and equipment that are not available at home.

Parents have a right to be involved with their child's education and care. They are the main carers in their child's life, and may be the main people the child has spent time with in the past. Remember that starting nursery or school can be a traumatic event for the parents as well as the child.

Parents, grandparents, aunts, in fact any member of a child's family, can enrich a nursery or school by contributing.

Joining the committee or parent-teacher group
Making new toys or storage
Making costumes for the concert
Helping a child to settle
Extra adults on outings
Reading stories
Listening to readers
Helping children bake
Fundraising
Baking for Christmas Fair
An extra pair of hands in the home corner

Figure 4.9 *Ways in which a parent can contribute to a nursery or school*

Parental involvement benefits both parent and child; parents may see alternative ways of helping their child, they will gain new ideas for activities, and children who are slow to settle in may be happier with a familiar adult around. Even if parents cannot or are unwilling to come to school or nursery, it is still important to work with them. Do not assume that parents who are not in contact or helping in nursery or school are not interested in their child. Very often, parents feel intimidated by schools. Parents are very important when a child is moving to another room or class. They can help in preparing a child for the change by talking about it at home, or reading appropriate books to their child.

THINK IT THROUGH

Consider your current work placement. Discuss the level of parental involvement with your supervisor, and make a list of points about this. Now think of any ideas as to how parents could be involved to a greater extent.

Communicating with parents is no different from communicating with other adults. Think about how you would communicate generally, and use those skills.

- Use the names parents wish you to use. Never assume that Jane Smith's mother is called Mrs Smith. Different cultures have different formats for family names. If in doubt, ask what you should call someone.

- Acknowledge when a parent is there. You may be busy with a child or talking to someone, but a brief turn of your head and a welcoming smile shows you have seen the parent.

- Give parents feedback about their child, e.g. 'Lia did a lovely painting today'.

- If you do not share the same language with parents, make sure that information is translated for them. You may both speak English, but it is very easy to use technical jargon that outsiders do not understand; *you* know that ELGs means early learning goals, but a parent may not.

- Make sure parents receive regular written information, e.g. letters, posters displayed in the setting, etc.

- Always make sure that written information is in a language the parent can read. If you are not sure if parents can read, it is better to speak to them to make sure vital information is received. Do not rely on a child to pass on written information; sometimes using the postal service might be a more reliable way.

- Be sensitive about conversations that may be embarrassing. If a parent is uncomfortable talking to you in the corridor, take the parent into an empty classroom or staff room to ensure privacy.

- Try not to appear shocked if you hear information that surprises you. You will alienate the parent, and you should not be making judgements.

- Remember that as a student you should not be dealing with difficult situations with parents, but should pass them on to a more senior member of staff.

THINK IT THROUGH

If possible, ask some parents of children about communications they receive from their child's nursery or school. Write down the details of letters and discussions they may have had, and ask if they were happy with them. If so, why? If not, what do they feel should have been said or written?

ASSESSMENT ACTIVITY

This assessment activity requires you to draw on your knowledge across all aspects of your work. It does not apply to just this unit. You need to review activities from other units to show most effectively your understanding of this important aspect of your role.

1. Describe the role and responsibilities of an adult working in early years settings

2. Explain the need for the worker to work in partnership with parents.

To achieve a **merit grade** you will need to use examples to suggest ways in which workers and parents can work together to promote children's development.

To achieve a **distinction grade** you will need to analyse the advantage to the child of parents and carers working in partnership.

CHILDREN'S ACTIVITIES AND PLAY

You have looked at children's development in detail, and at some specific activities to promote areas of development. This unit provides you with the opportunities to develop the practical skills required to work with children. You are now going to explore the range of activities that you can do with children. You will use your knowledge and understanding of milestones of development to plan, carry out and evaluate a series of activities. You will also identify ways of adapting the activities for children with additional needs. These are some of the fundamental tools of an effective child care worker.

In this unit you will learn about:

- practical activities for use with children
- activities for promoting development
- carrying out planned activities.

Practical activities for use with children

It is not enough to simply tell a child to play. Play can take many forms and can be of different qualities. As an early years worker you need to effectively plan and organise the play, and provide suitable materials in a suitable environment, to make sure that children have good experiences of play. You should ensure the activity is appropriate for the stage of development of the child. Also, you need to be there to support the children in the activity. You need to think about the following in your planning and preparation stage.

DID YOU KNOW?

John Locke writing about child care and planning for children's play in 1693 stated that children should have lots of different 'playthings'. He thought that children should only be allowed to use one toy at a time so that they would learn to look after them. He also felt that rather than buying toys, children should be encouraged to invent their own 'playthings' – for example, when they were given a toy like a top, children should be encouraged to make the stick and leather strap with which to spin the top.

Layout of the area
■ Is the area big enough for the planned activity? (Think about floor space, table space, sand or water tray if used.)

■ Are chairs, tables or any other equipment arranged to encourage children to work together (or alone – depending on the intended aim)?

■ Is there enough space for children to move about safely?

■ Are support facilities nearby if needed, e.g. sinks?

Equipment
■ Is the equipment suitable for the activity?

■ Is it suitable for the stage of development of the children?

■ Is the equipment safe and clean (no breakages, tears, incomplete equipment)?

■ Is there enough equipment for the children involved? (Think about aprons, cloths, brushes for cleaning up, protective coverings for floor, etc.)

Preparation
■ Make sure all the necessary equipment is put out or readily available.

■ Can the children reach everything they need?

■ Does the area look exciting and inviting to the children?

- Is everything on hand for adults to support (e.g. drying lines for paintings)?

- Have you got plans to follow on after the activity? (For example, does it lead into snack time? If so you will need to allow time for hand washing.)

- Does everyone involved know what is happening and what they need to do?

- Do other staff know of the plans and when the activity will finish?

- Do you have 'back up' plans? (For example, what if one child cannot do the activity? How will you adapt? If some children finish early do you have an extension planned?)

Support for play

- Be ready to offer help if a child needs or asks for it.

- Support does not mean taking over; ask questions about helping rather than be directive.

- Offer lots of praise and encouragement.

- Be ready with extra materials if appropriate, e.g. paint, paper.

- Withdraw from offering support if it is not needed.

- Be ready to guide less confident children into an activity if needed.

- Help with encouraging group activities.

- Encourage sharing of the activity through talking and listening to the children.

- Be ready to intervene if children are at risk of hurting themselves or others.

- Be ready to intervene if children are running out of ideas.

- Intervene if a learning opportunity arises that is too good to miss.

Finishing the activity

- Plan the ending of the activity as carefully as the main event.

- Have you got an area to display creative results?

- Have you planned time to clear up spilt sand or water, clean paintbrushes, tidy away dressing up toys, building materials, etc.?

- How will you ensure the area is clean, tidy and ready for the next person who uses it?

- Always involve the children in clearing away and tidying; it helps to develop their responsibility.

THINK IT THROUGH

Can you think of examples of an activity you have observed or planned that has not been well planned and supported by the adults? What happened and why do you think it happened? Looking at the guidelines above, what could have been done differently?

Language activities

Language development is a crucial part of a child's progress. Without communicating through language, reading and writing, it is very difficult to progress in life. Children learn language skills from before birth, by hearing

the sound of the mother's voice in the uterus. This continues through adults' constant communication with children, and you have a vital role to play in this. Reading stories, repeating rhymes and singing are an important part of your job as a child care worker.

When you are reading a story to a child or group of children, you need to give careful thought to the type of book you choose.

- Does it have a theme that will interest them, and that they can relate to?

- Are there attractive pictures to look at?

- Is the length appropriate to their age? Very young children need short stories that hold their attention, while older children may enjoy a story that can be read in a few instalments.

- Can you develop other activities from the story, e.g. rhymes, songs, paintings and so on?

Look in a good bookshop or the children's section of the library. You will see a selection of the following types of books:

- pop-up and flap books

- feely books

- dual-language books

- joke books

- books based on TV programmes and characters

- factual books about events such as the arrival of a new baby, or starting school.

Before selecting a book for use, make sure that it does not portray stereotypes of particular groups, e.g. always shows girls playing with dolls, or older people in rocking chairs. Books should reflect a mix of cultures, both ones that are familiar to the children and ones that offer new experiences.

Music activities

Music is a language common to all children. All children are exposed to music in some form, even if it is only on the radio or television. Music can be a very useful way to soothe a distressed baby, and in their first year babies will enjoy joining in by clapping hands and imitating the singing, accompanied by body movements. From the age of two, they enjoy singing with other children and can learn the words and tunes of songs. Music can allow children to explore their feelings and ideas, to develop their physical skills and co-ordination through dance, and their manipulative skills by playing instruments. Young children will enjoy music when:

- it has meaning in relation to things they know about, e.g. weather, time of year, festivities

- they can choose some of the music

- songs have accompanying actions

- they can accompany songs with instruments.

Musical instruments come in many types, and can be purchased or home-made. Simple instruments are those that involve:

- banging, e.g. drums, triangles, xylophones, tambourines

- shaking, e.g. maracas

- blowing, e.g. whistles.

Some of these are easy to make, for example shakers can be made from an empty container filled with a few dried beans or lentils, and drums can consist of a bowl with several layers of greaseproof paper or cling film, or a simple wooden box. Children can begin to learn simple scientific principles if they are shown the use of different-sized instruments, fillings, materials, etc.

Older children respond to the use of more sophisticated instruments such as recorders and keyboards. Children as

Plastic bottle containing pasta or beans for shaking

Blocks of wood to rub or knock together

Empty biscuit tin and wooden spoons make a 'drum'

Figure 5.1 *Some home-made musical instruments*

young as five can begin learning to play instruments in which they are interested. Parents need to be careful not to push the child too hard, or they may lose interest and confidence.

DID YOU KNOW?

By the age of three Wolfgang Amadeus Mozart was picking out tunes by ear on the piano and by the age of six was composing music.

Carrying out music and language activities

If you are reading to just one or two children, a quiet corner with comfortable seating is all you need. Ideally, you should be free from interruptions. Reading, singing or playing music to a group requires a little more thought to be given to the arrangement of the room.

- All the children should be able to sit comfortably and see what you are doing.

- Make sure there is adequate lighting.

- Try to use appropriate body language and expression to add interest to the book or songs. You may find it amuses the children if you use props such as hats and glasses, or different voices.

- Find points where the children can join in or repeat lines, to add to their interest.

- After you have finished, try to develop a discussion about the story or song, asking for the children's opinions or experiences.

THINK IT THROUGH

Have a look at two different stories with linked songs. What is each one about? How would you use them with children? If possible try using one pair with the children in your placement and write a short report on the project.

Prepared and improvised games, physical activities and role plays

Games are an excellent way of developing children's social skills; even young babies playing peek-a-boo are learning valuable skills. Older children learn about turn taking and rules through games. When you choose games to play with children, remember that a child under three cannot sit still for very long, and does not understand rules. A visit to a toy shop will show you a wide range of games, many of them expensive to buy, but it is possible to play games that cost very little or nothing.

Types of game	Examples of games
Table-top	Snap, pairs, lotto, matching games, counting games, Kim's game, Monopoly, Jenga
Physical games	Hide-and-seek, musical statues, football, rounders, hopscotch, obstacle races
Party games	Oranges and lemons, hunt the thimble, pass the parcel, musical chairs, sleeping lions

If you are playing games with children, especially younger ones, make sure that all the children have a go, and discourage serious competitiveness. Once they understand the rules, children are usually fiercely defensive of them and do not react well to 'cheats'. You will need to unobtrusively organise the games for younger children, as they will need help to take turns and understand what they have to do. Children will often enjoy playing an individual game such as snap with an adult, especially if they occasionally win.

Role-playing can be part of a game, involving dressing up and pretending to be someone else. Children can explore and express their feelings through role-play. They can use:

- everyday materials such as dressing-up clothes and items found in the home corner

- pre-prepared resources, e.g. a shop or café set up in the school or nursery

- resources from outside the children's experience, e.g. from other cultures, from history, etc.

Care should be taken that materials conform to health and safety requirements, and they should be monitored to check whether they need cleaning or repair work. With role-play, as with any game, it is essential that you give careful thought to the children who are going to participate. Can they all take part? Do you need to make any changes to the organisation of the activity to suit the children's needs?

THINK IT THROUGH

Explore the games and role-play materials at your placement. Ask if you can plan and use a game with a group of children. Write a description of how you planned and arranged the game, how it worked and any changes you had to make to suit the needs of the children involved.

Cooking activities

Most children enjoy cooking. Part of the enjoyment is creating something from a mix of items and learning about the changes that occur, then there is the fun of eating your results. Some children may have experienced cooking with parents or carers at home, but many may not have done so. Adult supervision is essential, and because small groups are usual, there is an excellent opportunity to talk with the children about the task, where the food comes from or other issues. Let the children do as much as possible themselves to encourage a sense of achievement. Many parents feel comfortable about helping out with cooking activities in nursery or school. There is the added bonus that if you involve parents, you and the children will learn about other cultures, or different recipes and ideas. In choosing cooking activities, consider the following factors:

- the ages and size of the group

- equipment and ingredients that are available

- time available

- the level of involvement of the children

- learning outcomes (such as science or numbers)

- dietary considerations: cultural and health matters (e.g. nut allergies) as well as personal preferences

- trying the recipe out first at home.

You do not need to confine cooking activities to making buns or rice crispy cakes. Cooking can also be 'cold cooking'. Think about involving children in making snacks such as sandwiches, toast, fruit or pizzas. Making jellies or milky whips involves changing textures and producing tasty results.

You need to think about the following issues when you are cooking with children:

- the safety of the children: access to hot surfaces, knives, etc.

- ease of access for the children to work comfortably and safely

- numbers of children who can work at one time

- hygiene: hand washing, etc.

- protection of clothing: aprons

- access to cleaning facilities: sink, washing up liquid

- safe storage of food.

THINK IT THROUGH

Plan a morning of cooking with a group of five-year-old children. You have been asked to choose something with a theme, e.g. Christmas, or a country. Write out your plan, describing the items needed, how you will involve the children and safety considerations.

Creating and using interest tables

Anything that can be put on a table or shelf can contribute to an interest table. Adults and children can provide items, and the main focus of an interest table is to allow children to touch and see objects of interest.

Good practice: interest tables

- Ensure that small children cannot pick up items they can swallow or chew.

- Place the table in a position where it will not be knocked over.

- Avoid food items that may spoil or present a health hazard if eaten.

- Discourage the presentation of insects, small animals, etc.

Interest tables usually have a theme, for example colours, toys, a country or holidays. It is possible to create a 'growing' table by planting bulbs, seeds or plants that can be observed in progress.

THINK IT THROUGH

With a partner, brainstorm as many themes for an interest table as possible.

Displaying items to their advantage and stimulating discussion is a task that needs to be thought through. The following steps will help.

- Cover the table with a plain cloth or fabric. Choose a colour that complements the objects to be placed on it.

- Use boxes and books under the cover to raise certain items above the level of the table.

- Do not include precious objects that could be lost or spoiled.

- Arrange objects so that children can see and touch them.

- Label objects neatly, and make sure the names of their providers are on them.

- Encourage the inclusion of everyday objects from home; contributions do not have to be exotic.

- Beware of inadvertently encouraging the picking of wild flowers or plants from gardens.

- Try to add additional material such as books or pictures relevant to the theme.

- Take a photograph of the finished table.

Once constructed, the interest table is a focus of attention and can be used to:

- stimulate discussion about the objects – what they are, where they are from, what they are used for, etc.

- stimulate creative activities – paintings, stories, model-making

- promote learning in areas of science, literacy and numeracy, and interest in the world at large.

THINK IT THROUGH

Using an idea that fits in with the aims of your placement, plan and prepare an interest table. Write about your experience, including details of the items shown, the use made of the table and any problems encountered. If possible, include a photograph of the finished display.

Activities involving plants and animals

Plants and animals both offer children many valuable opportunities including watching something grow and develop responsibility for care. There are, however, serious issues to consider for both plants and animals in an early years setting.

Plants

- Are any plants poisonous?

- Will they survive potentially rough handling?

- Do they grow quickly?

- What will the children learn from them?

- Can links be made to other activities?

DID YOU KNOW?

Of the many thousands of plants that exist, just over 100 have been proved to be poisonous or cause severe skin irritation.

Growing plants from seed is an excellent way of children seeing the change from a small seed or bulb into the final plant. Spring bulbs such as hyacinths are good for this. A hyacinth bulb can grow in a special glass vase and the root system can be seen as it develops. Growing seeds from beans is rapid and can be linked to stories such as Jack and the Beanstalk.

Pets

Pets obviously need much more care than plants, and need someone to look after them in the holidays and even weekends. A pet will usually be the first opportunity a child has to care for some other living being, and is a good way of encouraging the responsibility of feeding and caring. The age of the children is important; children who are too young cannot be expected to take a big role in their care. Small animals such as hamsters or gerbils are not good for very small children as they move too quickly, spend most of the day asleep and tend to bite easily. Issues to consider include the following:

- the age of the children
- children with allergies
- good hygiene practice: hand washing after handling the animals, cleaning up excreta quickly
- always supervising children when they are with the animals
- taking great care not to mix feeding bowls with human feeding plates, etc.
- encouraging a mature approach to animals from the children, e.g. they are not toys and may not always like to be handled.

Although animals give a lot of enjoyment to children, they can also pass on some serious diseases and injuries.

- Bites can cause infections, and dog bites can cause serious shock.
- Toxocaris are found in dog and cat faeces and can cause blindness or visual impairment.
- Fleas are found in dogs and cats.
- Ringworm is a fungal skin disease that can be caught from many animals.
- Salmonella can be caught from terrapins.

Equipment for activities

Materials for creative activities

Creative play allows children to express themselves and to discover the physical properties of the materials they are using. The role of the adult is to provide a range of materials and encourage experimentation. With creative activities, the process is far more important than the end product. Most creative play is potentially messy, and good preparation is necessary to avoid children spoiling their clothes or their surroundings; this takes away any anxiety from the activity. Consider safety aspects carefully, especially with young children who may put everything in their mouths. Be careful that dyes and colours are not poisonous. Some children may need encouragement to get their hands wet, dirty or covered in paint.

Activity	Materials and preparation
Painting and drawing	Tables, easels or the floor with adequate covering Different paints – poster, acrylic, ready-mixed, finger paints Chalks, pastels, wax crayons, glitter, felt tip pens Paper, card, brushes, rollers, sponges, potato shapes for printing
Junk modelling and collage	A wide range of boxes, containers, papers, materials, pasta, sawdust and shavings, sweet wrappers, sequins Scissors, glue, aprons
Sand and water	Both can be indoor or outdoor, and need attention to safety Purpose-built trays, mix of wet and dry sand Water with different coloured dyes, soapy suds, bottles, jugs, funnels, sponges, objects that sink and float Sand scoops, sieves, spades, buckets, toy cars
Clay, dough and plasticine	Home-made or bought dough of different consistencies, colours and smells Plasticine and clay Rolling pins, cutters, scissors, boards, plates, modelling tools

Most creative activities will stimulate all areas of a child's development. Hand–eye co-ordination is promoted, along with manipulative skills, language in talking about the work, emotional expression, pride in seeing work displayed or completed, and social skills in turn taking. When you are selecting activities for children, make sure that they will all be capable of carrying out the activity. If you have to help them with everything, there will be little sense of achievement and they will soon lose interest.

Always recognise a child's efforts at creative activities, and ask the child to tell you about what has been made or done. If possible, write a short statement of this to attach to the work. Make sure that the child's name is on the work, and that unless it is going on display it is given to the child to take home.

THINK IT THROUGH

Spend some time looking through the resources in your placement and reading catalogues to find out about the wide range of creative materials available. Ask if you can have small samples and make notes on their uses. Put your findings into a file to make a personal catalogue of resources for creative activities. Every time you develop a creative activity, put a sample in your file, with a note of the materials needed and instructions for use.

Indoor and outdoor play equipment

Large and small play equipment can be used to encourage children's physical development. Large-scale equipment will enhance gross motor development and co-ordination, while small play equipment encourages manipulative and fine motor skills.

Which of the following equipment is in use in your placement:

- climbing frames
- play tunnels
- swings
- slides
- trampolines
- seesaws
- ropes and rope ladders
- sit-and-ride toys
- bicycles and tricycles
- large balls, hoops, beanbags?

All large equipment needs plenty of space if it is to be used safely. Children will enjoy using it either indoors or out of doors, but wherever it is used you must think about:

- protective matting for the floor in case of falls, and avoiding the risk of falls onto dangerous objects
- adequate adult supervision
- avoiding too many children trying to use the equipment at once
- adaptations and support for children with physical disabilities.

If your placement has a wide selection of equipment, try to find out how the adults decide which item is to be used. Children enjoy variety in activities, and keeping a piece of equipment for occasional use will make it a treat. For example, a trampoline needs close supervision, so it can be used only at certain times. Large-scale equipment needs careful checking before use for loose parts, broken sections and cleanliness. If it is kept outside, covers should be put over it. If possible, equipment should be stored indoors to prevent spoilage.

Small equipment has fewer potential hazards and requires less space. It offers great potential for children to develop their self-esteem, as results are almost instantaneous. An important rule about selecting suitable small equipment is that smaller children need bigger pieces, while larger (older) children enjoy smaller pieces. The safety issues are obvious: small children can and will put small items in their mouths, and may choke.

Smaller children should also be kept away from older children's construction and modelling work to avoid the accidental destruction of their efforts. Small play equipment includes:

- stacking beakers
- Duplo
- jigsaws of many types
- foam blocks
- construction straws, stickle bricks, Meccano, etc.

- posting boxes
- Lego
- interlocking train sets
- wooden blocks

THINK IT THROUGH

For which age group might small equipment be suitable? Put an approximate age range against each type of equipment listed above.

As with large play equipment, you need to be selective in the amount of equipment you put out. Small play materials need to be carefully stored in boxes or trays, keeping different sized pieces separate. Tables should be arranged to confine each type to a separate area. In this way, toys will be kept in good condition and not get mixed up or lost.

DID YOU KNOW?

When Maria Edgeworth was writing in 1789 she thought that a nursery should be filled with toys that led to experimenting. These included sturdy carts, gardening tools, printing presses, looms and furniture that can be taken to pieces and put together again, pencils, scissors, tools and workbenches. How does this compare with the toys and equipment at your placement?

THINK IT THROUGH

1 You have been asked to set up the small play equipment area for the morning session in a nursery for three- and four-year-olds. How would you approach this? What types of toys would you put out? What safety considerations would you have to bear in mind?

2 How does your placement provide opportunities for using large play equipment? What are the most popular items? How are safety issues managed?

Activities for promoting development

All early years centres should provide plenty of opportunities to learn and develop skills. This should be in a safe environment, but one that is exciting and encourages the children to try out new activities and skills, as well as the familiar activities that they feel comfortable with. The emphasis of Sure Start is to actively promote children's development through attention to all contributing factors. This aim is one that should be shared in all early years settings and for all ages of young children and babies.

Planning activities

The planning of activities will take place at several levels:

- for the overall setting, for all children

- within sections of the setting, e.g. different age groups

- on a long-term basis, e.g. each term or three-month time spell

- monthly

- weekly

- daily.

As a trainee early years worker you may be lucky enough to be at meetings where the overall plan and themes are being decided, at least in the department you are working in. You certainly should be able to see the plan for the coming weeks, and look at where you could plan some individual activities within that. There are different ways of planning an activity, even within the early years curriculum. Remember that:

- children need the chance to explore and experiment without a very structured activity; to learn by experience

- children need direction to achieve certain outcomes for their overall development

- children can learn many different skills from one activity.

Unstructured planning occurs when an adult provides an activity for children to use in their own way. The outcomes may be very different from the intention of the adult. For example, a water play activity with different containers for different volumes and density may result in the children discarding the heavier items and larger containers and using the smaller, lighter ones as boats. A structured activity is planned by the adults with a specific learning outcome as the focus, for example, a cooking activity to investigate ingredients, ask why things happen, aid personal, social and emotional development, and encourage working as part of a group and taking turns. An experiential activity uses the environment and expected or unexpected activities to learn from, for example the arrival of new-born lambs in the field adjoining the nursery; an adult or child going to the dentist. Thematic activities use a realistic activity relevant to a child's experience to provide opportunities to develop in several or all areas of the curriculum, for example a trip to the local park or a 'shop' inside the setting. A thematic plan is often split into the various areas of development to ensure a range of suitable activities are provided. Extension activities can then be included, for example if there are ducks on the pond in the park a suitable story and songs can be used back at the centre. Relevant creative work using images and experiences can be planned.

You may see a planning system that focuses on the five main areas of development as the one below shows.

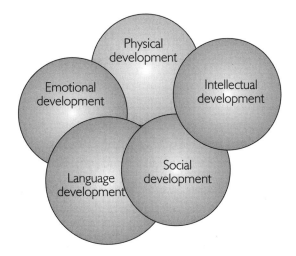

Another approach is to actively consider the six areas of learning within the foundation stage, as shown below.

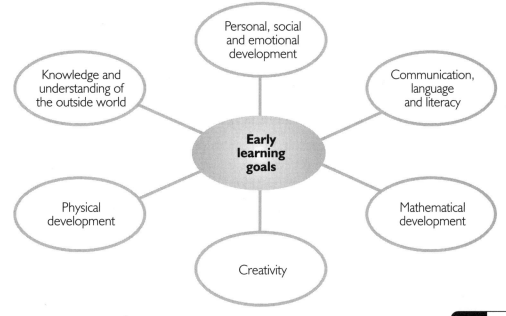

Things to think about when planning are different at the different levels of planning. Your supervisor will be thinking about some of the following points.

■ How will I check that the range of activities is balanced to support all aspects of development?

■ How will plans be adjusted for different needs and ages and for all the children?

■ How will learning and progression by the children be observed and recorded?

■ How will the activities be presented to the children?

■ What will the role be of staff in delivering the activities?

■ How will parents be informed, and where possible involved, in their children's learning?

Who should be consulted when planning activities?

As the children are the central characters in each activity you do, it is a good idea to consult older children (over the age of three). There is little point in developing an activity, at much expense of time and resources, only to discover the children are not interested in it. Working within the Early Years Curriculum, you are aiming for a well-balanced programme, facilitating all-round development. You will also have other aims in planning activities.

■ Do they fit in with the overall plan or theme of the setting?

■ Are they suitable for the time of year? There is little point in working on a theme of winter in March – far better to use spring.

■ Are the materials you need easily available and cost effective? Grand schemes using the entire materials budget for the term will not make you popular.

■ Will there be enough or too many children for the activity? Think about timing at the start and end of terms, holidays, etc.

■ Are there any cultural implications? Be careful not to offend children, parents or other carers. An activity based on food during the Muslim fasting period of Ramadan would be rather insensitive.

■ Is the activity planned for a suitable time in the nursery or school day? Try not to have a very boisterous activity just before rest time, or when the children have just come in from outdoor play.

■ Does your plan conflict with anyone else's? Children need diversity, and a repetition of an activity they have already done may not be a great success.

- If appropriate, will it be possible to display the results for parents and visitors to see?

- Are there any other constraints, e.g. other activities in the building, outside visits and so on?

- Can all the children join in? Some activities may exclude children with disabilities, illness, allergies, etc.

- Are there any health and safety implications?

- Are any permissions required, especially for trips out of school or nursery?

If you look carefully at the points above, the list of people you may have to consult should become apparent:

- head of your placement

- other child care staff

- parents

- for outside trips, the organisations you might be visiting, people involved in transport, etc.

- social service registration unit to check on staff ratios for visits

- kitchen staff if food is involved

- cleaning or care-taking staff if any mess is likely to be made.

> **THINK IT THROUGH**
>
> *Jason is planning a week of activities in the private nursery school where he works, around the colour red. He plans to read stories, set up an interest table, do some baking with the children, go for a walk in the park and the high street, and do some painting and modelling to be put on display.*
>
> *Make a list, giving reasons, showing who he will need to consult before he finalises his plans, and add notes explaining how he might do so.*

Planning for all – cultural differences and equal opportunities

It is essential that you always promote the interests of all the children in your activity. Careful consideration is needed to be sure that all children can join in, and that adaptations can be made to accommodate a child who may be shy or timid, have hearing impairments, or have poor co-ordination in his or her movements, in fact any particular need a child with. If you have children from a range of cultural backgrounds, it is your duty to be aware of any limitations that may affect your activity.

Research other cultures in depth. Involve parents or other members of the community to help, and celebrate the diversity of all our cultures in a fun and interesting way. Think of ways you can promote positive images of different cultures and social classes. Think about books, posters and materials that you use. Will any child feel excluded by them? For example, a story that concentrates on a family setting with both parents at home is fine, but you need to balance this by pictures of one-parent families.

Help !

If you ask children to bring items in for a topic or the interest table, be sure it will not cost too much for the family. Be sensitive to children when talking about festivals; families who are Jehovah's Witness do not celebrate Christmas or birthdays. The key factor to think about is to consider each individual child; always ask yourself the following questions.

- What are each child's needs?

- How are they different to the needs of another child?

- How might this activity need adapting to meet their need?

Areas you need to think about include:

- culture

- language

- social class

- family situation

- health

- disability

- stage of development.

Activities need careful thought to make them accessible to all. A child may have difficulty joining in because of:

- cultural issues, for example a Muslim girl may not be able to join in an activity requiring shorts to be worn

- religion, for example a Jehovah's Witness would not be able to join in activities that celebrate Christmas

- gender issues, for example boys may take over a construction activity because of poor attention to gender issues in the setting, or be pushed out of cooking activities by the girls

- an activity being too boisterous for a timid child

■ an activity requiring a skill level a child does not possess.

Reassessing an activity to make sure that it is suitable for all the children is often only a case of remembering the basic principles shown in the checklist below.

Good practice: planning activities

■ Make sure you have a thorough knowledge of the children in the group before you start planning.

■ Is there enough room for children to move around?

■ Is the equipment suitable for all children? Have you provided a range of sizes of paint brushes, for example?

■ Is there special equipment for particular children?

■ Can equipment be reached by all the children, to promote independence?

■ Do any of the children require practical assistance, e.g. putting on aprons, moving to the table?

■ Ask the children if they need help, rather than waiting for them to ask you.

When you are planning activities that develop a child's creative skills, do not make the mistake of basing your planning on your own cultural or gender identity. You will not meet all needs in this way. Look at the following examples.

■ When baking it would be easy to limit your ideas to those you are familiar with, especially as you want to be comfortable with the activity. A simple way of broadening it is to ask a parent from a culture other than yours to be involved.

■ Look for books or computer software that are in dual languages, e.g. English and Urdu, that will appeal to all children in your nursery or school.

■ When setting up an interest table, use the opportunity to focus on another culture or race.

■ Choose a topic that is popularly viewed as mainly female or male, and deliberately widen the appeal and interest to both genders.

DID YOU KNOW?

Recent research shows that boy and girl babies as young as nine months show preference for different types of toys. There are two explanations for this. The most common view is that children are influenced by adults but some other research suggests that it is because of biological differences between boys and girls. Whatever the reason, it is essential that both boys and girls should be encouraged to play with all toys.

THINK IT THROUGH

You have been looking for a book to read to the children that can be developed into an activity and you have chosen Cinderella. As you read it, you realise that it is based on gender and ability. The wicked stepmother is very stereotypical too. How could you adapt the story, and subsequent activities, to challenge these stereotypes?

The Early Years Curriculum

As you learned in Unit 4, the foundation stage has six areas of learning which form the basis of the foundation stage curriculum. Each area of learning has a set of early learning goals as targets for achievement by a child. Activities in the early years setting must be planned to cover all of the early learning goals with the following considerations.

- Personal, social and emotional development outcomes focus on children learning to work, play, co-operate with others and function in a group. They cover important aspects of personal, social, moral and spiritual development.

- Communication, language and literacy outcomes cover important aspects of language development and provide the foundation for literacy.

- Mathematical development outcomes cover important aspects of mathematical understanding and provide the foundation for numeracy.

- Knowledge and understanding of the world outcomes focus on children's developing knowledge and understanding of their environment, other people and features of the natural and made world.

- Physical development outcomes focus on children's developing physical control, mobility, awareness of space and manipulative skills.

- Creative development outcomes focus on the development of children's imagination and their ability to communicate and to express ideas and feelings.

Underlying the curriculum are some basic principles about how children learn.

- Children learn best when material suits the stage they have reached in their development.

- Attention needs to be given to the whole child, that is, to physical, moral and emotional needs as well as intellectual needs.

- Children learn in an integrated manner, they do not separate learning to speak from learning about numbers.

- Children learn best when they are allowed to try things out and make mistakes.

- Children need to have their efforts recognised and valued.

- You should always start with what a child can do, not what a child cannot do.

- Conditions for learning have to be positive to ensure the development of creativity and imagination; children need materials and encouragement.

- There are particular times when a child is ready to learn certain skills.

- A child's relationships with other children and adults are very important.

ASSESSMENT ACTIVITY

Demonstrate an understanding of the early learning goals.

Produce a simple explanatory sheet for parents of new entrants to nursery, explaining what the Foundation Stage Curriculum is.

To achieve a **merit grade** explain how activities in the nursery are linked to early learning goals and the Foundation Stage and the Key Stage 1 curriculum.

No extension to distinction is possible for this assessment.

Activities suitable for different children in different care settings

Effective planning can make all the difference to the success of an activity. You may have heard staff using the phrase 'planning cycle'. The planning cycle is a very useful tool in your work with young children.

Planning cycle

Planning happens at a variety of levels in a child care setting. It can be over a term, a month or a week ahead. The following flow chart demonstrates how a theme is developed, using the example of the theme of change.

Within the framework of the overall plan, there will be small-scale planning of individual activities to ensure that the needs of all children are met.

Activities such as baking lend themselves to being carried out in both group and home-based child care settings. In fact, the close link between home and school or nursery can be valuable. Children of all ages usually enjoy baking, and the complexity and involvement can be increased with older children at different stages of development. Different cultures and dietary requirements can be explored with baking, often with the help and support of parents and other adults from the community. Your planning sheet could include a note showing how you would use the activity with different age groups and in different settings.

Few, if any activities, can be enjoyed only by a narrow age range, or in only one setting. A well thought out plan, with attention to the skill level of the particular children you are working with, should ensure an activity is matched to the ability of the children.

Activity Planning Sheet	
Group Blue group	**No of children 8**

Age range   4 to $4\frac{1}{2}$

Planning activity   Baking fairy cakes

Outcomes	Learning about transformation of ingredients – science Finding out about why things happen – knowledge and understanding of the world Numeracy – weighing, counting, time Turn taking Manipulative skills – mixing, spooning into cases

Room Kitchen	**Date and time** Monday 12 October 11am

Resources

250 g self-raising flour
2 eggs
250 g margarine
250 g sugar
milk

Icing sugar, cherries, hundreds and thousands

Bun baking tray, bowls and wooden spoons, aprons, scales

Plan of action

1. Explain activity to children
2. Divide group into two – Mrs Smith will work with other half
3. Take children to wash hands and put on aprons
4. Explain need to be orderly, keep away from the oven, and for hygiene
5. Start baking – ask each child to weigh one ingredient, allow each to stir
6. Let children fill three bun cases each
7. Bake
8. Clear away and wash up – children to take the lead
9. Allow buns to cool, while other group bake
10. Mix icing and allow children to decorate buns
11. Identify owners of buns
12. Allow eating of one bun – take the other two home.

Points to consider

Safety in the kitchen
Conversation to explain process, what they can see happening
Asking for experiences at home, with grandparent, etc.
Ask about preference for buns, favourite foods, where else they get cakes.

THINK IT THROUGH

You have volunteered to do some baking with the children to show how flour, eggs, margarine and milk can change into buns to eat. You need to give a lot of thought to the task to make sure it works well. Using a planning sheet such as the one shown opposite will help your thought processes.

If you are working with a group of children with a wide range of skill levels, greater care will be needed. You may have to adapt the activity within the group to allow for this. For example, in a baking activity, some children may not be able to weigh the ingredients, due to lack of manual skills. They could be asked to put out the bun cases, and be more involved in stirring the mixture. Some children may be able to recognise the required weight on the scales, while others pour the flour into the scale pan.

THINK IT THROUGH

You have been asked to provide a creative activity for a group of six children aged four. Choose an activity – it could be one you have already used – and complete a planning sheet, indicating how you will allow for different skill levels and interests.

Skills required to perform planned activities

All the planning and preparation involved in a successful activity will be wasted if you have not thought about a vital question: have the children reached the required stage of development, and do they possess the skills necessary to take part in and enjoy the activity? A good understanding of child development and observation of children playing and working will help you to develop the knowledge you need to work out the answer to this question. Most activities are planned with the aim of extending children's skill levels, but skills cannot be extended or developed if the child is not ready for that next step. One example is the use of jigsaws. It requires quite a high degree of manipulative skill to put jigsaw pieces together, and children need to learn to use slot-in jigsaw boards first, where they can match the picture underneath. Next they move on to jigsaws with very large pieces, and gradually move to harder puzzles.

THINK IT THROUGH

Can you think of an activity you have prepared for which the child was not ready? What did you do in the situation?

The chart below should help you to choose activities matched to the age and stage of development of the children you are working with.

Age	Play needs of the child	Indoor equipment	Outdoor equipment
1–2	The child is mobile and gaining gross motor and fine manipulative skills. The child needs plenty of opportunities to strengthen muscles and develop co-ordination.	Push and pull toys Toys that make music Dolls Trolleys Building bricks Posting toys	Paddling pool Baby swing Small slide
2–3	Children are starting to notice and play with other children. Their language is increasing and much of their play is pretend play. Children are gaining confidence in physical movements and enjoy playing outside. Children of this age can be easily frustrated and have a short concentration span – less than 10 minutes – so they need opportunities to be independent in their play and range of activities. There should be plenty of equipment as children find it difficult to share with each other.	Dressing-up clothes Home corner equipment – e.g. tea sets, prams, cooking utensils, pretend telephones Building blocks Toy cars and garages Dolls and cuddly toys Dough Paint Jigsaw puzzles Musical instruments	Paddling pool Sand and water tray Slide Climbing frame Swings Sit and ride toys Tricycles
3–4	Children are starting to co-operate with each other and enjoy playing together. Most of their play is pretend play. Pieces of dough become cakes; tricycles become cars! Children enjoy physical activity, gaining confidence in being able to use large equipment – e.g. climbing frames. They are also developing fine manipulative skills and beginning to represent their world in picture form.	'Small world' play – e.g. playmobile, Duplo figures Dressing-up clothes Home corner and equipment Dough and other malleable materials Water and sand Construction toys such as train tracks, building bricks Jigsaw puzzles	Climbing frame Slide Paddling pool Tricycles Bicycles with stabilisers Balls and bean bags

Age	Play needs of the child	Indoor equipment	Outdoor equipment
4–6	Children are more interested in creating things – e.g. making a cake, drawing cards and planting seeds. Children enjoy being with other children although they may play in pairs. Children are beginning to express themselves through painting and drawing as well as through play. Children are enjoying using their physical skills in games and are confident when running and climbing.	Materials for junk modelling Cooking activities Dough and other malleable materials Jigsaws Home corner Construction toys Small world play – e.g. Duplo people Simple board games	Mini gardening tools Skipping ropes Hoops Climbing frame Slide Tricycles Different-sized balls
6–8	Children are confident and can play well with other children. Children are starting to have particular play friends and are able to share ideas about their play. Games that involve rules are played and rules are added and changed as necessary! Most children enjoy physical activity and play organised games. Sometimes this age can be very competitive. Children are also keen on making things – either of their own design or by following instructions.	Creative materials – e.g. junk modelling, crayons, pieces of card and paper Board games Jigsaw puzzles Complex construction toys Books Collections – e.g. stamps, stickers	Balls Hoops Bicycles Roller-skates Skipping ropes Climbing frames Slides Swings

THINK IT THROUGH

Think about at least three activities that you have carried out with children in your placement, all using different skills. Make a chart giving the age of the children you worked with, the skills the activities required, and notes on how the children coped with the activity. You should also indicate if you had to make any changes as a result of your observations.

Carrying out planned activities

Using equipment and space effectively

Children are cared for in a variety of settings:

- a childminder's home

- the child's home

- church halls and community halls e.g. playgroups or crèches

- classrooms in schools

- adapted buildings used as nurseries

- purpose-built nurseries

- parts of sports halls e.g. playgroups or crèches

- areas of shopping centres e.g. playgroups or crèches.

Some of these areas are easier to arrange for effective care and activities than others. A purpose-built unit will have tables, sinks, toilets, etc. all designed for children, and equipment will have suitable storage. Buildings that are used for other purposes, such as community centres, pose a challenge, as you will probably share storage space with other groups and have to adapt furniture and fittings. However, the size or quality of the space is less important than how it is used. Careful planning can make the most of the available space, and help to ensure that children's needs are met. Always make sure that:

- entrances and exits are kept clear (especially fire exits)

- the room is well ventilated and at a temperature of between 18 and 21°C

- the room is well lit and has good access to natural light

- there is enough space for the activities, and for the children to move around; if space is limited, it is good practice to set out fewer activities at a time

- there is room for wheelchair users to move around

- there are sinks near to 'messy' activities such as painting or dough, and the flooring and tables for these activities are protected or very easy to clean

- the book corner is well lit, with comfortable furniture or a carpet

- the room is easy to clean and is not cluttered with other equipment

- toys, games and equipment are stored effectively, and are easy for the children to access.

All settings must have a quiet area where a child can go to relax, perhaps listen to a story or go to sleep. The range of facilities for this will vary from a carpeted corner, a sofa or chairs, to a separate room with cots or beds.

Children should never be presented with toys or games that are broken, dirty or have parts missing. They will not enjoy playing with them, they could be dangerous, and a child will be frustrated with a jigsaw that has a piece missing. Your role is to check toys and equipment before the children have access to them. This should be done as they are put away and again as they are put out for use. Equipment that is broken should be attended to straight away, and broken toys should be thrown away. You should also ensure that everything that will be needed for a particular activity is available and ready for use.

Health and safety issues were discussed in detail in Unit 3. It is essential that you keep the principles of health and safety in mind when you are planning and carrying out activities. Remind yourself of the main points by using the following checklist.

Good practice: health and safety

- Is there adequate adult supervision? Are more adults needed for certain activities?

- Is the building secure, to prevent strangers from entering and children from wandering off?

- Are there any hidden dangers in the immediate area, e.g. tools, steep steps, badly protected pools?

- If outside, are there any poisonous plants or berries within children's reach?

- Are fire exits clear and extinguishers in place?

- Is the flooring safe: no frayed carpet edges, loose rugs, splinters in wooden floors?

- Is all basic furniture and equipment in good condition, and not liable to be pulled over?

- Are safety items in place, e.g. mats under climbing frames, safety gates, childproof locks and so on?

- Are all toys and games safe to use and clean?

- Are spills cleaned up immediately?

- Do adults understand they must not have hot drinks in an area where children are playing?

- Is there adequate provision for waste disposal?

- Is there a clear and practical routine for cleaning the setting and equipment?

Being constantly on the alert for possible dangers will help to prevent accidents and illnesses in children. As soon as you spot a potential hazard, do something about it. Remove a broken toy, mop up a spillage, and report anything that you cannot deal with to your supervisor. If you do not do so and a child is injured, you could be held responsible under the Health and Safety at Work legislation.

THINK IT THROUGH

How clear are the health and safety guidelines at your placement. Have you ever noticed something that needed fixing or cleaning up? Did you know what to do?

Providing guidance, support and supervision during activities

Children should not undertake any activity without the supervision and support of an adult. This is for many reasons, including the following:

- safety: to prevent accidents and ensure safe usage of equipment
- to help children to start an activity, by explaining to them what the activity involves and perhaps demonstrating it
- to provide help when children need it, e.g. when they encounter a difficulty or reach a natural pause in an activity
- to support children who need extra assistance
- to keep order in the group, facilitating turn taking and the sharing of equipment
- to help with the ending of the activity, displaying the work and tidying up
- to help the child to move on to the next activity, game or break.

There is a difference between offering guidance and support to children and taking over and doing things for them. The best way to learn this skill is to observe experienced people. Guidance and support is about:

- asking if you can help
- offering plenty of praise
- suggesting easier or alternative ways, by asking 'have you tried ...?'
- listening to children's thoughts and ideas, and asking questions to prompt them
- being a quiet presence during activities

■ observing from a distance to avoid intruding, but being ready to step in if needed.

Children need supervision so that they feel secure and protected. The presence of adults will give them the confidence to try activities that are new or difficult. Supervision of children in a care setting is a legal requirement, but it should also be common sense.

THINK IT THROUGH

If possible, spend one of your sessions in placement shadowing an experienced child care worker. Make notes on how the worker offers guidance and support to the children he or she is with, and how supervision is provided. Try to decide if the level of guidance and support is appropriate, or whether children sometimes seem 'lost' or over-supported. What are the skills the carer is using? Think about communication skills, practical assistance, demonstration techniques, etc.

Reviewing activity plans

Whenever you plan an activity for a child or group of children you should complete a planning sheet that also has space to allow you to review it later. Why should you review activities? Because reviewing allows you to reflect on the following points:

■ the success of the activity in achieving your aims

■ why it was successful or unsuccessful

■ any alterations you need to make next time

■ why you needed to make alterations, for example if it was too easy or too hard, or did not suit a child with a physical impairment

■ whether the time allowed was long enough or too long

■ whether the children enjoyed the activity

■ whether the equipment was suitable and adequate

■ safety issues

■ how the activity could be developed for older or younger children

■ how you would use the activity again in the future.

You will find it helpful to use a form with these headings, perhaps kept in a notebook or file, for the purpose of reviewing activities.

Case Study – Liam

Liam planned a game of snakes and ladders with four children aged five. This well-known game offers opportunities for number work, turn taking and sharing. After ten minutes, the game was in uproar, and one little girl was pushed over. The game had to be stopped. In his review, Liam recognised several issues.

- Four children were too many for the board size; a bigger board would have improved matters.

- The table he was using was too small to allow space for the children to spread out. A larger table was needed, with the children sitting down.

- There were long gaps between turns; two dice would have kept the pace moving.

- The dice he used was too small, and he only had one; a larger dice would be easier to see.

- He needed to have a better awareness of potential tensions between the children.

This example of the game of snakes and ladders shows how even simple activities can be improved. Reviewing a creative activity might need thought about materials, or even the basic plan. Can you think of anything else Liam could have done differently?

THINK IT THROUGH

Choose an activity the next time you are in your placement and write a detailed review of it, using the checklist above. What lessons have you learned from the review?

Reporting on outcomes

Virtually everything children do in school or nursery will have an impact on their skill levels in some way. As a child care worker you have a responsibility to report on the progress or lack of progress that you see in children, both to your supervisor and to parents or carers. Schools and nurseries are expected to assess children's progress against attainment targets for schoolchildren and desirable outcomes for pre-schoolers. Senior staff cannot do all the observation and work involved in assessing these attainments, and rely on their support staff for help and information.

It is also important for individual children that you report on outcomes. A child may be making exceptional progress in reading, for example, and need more challenging material, or may be having some difficulty and need easier material. A child may also need to be assessed for reasons other than academic progress, perhaps on behaviour or emotional reactions.

Make sure that you are aware of the feedback that will be required before you start an activity. If you are in doubt, ask. If a formal assessment sheet must be completed, make a copy of it and record your findings on the copy. You can then complete the sheet in a legible fashion. If there is no formal feedback form, you may find it easier to make notes in a small notebook as you work with the child, or immediately after the activity has finished. Always be factual in your reporting, 'Jolene has read very well today' is too vague. It would be far better to say 'Jolene read to page 12, and did not make any mistakes'. Reports of behaviour should be specific; try to avoid terms such as 'disruptive' or 'naughty'.

Carers who have left their children with other adults want feedback at the end of the session, because they are genuinely interested in what their child has been doing. Most parents like to hear positive things about their child, so always tell them something positive, even if it is only that the child ate all of his or her lunch. Most children do some positive work, e.g. painting a lovely picture, or building a big bridge with bricks. Unit 7 looks in greater depth at communicating with parents.

THINK IT THROUGH

Ask your supervisor about all the different reporting methods used in your placement. Using one of them, write a report on the activity you reviewed in the last section. You should show what you will report to your supervisor and what you will report to parents.

Planning outings

Children enjoy and benefit from outings of all descriptions, ranging from going to post a letter, to a full day trip to the seaside or country. Trips and visits fulfil many functions for children.

- They provide new experiences.
- They develop new awareness.
- They build on skills and abilities.

Taking children out from school or nursery is potentially a hazardous occupation. However, the biggest potential for problems lies in being too ambitious.

Choose a place to visit:

- that is not too far to travel
- that will not be too tiring for the adults or children
- with plenty of interest at a suitable level for the age of the children.

Popular places for trips include the following:

- local parks
- farms
- museums, particularly hands-on types
- fire stations
- behind the scenes in large shops
- the countryside for a picnic
- adventure playgrounds.

A successful outing requires a lot of planning, and all those involved should meet to discuss and plan the trip. Parents will want to be convinced that their children will be safe with you. A visit to check the facilities and the potential of the locations should be made before children or parents are told about the trip. When you are planning an outing you must consider all of the factors shown below.

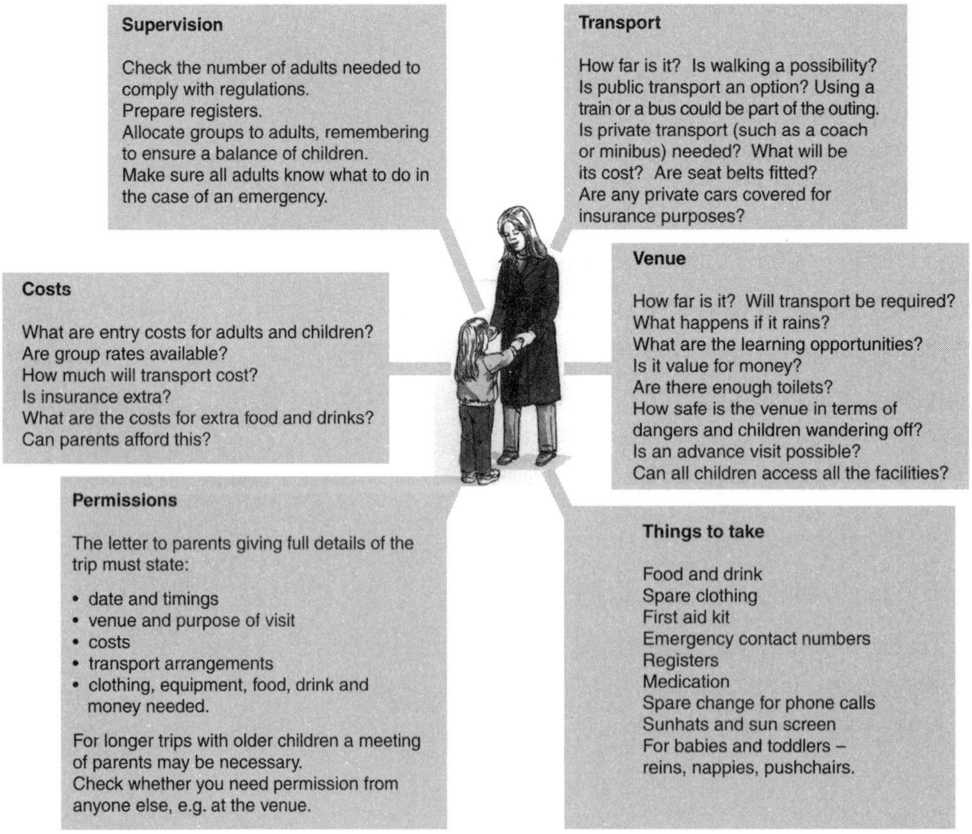

Supervision

Check the number of adults needed to comply with regulations.
Prepare registers.
Allocate groups to adults, remembering to ensure a balance of children.
Make sure all adults know what to do in the case of an emergency.

Transport

How far is it? Is walking a possibility? Is public transport an option? Using a train or a bus could be part of the outing. Is private transport (such as a coach or minibus) needed? What will be its cost? Are seat belts fitted? Are any private cars covered for insurance purposes?

Costs

What are entry costs for adults and children?
Are group rates available?
How much will transport cost?
Is insurance extra?
What are the costs for extra food and drinks?
Can parents afford this?

Venue

How far is it? Will transport be required? What happens if it rains?
What are the learning opportunities? Is it value for money?
Are there enough toilets?
How safe is the venue in terms of dangers and children wandering off?
Is an advance visit possible?
Can all children access all the facilities?

Permissions

The letter to parents giving full details of the trip must state:

- date and timings
- venue and purpose of visit
- costs
- transport arrangements
- clothing, equipment, food, drink and money needed.

For longer trips with older children a meeting of parents may be necessary.
Check whether you need permission from anyone else, e.g. at the venue.

Things to take

Food and drink
Spare clothing
First aid kit
Emergency contact numbers
Registers
Medication
Spare change for phone calls
Sunhats and sun screen
For babies and toddlers –
reins, nappies, pushchairs.

Figure 5.2 *Planning outings*

THINK IT THROUGH

In a group of three or four plan an outing for 12 children aged three and four. Choose somewhere local to you, so that you can visit it and assess all the points you have read about above.

Discuss what you would need to do if you were carrying this out; list all the tasks on a flip chart and compare with other groups.

ASSESSMENT ACTIVITY

This is the final summary activity that covers nearly all the knowledge and skills from this unit. It also requires you to think about a lot of information from most of the other units as well. If you have been completing the activities throughout this unit you will have already carried out much of the pass criteria. Now is the opportunity for you to reflect on your skills and achieve the merit and distinction grades.

The best way of approaching the assessment for this unit is to practise planning and delivering small-scale activities in your placement. When you are feeling confident, discuss with your supervisor two activities that you could plan, deliver and evaluate with a small group of children. One should be indoors, the other outdoors and they should be capable of covering more than one of the early learning goals. Keep notes of your planning and delivery and review the success; these will form the basis of your assessment. Keep it simple; do not be tempted to try to impress with a complex activity.

1   Plan and carry out an indoor and an outdoor activity for children at a specific developmental stage (e.g. children in your setting).

2   Describe ways to lay out indoor and outdoor play areas with special regard to the use of space and health and safety issues.

3   Describe the process of planning, reviewing and evaluating activities.

To achieve a **merit grade** you will need to undertake a review of your activity and suggest ways it could be improved. You will also need to explain the reasons why activities need to change for children at different developmental stages and explain your role in the activity.

To achieve a **distinction grade** you will need to evaluate your activity and show to what extent it achieved its aims. You will also need to evaluate your performance in the activity and propose a development plan to improve your skills.

UNIT SIX

CARE OF BABIES

This unit concentrates on the knowledge needed to help you work with babies under one year old. One of the best ways of learning how a baby develops is to observe a real one in action! If you know someone who has recently had a baby or there is a young baby in your placement, ask the parents if you could visit from time to time and ask questions about the baby as he or she progresses over the first year of life. Explain that you will keep all information confidential, and will share your notes, exercises, etc. with the parents. A log of your interviews and photographs can be used to create a guide to the baby's first year, and you might like to give it to the parents when you have finished your course. If you do have this opportunity, all of the assessment activities and exercises in this unit could be based on your study. Of course, using other examples too from time to time will enhance your work, and help you to understand the wide diversity seen in the growth and development of babies.

In this unit you will learn about:

- care routines for babies
- appropriate hygiene, health and safety procedures
- foods suitable for the nutritional requirements of babies
- creating a safe and stimulating environment for babies.

Stages of development up to 12 months

Babies' growth and development in their first year is at a greater pace than at any other time of their lives. Weight will triple on average, length or height will almost double, and head circumference will increase by 50 per cent. Most babies born at full term weigh between 2.5 and 4 kg and measure between 45 and 52 cm in length. Head circumference will be on average 33 to 37 cm.

Age	Weight (kg)	Height (cm)	Head circumference (cm)
Birth	2.5 to 4.0	45 to 52	33 to 37
3 months	4.5 to 6.5	54 to 64	38 to 43
6 months	6.0 to 9.0	60 to 72	42 to 46
9 months	7.0 to 10.5	65 to 74	43 to 48
12 months	8.0 to 12.0	68 to 78	45 to 49

Try plotting the figures from the table on page 189 on a graph to see the pattern shown by growth. Graphs have been made from the measurements of thousands of babies showing the average range babies should fall into if they are growing normally. These are called 'centile charts' and are a useful guide for child care professionals. If you have a baby to study, start a chart for each measurement of growth and plot the stages as you receive reports of each.

In Units 2 and 3, you looked at the developmental milestones of all children from birth to eight years of age. Look again at the principles and rates of development in Unit 2. The principles are the same for babies.

To specialise in the care of babies you need to know more detail about development in the first year of life. A thorough knowledge of development will help you to plan appropriate care routines for a baby.

Age of baby	Stage of development	Associated care routines
Birth to 4 weeks	**Physical** Lies supine with head to one side (tonic neck reflex) Large jerky movements of limbs Head lags when pulled up to sit All primitive reflexes present **Intellectual** Fixes on faces and bright objects Reacts to loud sounds **Social and emotional** Enjoys feeding and cuddling Needs to suck for comfort as well as food Quietens when picked up Sleeps most of the time	Needs firm but gentle handling, supporting neck Constant holding when awake Lots of cuddles, touch, talking and singing during and in addition to feeding, bathing, etc. Playing music Use bright colours and mobiles within 20–25 cm of face Feed on demand, no set routine – this will provide emotional security through cuddling in addition to providing food

Age of baby	Stage of development	Associated care routines
8 weeks	**Physical** Controlled movements starting to replace reflex responses Turns from side to back Starts to lift head when on front **Intellectual** Begins to respond to adult's voice, looks for sounds Smiles in response to adults, starts to coo and squeal with pleasure **Social and emotional** Cries can be identified for different needs Still enjoys sucking Recognises familiar face	Use baby chair or carry around to allow baby to watch everyday activity Put bright pictures near the cot, use mobiles and chimes Talk and sing to baby, allow time for response Still lots of physical contact, massage, etc. Feeding may have a pattern – probably still needing night feeds Starts immunisation programme
3 months	**Physical** Movements smoother and continuous Waves arms with hands open Kicks Head lag disappearing When placed on front, lifts head and upper chest **Intellectual** Visually very alert, moves head to gaze around Watches own hands and fingers Recognises feeding bottle Holds rattle placed in hand for a short time Vocalises well Quietens to sound of bell or rattle **Social and emotional** Sucks in response to feed preparation Fixes gaze on person feeding Reacts to familiar situations with coos and smiles Enjoys bathing and care routines	Will enjoy freedom of activity now – on changing mat without nappy, or on blanket Enjoys baby gym activity Introduce new noises, visual experiences, e.g. through music, animal noises Change pictures by cot, plays with different mobiles, show things around and outside the house, nursery Enjoys lots of conversation from carers and songs Starts to enjoy soft squeaky toys, range of textures and sounds from toys Starts to enjoy looking at picture books – adult pointing out names Will enjoy bathing, use of toys Still needs lots of physical contact, gentle rough and tumble games May start to sleep through the night, routine should be developing – daytime naps, evening bath, story time, etc. May start introduction of solid foods Second immunisation (third at 5 months)
6 months	**Physical** On back, lifts head to look at own feet Sits with support and turns head to look around Lifts arms up to be picked up Pulls self to sit up when holding hands Kicks strongly with alternate legs Rolls over from front to back and starting to roll from back to front May sit alone for a few seconds On front, lifts head and chest well up, upporting self on extended arms eld standing, bounces up and down	Attention to safety issues essential – start of mobility Look at safety gates, fireguards, plug covers, etc. Needs strapping into high chair, pram Development of physical play – activities to encourage rolling over Knee games – e.g. Humpty Dumpty Toys needing manipulation start to be enjoyed – activity centres Also enjoys play with everyday objects – pots and pans, empty boxes, rustly paper Bath best at night – starting to get grubby during the day from floor play and feeding Weaning well established, eating wide range of mashed foods, losing dependence on milk Enjoys outings to the shop, park

Age of baby	Stage of development	Associated care routines
	Intellectual Very curious, attention easily attracted Vocalises with sing-song and double syllables Laughs, chuckles and squeals Responds to different tones of voice Reaches for and grasps small toys Starting to use single hand Takes everything to mouth to explore Finds own feet interesting **Social and emotional** Pats breast or bottle with hand when feeding Reaches for offered toy immediately Passes objects from hand to hand regarding them closely Starting to show shyness with strangers – develops at about 7 months to stranger shyness Not happy when main carer is out of sight	Routines firmly established – clear daytime nap times May sleep all night
9 months	**Physical** Sits alone for up to 15 minutes Leans forward to pick up toys and can turn body sideways without falling over Rolls or squirms across the floor, may try to crawl Pulls self to standing on furniture, but cannot lower self When held standing, moves feet in steps **Intellectual** Reaches out to grasp objects with one hand, passes them from hand to hand Looks at new object before grasping Points at distant objects with index finger Holds string on toys, etc. in scissor fashion to pull Picks up small items with finger and thumb – 'inferior pincer grasp' Releases toy by dropping, cannot put down voluntarily Looks in right direction for falling toys – start of 'casting' Vocalises as communication, shouts to attract attention Babbles in long strings of syllables – e.g. dad-dad-dad Understands no and bye-bye Imitates coughs, 'brr' Immediately locates sounds in hearing tests (1m from ear) **Social and emotional** Can hold, bite and chew on finger food Tries to grasp spoon when being fed Throws back head and body when annoyed Very wary of strangers, clings to familiar people Plays peep-bo, and tries to clap hands Holds out toy to adult but cannot let go yet Finds toy that is partly hidden while watching – very early stage of concept of object permanence	Safety aspects increasing in importance – very mobile Allow use of feeder cup alone, offer spoon when feeding As many finger foods as possible Do not rush in practising activities Allow choice of activity, e.g. building bricks, post it boxes, play with safe household objects Give plenty of chance to copy activities – building bricks, finger and hand games Offer changing variety of items and activities to stack, bang, build, roll on, look at, listen to Continue to widen experience of the world – feeding the ducks, visits to farms, walks in the country Respect child's fear of strangers – do not force to accept new people Respect lack of concept of object permanence – has not yet grasped that if carer goes out of room he or she has not gone forever – will be distressed, so take child with you if possible Continue to widen range of foods, tastes in diet

Age of baby	Stage of development	Associated care routines
12 months	**Physical** Sits alone indefinitely, can rise to sitting from lying down Crawls or shuffles rapidly Pulls to stand and walks round furniture, side stepping (cruising) Can drop to sitting Walks with one or both hands held May stand, walk alone or crawl upstairs – at average age 13 to 14 months	Keep thinking of safety Encourage walking skills – push-along toys, furniture for cruising Use of sand, water and paint with supervision Offer books with thick pages – will enjoy turning Continue to extend and explore language, music with stories, songs, rhymes Encourage displays of affection Encourage self-feeding using cup and spoon May start to lose interest in food with increasing mobility
	Intellectual Has neat pincer grip for tiny objects Drops and throws toys deliberately and watches them fall – 'casting' Looks in the right place for toys that have rolled out of sight Points with index finger at items of interest Recognises familiar people from 6m Uses both hands freely, starting to show preference for one hand Holds cube in each hand and bangs them together Knows own name Jargons loudly in conversational tones – containing most vowels and many consonants Understands several words in context – dog, dinner, walk, and simple instructions with gestures, such as 'come to daddy', 'say bye-bye'	Distract wherever possible from undesired behaviour Use a firm 'no' if necessary Make a game of dressing Offer range of experiences through feely-type toys, toys that make things disappear, such as posting objects Lots of songs and action games, with singing and hand movements
	Social and emotional Drinks from cup with little help, holds spoon and tries to use it Holds out arm to put in sleeve and foot in shoe when being dressed Mouthing becomes less frequent Puts bricks into box when shown, rattles spoon in cup without being shown Gives toys to adults on request Plays pat-a-cake, waves bye-bye on request and later without prompting Sits or stands without support when being dressed Likes to be within sight and sound of familiar adults	

ASSESSMENT ACTIVITY

Describe the stages of development of a baby (0–12 months).

Describe the main changes you would expect to see in a baby, from birth to 12 months. You should look at changes from birth to three months, then to six months, then to one year. Base your observations on a real child if possible.

No extension to merit or distinction is possible for this unit.

Care routines for babies

In their first year, babies' routines are weighted towards their physical care needs. Providing for their intellectual, social and emotional needs is a natural development from providing physical care. It is almost impossible to think of feeding or changing a baby without interacting with the baby, playing games or showing him or her interesting things to look at. A routine for a baby is not a fixed plan. In an average day a baby will eat, sleep, get rid of bodily waste, be kept clean, be dressed, or have some fresh air, have an outing, will go to the clinic for weighing, will play, have plenty of cuddles and attention.

In Unit 2 we saw that all children do not have the same routines. In the first year babies' routines will change dramatically due to their changing needs. In the first few weeks of life a baby may need to be fed, changed and allowed to sleep. By 12 months, a baby spends more than 12 hours awake and is actively learning new skills, demanding entertainment and socialising. The routine is likely to be very different from when the baby was a few weeks old.

Planning a routine may appear to be much easier if you are starting from the basis of the nursery where you work, as nurseries have routines of their own. However, always remember that each baby is an individual. It is no use trying to make a baby fit into the routine of the baby room if his or her needs do not match it. The result will be a miserable baby and desperate staff.

When planning routines for babies, it is important to take the following into consideration:

- feeding requirements
- sleeping requirements
- home-based, childminder or nursery care
- the time parents go to work
- family mealtimes
- carer's routine
- visits to clinic
- needs of other children
- routine of nursery
- time for play
- bath time
- nature of the child – is he or she more lively in the morning or evening?
- parents or carer's wishes
- changes – such as illnesses.

How the stage of a baby's development relates to safety considerations

By now you should be aware of the huge steps in development that take place in the first year of a baby's life. It will not surprise you that it is essential to mirror those changes in considering a baby's safety and play needs.

The table below shows toys and activities that may be suitable at each stage of development.

Age and stages	Toys and activities
Birth to 3 months Reacts to light, noise and touch Field of vision 20–25 cm	Cuddles, singing and talking Mobiles hung over cot, chair, changing mat Brightly coloured pictures and objects
3 to 6 months Able to hold objects Visual field expanding Mouthing Voluntary movements replacing reflex actions Kicking becoming vigorous Communication developing	Objects to hold and look at – range of textures, ideally sound-making toys such as rattles Over the cot, rods with range of objects on strings, cords Watching trees in the wind Time to enjoy freedom for kicking in the bath, on a changing mat without a nappy Noisy paper to kick against Finger games – e.g. 'This little piggy' Songs and movement
6 to 12 months Sitting with support, moving alone Increasing mobility – may be crawling to walking Anxious when carer is missing Enjoys exploring Start of imitative play Developing sense of self Interested in outside world	Great enjoyment of water play – in the bath with toys, in small washing up bowl Household opportunities – pots and pans, boxes, cans Building stacks and knocking them down – toy bricks, boxes Games cleaning teeth, brushing hair Mirrors Outdoor trips to the park, shops, to see the cows … will enjoy repetition of these outings A treasure box made from a strong cardboard box, with changing items aimed at different senses Big, easy-to-hold crayons with big sheets of card to scribble on Push and pull toys, toys that make sounds or pop up when a button is pressed, etc.

THINK IT THROUGH

Thinking about physical, intellectual, emotional and social development, plan at least one activity covering each aspect for a child at two months, six months and ten months. What safety issues will you have to consider in your plans?

Safety considerations must be at least one, and preferably two or three, steps ahead of the baby. Provide a safety gate for the stairs before the baby starts to crawl, always look at toys for loose parts, look for strings that could wrap around necks, and always use a safety harness from the start of using a high chair, etc.

Communicating with parents

The reasons a baby is receiving day care will vary, but very often the only parent or both of the parents are working. You will see and hear various 'authorities' stating their opinions on the issue of the working mother or single parents, and you will have your own views. Part of your professional skill is to make sure that your own views, even if they conflict with the situation, are not made apparent.

Parents who use the services of child care professionals to look after their baby may feel guilty that they are not caring for the baby themselves. Leaving a baby with a carer for the first time is a very difficult step to take for many parents. You need to be sensitive to this and think of ways to involve the parents as much as possible.

Good practice: working with parents

- Before the baby starts in nursery, or before you start as a nanny, ask the parents for the baby's routine.

- Ask about feeding patterns, sleep times, favourite play activities and so on.

- Check with parents about their views on diet if the baby is weaning, the use of TV for entertainment, and any cultural issues that may affect the baby, such as soya milk feeds for babies of vegan parents.

- Always ask permission for intended outings and visits before the event.

- Keep a chart or other record detailing everything the baby has done that day, e.g. feeds taken, sleep time, number of dirty nappies, outings, toys played with and so on.

> ### Good practice: working with parents (*cont.*)
>
> - Always record any change from the norm, particularly any sign of illness or unusual behaviour, however trivial this may seem, and tell the parents.
>
> - At the start of your time with the baby, ask the parents what sort of night the baby has had. Did the baby take all of his or her feed, seem comfortable, have a dirty nappy, etc.
>
> - Before you finish your shift, give verbal feedback to the parents on the type of day the baby has had, any changes in routines, etc.
>
> - If possible, have a camera on hand to record anything that will interest the parents, such as activities in the nursery and outings.

Particularly in the early weeks of leaving their baby with a carer, parents may feel that they want to telephone during the day to ask about their child. This is perfectly normal and acceptable; never feel that you are being checked up on in any way. When parents are comfortable with the care arrangements, phone calls will reflect only their wish to keep in contact with their child's day.

There are times when you should contact the baby's parents, for example:

- if the baby is ill

- if the baby is behaving out of character in any way

- if there is an unplanned outing, and the parents would be anxious if they telephoned while you were out.

Communication with parents is all about mutual respect. You will maintain respect for them as the main people in the baby's life, who must be kept in touch with everything happening in his or her life. They will respect you as a person important to their baby, who is concerned for the baby's welfare, and as a child care professional.

THINK IT THROUGH

If you have a baby to study, ask the parents what information they would like to receive from their baby's carers, and what information they already receive. Devise a chart or booklet that could be used to help communicate with the parents of a baby you were caring for, either at home or in a nursery.

Appropriate hygiene, health and safety procedures

Organising babies' environments

As a child care worker you are responsible for the health and safety of babies and children in your care. Some basic, essential rules should always be in your thoughts when working with any child, but are particularly important with babies.

1   You must always wash your hands to avoid cross infection:
    - before picking up a baby
    - before preparing or giving feeds
    - after changing a baby
    - after taking older children or yourself to the toilet
    - after playing with pets.

2   Strict hygiene and care is essential with babies' feeds, and you must:
    - never reuse a partly finished bottle of feed
    - never leave a bottle of feed out at room temperature
    - always keep bottle teats covered when not in use
    - never test the temperature of a bottle by tasting a drop yourself; check it on the back of your hand
    - not allow other children or pets to touch spoons or dishes that are for a baby's food
    - never prop feed a baby, that is, leave a baby in a pram or seat with the bottle propped up on a pillow, etc. (the baby could choke)
    - never thicken a baby's bottle with rice or rusk; solids should be given by spoon, otherwise babies may choke
    - always supervise an older baby when eating, particularly hard foods such as rusks or apple.

3   Always remember that young children, and babies in particular, have no sense of danger. They need protecting from:
    - animals, even family pets
    - dangers from heat, household objects, etc.
    - falls, as they become more mobile; a baby should never be left alone on a surface above ground level
    - other children, who may injure them through exuberance or jealousy.

4   You should try not to expose babies to known infections, although this is not always easy, as many conditions are infectious before symptoms appear.

5   Always put a baby to sleep on his or her back, with the feet at the bottom of the cot, and use blankets that can be tucked in and will not billow over the face. This will help to prevent sudden infant death syndrome (cot death).

6   Never smoke in a room where a baby may be cared for or anywhere near to a baby or child. Apart from the risks associated with passive smoking, the effects of smoking by a baby's carers is a high risk factor involved in sudden infant death syndrome.

7   Never be tempted to leave any child alone in a house even for a few moments.

The dangers to babies change as they move through their first year. The chart below shows the dangers they face and how to prevent accidents or illness.

Age range	Danger	Prevention
Birth until crawling or cruising	Injury from cold or overheating	Attention to room temperature and clothing Room temperature between 18° and 21°C
	Gastro-enteritis	Strict hygiene and bottle care
	Injury from other children	Avoid leaving toddlers alone with babies
	Sudden infant death syndrome	do not allow smoking anywhere near or in the same room as a child Put child to sleep on back Avoid overheating
	Choking	Care when feeding, milk only in bottles Attention to ribbons, etc. on clothing Avoid leaving small toys or other items in reach
	Illness	Avoid people with known illness Ensure child has appropriate immunisations
When a child becomes mobile – crawling, shuffling	*All the above*, plus: Falls	 Use baby gates, play pens, closed doors
	Injury from pulling objects onto self	Attention to wires, cords, any dangling objects, tablecloths
	Burns and scalds	Care with hot drinks, kettle flexes and bath temperatures Use of fire and cooker guards
	Electrocution from plug sockets	Use plug covers
	Poisoning	All cleaners, chemicals, paints, medications, etc. kept securely locked or in high cupboards

Case Study – Justine

Justine is working as a nanny looking after Melanie who is four months and Sam who is two years old. This morning Sam has been sick and Melanie is crying because it is past the time for her feed and she is hungry. Justine cleans Sam up, changes his clothes and settles him down on the sofa with a blanket. Melanie is still crying. Justine goes through to the kitchen and drops Sam's dirty clothes by the washing machine before collecting a bottle from the fridge for Melanie. Melanie is exhausted by crying and falls asleep before she has finished her bottle. Justine puts her down in her cot thinking she will change her nappy later. Justine decides that as Sam seems ill, she will slip down to the chemist at the corner of the road to get some medicine before the children wake up. Fortunately the children are still asleep when she gets back so she decides to have a quick smoke before dealing with Sam's dirty clothes. She opens the patio doors to make sure that the smoke does not come in the house. 'I think I need this, it is obviously going to be a very bad day…

1) List five things that Justine has done wrong this morning.

2) What might happen to these children as a result of Justine's mistakes?

THINK IT THROUGH

Describe how to organise a baby's environment for hygiene, health and safety procedures:

1   Visit a selection of baby-care shops and, if possible, collect catalogues. Look at the equipment available in the safety section and re-read the information on safety in Unit 3.

2   Produce a simple and easy-to-understand booklet describing how carers can protect children in their care at home from injury or ill-health during the first year of life.

Selecting and dealing with clothing

All children's clothes shops and most department stores have a wide range of clothing suitable for all ages and activities. Prices range from inexpensive to designer label levels. Babies do not mind what they are dressed in, as long as they are warm and comfortable. The wide range of styles is aimed to appeal to carers, and for the manufacturers' profits. A few basic points about baby clothes are important to remember.

■ Natural fibres are more comfortable to wear as they absorb perspiration.

■ Two or three thin layers of clothing are better than one very thick layer; clothing can then be adjusted to suit the temperature.

- Overheating can be dangerous for a baby, more so than being a little cool.

- Clothes that are machine washable are easier to care for.

- Clothes should be loose and easy to put on and take off.

- Avoid ribbons and cords that could easily cut off the circulation around a finger or neck.

- All materials should be flame resistant.

- Care should be taken with clothes that have feet in them, e.g. stretch 'babygro' suits. It is important to check frequently that there is enough room for the baby's feet to move, as wearing too tight a suit will damage the soft, growing bones of the feet.

Choice of clothing

Encourage parents to use second-hand clothes from other babies. The list of essential clothing for a new baby is quite short, and includes:

- stretch suits/babygro

- vests, with an envelope neck for easy application

- cardigans for cooler days

- mittens for cold days

- socks or booties for cold days

- hat or bonnet, essential for cool weather, and a sun hat for days when the sun is out

- shawl for extra warmth.

An older baby who has started to be mobile through crawling or shuffling needs very practical clothes. Dresses get in the way of crawling, and pale-coloured, delicate fabrics quickly get dirty. Dungarees or stretch trousers with a similar top are practical and easy to wear. 'Snow suits' or jackets are essential for cold weather when a baby is in a pushchair or papoose carrier. Remember that in cold weather a baby is not moving around in the same way as you are, and needs additional layers of clothing.

Caring for baby clothes

A daily change of clothes is usually necessary, as the baby will perspire and may posset (bring back up) small amounts of food. If clothes have been well chosen they should be easy to wash, preferably in a washing machine. It is important to be familiar with the fabric care symbols on clothing. Choice of washing powder is an important factor. Babies have skin that is much more sensitive than that of most adults. Biological powders may irritate the skin and should be avoided. Fabric conditioners should be used with care, and they can cause serious irritation. This is a particular problem if clothing becomes soaked in urine, due to a leaking nappy. Urine reacts very badly with most fabric conditioners and can produce a serious rash. It is advisable to look for the special conditioners for babies that avoid this problem. Clothes that have become soiled with faeces or vomit need to be soaked in cold water after the solid residue has been disposed of into the toilet.

Nappy changing and common skin problems

Ask your parents what type of nappies you used to wear. Were they disposable, terry towelling or a mixture depending on the activities for the day? If you ask your grandparents what type they used for your parents, the answer will undoubtedly be terry towelling.

Disposable nappies have taken over in the past 20 years, with the result that millions of dirty paper and plastic nappies must be destroyed daily. Disposable nappies are convenient, do not require washing or carrying around if you are out, but they are very expensive and present society with the big problem of disposal. A move back to using terry nappies is slowly gaining ground. You may find yourself caring for a baby who uses them, so being able to change one is a useful skill.

Changing nappies

DID YOU KNOW?

When William Cadogen was writing about childcare in 1748 he suggested babies should be changed just once a day!

Whichever type of nappy you have to change, there are several important points to consider.

- Always gather all your equipment together first.
- Have some means of cleaning the baby's bottom, e.g. water and cotton wool, or baby wipes.
- Have a bin or bag ready to receive the dirty nappy.
- Immediately you finish the task, clear the rubbish away and then wash your hands thoroughly.
- Never leave the baby unattended on a changing table or at any height above the floor.

The best way to learn the mechanics of changing a nappy is to watch a competent person. The folding of terry nappies is almost an art form, and there are many ways to do it depending on the size and sex of the baby. This is one of their advantages, as the nappy can be folded to be thickest at the position of urination. The same sized terry serves a tiny 3 kg baby and a bouncing two-year-old. They need to be covered with some form of plastic outer to prevent wetness coming through, and are often used with a thin paper lining to make the disposal of faeces easier. Disposable nappies come in many different sizes and shapes with a range of special compounds to absorb wetness, built-in cream to prevent soreness, etc.

The aim of changing a nappy is to put the baby into a clean, dry nappy with a clean, dry bottom. The following procedure is recommended.

1 Collect all your equipment first: nappy, water, soap and cotton wool or baby wipes, cream, changing mat, bucket or bag for the dirty nappy.

2 Always wear gloves and follow the policy of the setting. After removing the nappy, clean the baby's bottom. If the nappy is a dirty one this will need greater care than if the nappy is wet. When cleaning female babies, always clean from front to back to avoid introducing infection into the vagina. With boys, try to avoid soiling the foreskin area. Using clean water is fine, but baby wipes contain a solution to neutralise ammonia and so help to prevent nappy rash.

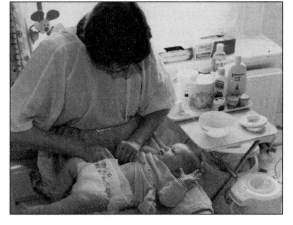

3 Apply a protective barrier cream if used. Be careful not to get cream on the adhesive fixings of a disposable nappy; if you do they will not stick.

4 Put the nappy on, being very careful with nappy pins if used, and dress the baby.

5 Dispose of the soiled nappy. Roll it up and put it into a nappy sack if disposable. If it is a terry nappy, dispose of the paper liner and put the nappy into a bucket of sterilising solution.

6 Wash your hands.

Terry nappies should be washed after soaking in solution, at a temperature of at least 60°C and in non-biological powder. They should be rinsed thoroughly.

Nappy rash

Nappy rash appears as a red, sore area over the buttocks. In severe cases it can look like chafing. Sometimes a baby can develop thrush on the buttocks; this can be seen as small outbreaks of spot-type lesions away from the main red area. Medical advice is needed to deal with a nappy rash caused by thrush.

A barrier cream applied to the napkin area is useful to prevent nappy rash, and petroleum jelly is a good standby. There are many different creams on the market, all claiming efficiency, but few babies will reach the age of two without ever having a nappy rash. The first defence to prevent nappy rash is not to allow a baby to spend too long in a wet nappy, and certainly never leaving a baby in a wet and dirty nappy. Applying a barrier cream is a second defence. All babies will benefit from spending some time each day without a nappy on. A warm room and a covered mat on the floor are a suitable place to let the child have time without a nappy.

Babies are prone to other types of minor health problems that can cause concern to parents. They are described in the table below.

Problem	Description	Cause	Treatment
Sweat rash (milaria)	Rash of small red spots on face, chest	Overheating Immature sweat glands	Cool child down by removing clothes. Use cotton next to skin, avoid synthetic fibres. Avoid overheating with clothes and room heating.
Cradle cap	Yellow/brown crusting on the scalp, particularly on anterior fontanelle	Build-up of sebum, failure to wash and rinse area properly	Soften with olive oil, baby shampoo and rinse well – special shampoos available.
Chafing	Soreness in body creases – neck, groin and armpits	Insufficient washing and drying of skin Excessive sweating	Prevent by good skin care, especially in the neck area due to baby dribbling. Apply mild cream – e.g. zinc and castor oil.
Eczema	Sore red rash, may affect face or any part of the body, particularly skin folds Can be very severe, with bleeding and weeping	Usually an allergic response – possibly to cows' milk	Requires medical treatment. Avoid soap and using detergents for washing clothes. Keep nails short to stop scratching. Use emulsifiers in the bath. Breast feeding helps to lessen severity and delay onset.
Constipation	Very hard, dry faeces, baby may cry on passing them	Insufficient liquids, especially water, and dehydration in warm weather	Try to ensure that the baby drinks enough water or diluted fruit juice.
Diarrhoea	Very smelly, loose faeces, at frequent intervals	Over-rich formula feeds Poor hygiene in making feeds Infection	Lots of water to drink. If it continues longer than 24 hours, seek medical help.
Urine infection	Smelly nappy, even when only wet Often produces a nappy rash	Infection	Seek medical advice.

Bathing a baby

Bathing a tiny baby can be a frightening experience; holding a wet, soapy, wriggling baby is rather like trying to hold a wriggling fish. It can also be most enjoyable, and provide a natural opportunity to play with a baby and introduce new toys as the baby gets older. Good preparation is vital. Suddenly remembering that you have forgotten a towel is not very helpful when you have the baby in the bath – leaving the baby to go and fetch one is not possible in any circumstance; the risk of drowning is too great Expensive, special baby baths are not necessary; a tiny baby can be bathed in a washing-up bowl until he or she is big enough to go into a normal, family-sized bath.

- Make sure the room is warm and draught free, as babies rapidly lose heat. An ideal temperature is 20°C.

- Gather all the necessary equipment, e.g. towel, mild soap or baby bath liquid, cotton wool, clean clothes and nappy.

- Fill the bath with water at body temperature (37°C), always putting the cold water in first. This will avoid potential accidents with older children putting their hands into hot water, or climbing into baths. This is a routine that should always be followed, to avoid any risk of scalding.

Figure 6.1 *Some items you will need when bathing a baby*

- Check the temperature with your elbow.

The best way, as with nappy changing, to learn how to bath a baby is to watch someone who is experienced. Guidance is given below.

1 Undress the baby down to the nappy, and wrap in a warm towel. Do this on the floor or in another safe area.

2 Check the water temperature and adjust if necessary.

3 Hold the baby gently but securely in the towel. Using cotton wool, wash the face. Do not use soap on the face. Use a separate piece of cotton wool for each eye, moving from the inner corner to the outer.

4 Hold the baby over the bath and wash the head with water or gentle soap or shampoo, twice per week. Make sure that the fontanelle (the 'soft spot') is washed and rinsed properly to prevent cradle cap.

5 On a firm, safe surface, unwrap the baby and remove the nappy. Clean the nappy area with wet cotton wool.

6 Holding the baby safely, with your arm under the shoulder supporting the head, gently lower into the water. Soap the baby all over the body if using soap, and then rinse thoroughly. Using baby bath liquid avoids the need for this. This is the ideal time for some gentle play and splashing, depending on the baby's level of enjoyment.

7 Lift the baby out of the bath and gently pat the skin dry. Be particularly careful that creases are well dried. Apply any moisturising lotion if the baby has dry skin.

8 Dress and put the baby into a cot, pram etc. before cleaning the bath and clearing away equipment.

Wrap the baby gently but securely in a towel, so that the arms are tucked in. Wash the face with moist cotton wool.

Hold the baby over the bath and wash the head and hair.

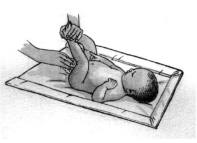

Put the baby on a flat surface, undress him or her and take off the nappy. Clean the nappy area.

Take off the towel. Holding the baby securely under the head and around the arm, lift him or her into the water

Use your spare hand to wash the baby

Lift the baby out of the bath supporting under the bottom, and quickly wrap him or her in a warm towel.

Figure 6.2 *The stages in bathing a baby*

Two notes of caution: never poke around in any child's ears, especially babies', with cotton buds. Just clean around the outside with cotton wool if necessary. Secondly, baby boys' foreskins should be left alone, and they should not be pulled back at this age.

Some babies are not happy with bath time at any age. This can be due to all sorts of reasons Do not be tempted to carry on regardless if you are bathing a baby who is not happy with the activity. Most babies do not need a bath every day if they are not happy about it. Hands, faces and nappy areas must be cleaned regularly, and in hot weather skin creases need attention.

Younger babies

Very young babies may not be happy having a bath. This may be because of a sense of insecurity when they are undressed and exposed; tiny babies are happier wrapped up and feeling cosy. If a baby is not happy having a bath, then 'topping and tailing' can be done on several days a week. The face, head, hands and feet can be washed with cotton wool, and the baby's bottom can be washed with soapy water. Attention should also be paid to the skin creases, to check for signs of redness.

Older babies

Older babies usually thoroughly enjoy their baths, taking advantage of the chance to kick and splash. As soon as it is possible, and certainly by the time they are sitting with support at around five months, babies will enjoy going into a full-size bath, if possible with older siblings or a parent. A firm, non-slip mat should be placed in the bottom of the bath. Of course, you should never leave any child alone in the bath even for a second; a child can slip and drown in a few centimetres of water.

If you are bathing an older baby in a baby bath, preparations should include protecting the surrounding floor areas from splashing. There is huge scope for play in the bath with an older baby. Commercial toys are available that fit on or in the bath, or you can use plastic containers, ducks, sponges, plastic bricks and simply splash.

THINK IT THROUGH

You are caring for a baby of six months who is not keen on being bathed. How could you make bath time an enjoyable experience for you and the baby?

Care of teeth

Good dental care starts from the beginning of a child's life. The health and condition of our teeth is dictated from conception. Even before the first teeth emerge, certain factors can affect their future appearance and health. Tetracycline, a common antibiotic, can cause tooth discolouration if used by expectant or breast-feeding mothers.

Since the first teeth usually emerge around six months of age, tooth care activities like brushing and flossing are not needed for very young babies. However, babies' emerging teeth do need protecting. Baby bottle decay is caused by frequent exposure, over time, to drinks containing sugars. These include milk and fruit juices. The liquids can pool around the teeth for long periods of time leading to decay to the teeth that are developing. For this reason, you should not let a baby fall asleep with a bottle of juice or milk in his or her mouth. A bottle or pacifier filled with water should be given before a sleep.

As soon as a baby starts to get teeth, you should start to clean them. Using a very soft baby toothbrush will be something of a game to the baby to start with. If the baby does not like the brush, you can use a soft piece of cloth with a tiny amount of toothpaste. Prevention is better than cure with dental care. Avoid giving a baby fruit drinks through a teat, or dipping a dummy in juice or honey.

The role of the carer

Babies are unable to protect themselves from risks of injury or illness. Everyone who has any dealings with a baby is responsible for the baby's safety. Thought needs to be given to all of the following points.

- Adequate clothing must be provided, suitable to the climate and room temperature, and it must be kept clean and maintained.

- The baby's surroundings should have appropriate levels of heating, light and cleanliness. An ideal temperature for a baby is one that you also feel comfortable in.

- Older children are naturally jealous of a new baby in the family; they feel that they will not be receiving as much attention. Even without intending any harm, toddlers can give cuddles that are over-zealous and could cause harm, or may 'offer' toys to the baby by throwing them into the pram.

- Animals can carry diseases that may be transmitted to humans. Never allow a dog or cat to lick a baby or the equipment the baby will use. Never leave a dog or cat alone with a baby; they can be as jealous as children.

- Protect the baby from illness. Avoid contact with people who are ill. People are often infectious before symptoms show, so this is not always possible. Do not go to work if you are ill yourself to avoid distributing an infection.

Hygiene

Careful attention to your own personal health and hygiene is the first step; remember the rules of hand washing, clean clothing and the use of aprons for dirty jobs. There should be a regular routine at nursery or the baby's home to ensure that the environment is clean and hygienic. Equipment and toys need regular washing and inspection for safety on a rota basis and also at any time you feel is necessary.

Safety

All equipment used with any child, including babies, should be checked daily for safety. The table below provides a safety checklist.

Item	Checks
Prams	Brakes working, catches to keep the pram opened working Harness safe and in use Shopping and other bags carried only in special carriers, not on the handles
Cots	Safety catches working, bars no more than 7 cm apart, mattress fits snugly Cot feels stable when gently shaken
Transport in cars, mini buses, etc.	Suitable safety seat provided, firmly fixed to body of vehicle – has BSI logo No wear on straps Straps adjusted to fit baby snugly
High chairs	Stable on the floor, cannot be easily tipped Have anchor points for harness – always used Tray firmly fixed, no cracks or chips
Safety gates	Good fit to size of opening When fixed and locked cannot be moved No horizontal bars to climb over
Fire guards	Firmly fixed to the wall Nothing to poke through into the fire No clothes on the guard for drying
Bouncing chairs, baby seats for use indoors	Harness or safety straps in use Never left unattended on a high surface
Baby walkers, bouncing swings	Seat adjusted to allow feet to sit flat on the floor Wheels and fixings safe
Toys	Check for cracks, breaks or loose parts Ensure nothing can be torn or pulled off and that there are no tears in fabric allowing fillings to escape

Good practice when looking at baby equipment is to check that it has a British Safety Institute kitemark or CE symbols attached, showing that it has been tested and meets safety requirements. Make yourself familiar with safety marks, and never use a toy or piece of equipment that does not have the appropriate mark. These safety marks are shown on page 119.

Buying second-hand items is a sensible step in terms of cost, and for items that do not receive a lot of use. Care needs to be taken, however, that the previous owners have not altered the item at all, making it unsafe. For example, a second-hand cot might have been repainted with a lead-based paint, or have transfers that will peel off.

THINK IT THROUGH

How safe is your placement?

Carry out a safety audit of all the equipment at your placement. List each item and the points that you feel need checking for safety. Briefly explain the routines at your placement relating to hygiene and safety.

Respecting parents' wishes

Increased marketing by companies promoting new products to parents may mean that you are faced with new ideas about hygiene matters. As long as these ideas are not in opposition to basic safety and hygiene requirements, you should always respect parents' requirements. Examples of different ideas are to have bath time in the morning rather than before bed, using terry nappies instead of disposables, and different methods of sterilising feeding equipment. In some cases you may feel that the routines or techniques parents are using are not safe, putting you in a difficult position.

THINK IT THROUGH

Often caring for a young baby takes place in the home of the child, e.g. you may be employed as a nanny. Working in a nursery with a baby unit is very different to working with older children. New parents can be very anxious when leaving their new baby in another person's care, no matter how experienced they are.

Think about how you might deal with some of these situations:

- *Sam, aged three months, arrives at nursery with a new type of nappy; it looks like a shaped terry nappy with a sheet of plastic, and seems to need advanced skills in order to apply it.*
- *Francis, aged two months, has not been sleeping very well. When you arrive to look after him for the evening his mother tells you to put a rusk in his bottle to help him sleep.*
- *You are bathing a baby on a home placement and the telephone rings. The baby's mother is busy in the kitchen and calls you to answer the phone. She says the baby will be OK on the changing table for a minute.*
- *A mother gives you some cotton buds and asks you to clean out her baby's ears inside, as they have been very waxy.*
- *When you arrive to care for a new baby for the day, you are shown a bottle of milk that has been half consumed and then put on top of the*

gas fire to keep warm. It is suggested that you finish it off with the baby if she needs it before her next full feed is due.

Discuss these scenarios with a partner. Are the parents correct in their advice to you? What do you think you should do about these situations? Make notes on your ideas.

DID YOU KNOW?

Research has found that the most common source of information on child care is the child's grandmother or aunt, closely followed by friends of the mother.

ASSESSMENT ACTIVITY

Plan safe, stimulating care routines, appropriate for babies at three different stages of development.

Plan a routine for a baby at birth, three months and nine months, highlighting the changes taking place in the baby's needs and requirements. You should include physical care, play needs and emotional and social care. It would be ideal if you could describe the exact routine of a particular child, for example the baby in your baby study.

To achieve a **merit grade** you must explain how the routines you have planned are related to the developmental stages of the babies concerned.

No extension to distinction is possible for this assignment.

Foods suitable for the nutritional requirements of babies

National guidelines relating to the feeding of babies clearly state that breast feeding is best for babies until they are at least six months old. From three to four months, solids may be gradually introduced, avoiding cows' milk, wheat, nuts, eggs, salt and sugar. Weaning is dealt with in greater detail later in this unit. The debate between breast and bottle feeding has raged on for many years. Until modern baby milks were produced, babies who could not be breast fed had to be fed on cows' milk, which is totally unsuitable for babies under one year. Modern infant formula milks are scientifically modified to make them as near to human milk as possible.

DID YOU KNOW?

As milk was often contaminated before the mid twentieth century, many babies died if they were not breast fed. Wealthy families used 'wet nurses', working class women who were prepared to feed someone else's baby as well as, or instead of, their own baby. It was not until the early 1900s that milk started to be treated to make it free of bacteria and viruses.

Advantages of breast feeding

The main advantages of breast feeding are the following.

- Breast milk contains the right amounts of nutrients, at the right temperature, and is always available without risk of contamination.

- Breast milk contains antibodies to boost the immunity gained in the uterus.

- It is less likely to result in an overweight baby.

- It helps delay or avoid eczema.

- It has little additional cost.

- It helps in the bonding process.

- It helps the uterus shrink more quickly.

- It delays the return of the mother's periods.

Although breast feeding is the ideal way of infant feeding, not all mothers wish to use this method, or they may not be able to breast feed, for example if they are taking prescription medication. Bottle feeding does have some advantages in comparison to breast feeding.

- It is obvious how much milk the baby is taking.

- There is no risk of embarrassment with public feeding.

- Other people can feed the baby such as the father.

- It helps the mother who is returning to work.

Your role in the choice between breast and bottle feeding is only to give impartial information if asked, and then support the parents in their choice. The choice about feeding is a personal one for the parents of the baby, with support from midwives, health visitors and doctors.

Breast feeding is one of the most natural functions of motherhood and when established is an immensely satisfying experience for all. It can take some time to establish a good feeding pattern and milk supply. Mothers who are breast feeding need support to ensure they have enough rest and a good diet to promote good milk production.

Mothers who are breast feeding may need help to find some privacy when feeding their baby. Discreet public feeding is possible, as mothers can usually find a quiet corner away from the public gaze, and if some thought is given to clothing it is quite possible to feed a baby without anyone really being aware. As a child care worker you have a role to play in promoting breast feeding, and challenging any negative views. Never suggest or support a suggestion that a mother could use a public toilet to feed; would you like to have your lunch in such a place? Being informed about breast feeding and offering support is a role of child care workers.

Returning to work can prove difficult if a baby is being breast fed. Some enlightened employers are supportive of mothers taking feeding breaks if the baby is near to mum's place of work. Working mothers can express milk and may use a breast pump. The milk can be kept in a bottle in the fridge until needed and then warmed and bottle fed to the baby. Some babies find it very difficult to adapt to taking milk from a rubber teat – a very different prospect to a human nipple. You also need to make sure that all the usual hygiene rules are followed to avoid the risk of contamination and infection.

Preparing formula feeds

Current formula infant feeds are almost a replica of breast milk; they are manufactured to match the protein and salts in breast milk. In one important respect, however, formula feeds cannot match breast milk: the antibodies that are passed on from mother to baby in breast milk cannot be replaced in formula milk. A well-prepared formula bottle given in a caring environment with close interaction between baby and feeder can be a satisfying experience for both parties.

Bottle feeding can, however, be dangerous and unsatisfying for a baby. Poor hygiene and preparation of bottle feeds can lead to potentially fatal gastro-enteritis. 'Prop' feeding can result in choking, and not stimulating the bond between carer and baby can lead to emotional problems.

Equipment for feeding

Large chemists and baby shops have a wide range of bottles, sterilisers and associated equipment that, if added together, would be very expensive. There are some essentials for formula feeding:

- feeding bottles: up to 12 to allow rotation and advance preparation
- teats with holes of a suitable size to allow milk to flow without choking the baby
- covers for the teats, usually a top for the bottle that allows the teat to be put upside down in the bottle during storage in the fridge
- bottle brush and teat cleaner
- sterilising equipment
- clean surface to prepare feeds.

Sterilising the bottles and equipment used in bottle feeding is essential to kill the bacteria that thrive in warm milk. There is no substitute for sterilising and it must be done after each use of a bottle and teat. The first stage in sterilising is a thorough wash in hot soapy water, paying particular attention to the inside of

the teat and the curves and edges of the bottle using a bottle brush. After rinsing, the equipment then needs sterilising.

There are several methods of sterilising.

- Steaming, using a special device, takes about ten minutes. Equipment is then sterile for up to three hours.

- Cold water sterilising uses a solution made from tablets or concentrated solution. Bottles are soaked for a minimum time, usually 30 minutes, and remain sterile for up to 24 hours.

- Boiling for at least five minutes tends to damage plastic bottles if used regularly. Equipment will need re-sterilising if not used within three hours.

- Microwaving, using a special unit that fits in the microwave, takes about ten minutes. The effect lasts for two to three hours.

Following the common sense rules of hygiene is the first step on the road to safe feeding. The table below examines the principles of good practice.

Subject	Action required	Comments
Environment (kitchen)	Clean, dry worktops No other foodstuffs around Keep pets, etc. from surfaces	Contamination can easily occur due to carelessness
Operator (person preparing feed)	Always wash hands before starting work Do not touch any surface or equipment that will come into contact with milk Avoid touching the head, face, etc. during preparation Carefully read and follow the exact instructions on formula and sterilising solution packets Exact quantities of milk powder and water should be used	Risk of contamination, introduction of bacteria Very easy to make a feed that is too strong or too weak, as proportions are carefully calculated by the manufacturer
Equipment (bottles, teats, etc.)	All should be assembled before the start of preparation All bottles, teats, jugs, spoons must be thoroughly cleaned in hot soapy water, rinsed and left fully immersed in sterilising solution for minimum recommended time Formula should be checked as fresh and within date of use on packet Check that the water supply is a safe supply, and water is boiled before use	Milk and milk residue is an ideal medium for bacteria to breed Even a tiny amount of residue under the rim of a bottle can be enough to cause serious illness in a baby if bacteria multiply Any food stuff deteriorates with age and may cause harm if not within the use-by date Water supplies can carry bacteria that will cause gastro-enteritis – this kills small babies due to the dehydration caused by vomiting and diarrhoea

Subject	Action required	Comments
Storage	Packets of formula should be kept in a dry cupboard, tops safely and securely closed Bottles should be kept in refrigerator when made, teats covered Bottles should never be left out at room temperature Contents of part-used bottles should be disposed of	All vital practice to prevent contamination and potential gastro-enteritis

Another potential risk to babies is making up the feed with the wrong amounts of water or formula. Giving a baby stronger feed is dangerous because the feed will contain too much protein and too many salts; a baby's body cannot cope with this and convulsions and brain damage could occur as the body dehydrates. Too high a concentration of salts can lead to kidney damage. To avoid accidentally making the feed too strong:

- always check the number of scoops of powder that are needed
- only use the scoop provided in the packet
- do not be tempted to use heaped scoops; level off the powder with a plastic knife
- always read and follow the directions on the packet.

Too weak a feed will mean the baby is under-nourished, and will not thrive or develop to full potential.

Most people find it convenient to make up a supply of feeds for 24 hours and then store them in the fridge. Provided there are enough bottles, this is good practice. All the bottles that are going to be used for the next batch of feeds must have had enough time in the steriliser before they are re-used.

Giving the feed

There is no nutritional benefit in warming a bottle feed, but if it is heated to a suitable temperature it will be more enjoyable for the baby. Heating can be in a commercial bottle warmer or in a jug of water. Never use a microwave oven; there is a serious risk of hot spots in the milk in the bottle that will scald the baby's mouth and digestive tract.

It is vital that the temperature is correct and not too hot. A test of the temperature should always be carried out (not by having a sample yourself). Your inner wrist is a sensitive area of skin and this should be used for testing purposes. The feed is at the correct temperature if a few drops sprinkled on the inside of your wrist feel comfortable.

When feeding, the bottle should be tilted to ensure the teat is filled with milk – this will prevent air being swallowed with the milk. If the baby swallows a lot of air the resulting wind and pain will disrupt the feed. However, some air is needed in the bottle as the feed is taken, because as the milk is taken in by the baby a vacuum (no air) results in the bottle and it can be very difficult for the baby to take the milk in. So, after a few minutes remove the teat from the baby's mouth and allow air into the bottle to prevent a vacuum forming.

Whenever possible, the baby should be fed by the main carers, so that the same bonding will take place that breast feeding promotes. Whoever feeds the baby, it should be done in a comfortable position that allows for eye contact and close bodily contact. Talking and smiling to the baby is an important part of the feeding experience. Remember that a baby should never be left alone to feed from a bottle that has been propped up, because:

- there is a high risk of choking
- the baby is being deprived of important contact with the carer
- too much air will be taken in.

Case Study – Charlene

Charlene has slept in this morning. She is supposed to be meeting her friend in town for a day's shopping and is very late. Her baby is crying, so she rushes down to the kitchen and takes the last bottle of milk out of the fridge. She pops it in the microwave to heat and then props the bottle up with a pillow so that her baby can reach the teat and take her feed while Charlene makes another bottle to take out with her. She puts the kettle on, grabs a bottle from the pile of dirty dishes beside the sink and gives it a quick rinse under the hot tap. She finds the formula but can not find a measuring spoon so she scoops a few teaspoons of powder into the bottle before adding the boiling water. She quickly packs a couple of nappies and the newly made bottle into a bag before putting the baby into her pram and setting off to meet her friend and have a good day out at the shops.

1) Make a list of all the mistakes that Charlene has made.

2) What might happen as a result of these mistakes?

Weaning

Weaning is the term used to describe the process of changing a child's feeding from being dependent on milk to eating family foods. A new-born baby does not have the digestive system to cope with solid foods. A baby of one year has a more mature system able to cope with different foods. The process of learning to enjoy a wide range of foods can be a simple, easy one, or it can be difficult for carers and the baby alike.

There are many fashions related to weaning. Ask your parents and grandparents when they weaned their children and what foods they used, and you will probably receive several different answers. Parents in the UK may say they started their child on baby rice, while parents in Israel may have used avocado pear as a first weaning food.

The important thing to remember about weaning is the purpose of it, that is to safely introduce children into the normal eating patterns of their family which involves familiarising them with a wide range of new tastes. Trying to rush the process can at best overwhelm a child's taste buds, and at worst cause health problems through the use of inappropriate foods. It is very easy for carers of children to transfer their own food dislikes to them. How difficult is it to feed a baby with something you dislike? Think about your body language and facial expressions if you are in that situation.

When should a baby start to be weaned?

There are national guidelines relating to the start of weaning, and it is a good idea to try to collect some government leaflets from baby clinics to check on the latest guidelines. The UK and Irish Department of Health guidelines of May 2003 recommend that a baby should have nothing but infant milk for the first six months of life. The guidelines recognise that all babies develop at a different rate but advise that it is not a good idea to introduce solid food before they are four months old because the digestive system and kidneys are too immature to cope.

A baby could thrive very well on milk alone until the age of 12 months. At this age, the iron stores from birth will be diminishing and the baby will be at risk of becoming anaemic. We could say therefore that weaning should start between four and 12 months. Leaving the start as late as 12 months could make it difficult for a baby to make the change from a breast or bottle to eating from a spoon.

Within the guidelines, the best judge of when to wean a baby is the baby himself or herself. If a baby is still hungry after feeds, wants feeding more often and starts to wake at night for a feed again, then he or she may be ready to start having more to eat. Sucking the fists is not a sign of being ready for weaning; this is a normal part of development as the baby has found these interesting objects. There are several stages involved in weaning, as shown in the table below.

Weaning stage	Suggested foods
First stage (ideally from 6 months) Sloppy, slightly thicker than milk foods	**Bland tastes** Thickened milk – baby rice Puréed or stewed apple, banana, avocado

Weaning stage	Suggested foods
Second stage Thickness increasing, but no lumps	**Increase variety and strength of taste** First stage commercial foods Home-made puréed vegetables with gravy, e.g. carrots, yam, sweet potato Fruit and custard
Third stage Food less puréed – coping with thicker texture and some lumpiness Starting to finger feed	**Introducing slightly lumpier texture** Home-made food mashed with fork: potatoes, vegetables, fish, fruits Rusks, bread crusts, peeled pieces of apple, banana or mango Cubes of cheese
Fourth stage (by 12 months) Eating most family foods	**Using family foods, avoiding tough or stringy textures** Very little that cannot be offered

There are a few safety rules about foods to avoid that should be kept in mind during the weaning process.

- Never give a child nuts of any description until the age of five years; there is a strong risk of allergy and also of choking.

- Do not introduce cows' milk until one year old and then always use full-cream, pasteurised milk to ensure full calcium and vitamin levels. Follow-on milks are recommended from six to 12 months as they contain higher levels of vitamins, minerals and essential fatty acids than cows' milk.

- Products containing wheat are best avoided until at least six months of age. Some babies are allergic to the gluten in wheat, resulting in coeliac disease.

- Avoid fatty foods at all ages to help reduce unnecessary fat intake.

The foods listed below can harm a child's health if given too soon.

Food to avoid	When it can be introduced
Gluten (wheat, rye, barley and oats)	6 months
Shellfish	6 months
Citrus fruits	6 months
Eggs	6–9 months (well cooked)
Salt and salty foods, e.g. processed foods and crisps	Limited amount from 12 months, though added salt is never needed
Sugar and sugary foods, e.g. cakes and sweets	Limited amount from 12 months
Whole cows' milk as the main drink	12 months
Honey	12 months
Soft cheeses/blue cheeses, e.g. Brie and Danish Blue	12 months
Unprocessed bran	5 years

THINK IT THROUGH

Investigate all the different commercial weaning foods available in supermarkets, chemist's shops, etc. How easy do you think it would be to provide similar foods at home?

Nutritionally there is little difference between commercial baby foods in jars or packets and home produced weaning food. There is no one correct approach to the use of commercial foods. They are expensive and the consistency is often unlike ordinary food. Some parents will only feed a baby home produced food. This is fine, but can be difficult if the family is out for the day, or the rest of the family are having a meal that is spicy or otherwise unsuitable. A sensible mix of commercial and home foods is a good compromise. Home produced weaning foods are nearer in texture and taste to the child's eventual diet, but can take time and effort to prepare.

How to start weaning

Try offering the first spoonfuls of a bland, very liquid mix, part way through a milk feed, or near the end, when the first pangs of hunger have been satisfied. It takes some time for a baby to recognise that nourishment can come from a hard plastic object that has strange tastes on it, rather than from a soft, warm breast or rubber teat.

In the weaning process new tastes should be introduced gradually. Babies are fairly conservative about new tastes, and trying too many in a short space of time will usually result in rejection and confuse their taste. Offer only one new taste a day in the first months of weaning, and if a new food is rejected one day, try it again later; it may then be accepted with pleasure. Initially food should be strained or liquidised and only be slightly thicker than milk.

Gradually over a few months, food can be thickened in consistency, and eventually mashed with a fork with a mix of foods on the dish. As the amounts of solids taken increase, the amount of milk feed offered should be reduced. By the time a baby is eating three substantial meals of solids a day, milk feeds should be reduced to night-time, with water or fresh juice at and between meals.

As soon as the baby starts trying, let him or her join in feeding, even though everything will fall off the spoon, and it will go anywhere but in the mouth. Offer finger foods as much as possible, as it all helps independence. It is no coincidence that a baby is ready to start self-feeding when his or her gross and fine motor skills have reached the stage of sitting up and a pincer grip. At nine months a baby can pick up small items between finger and thumb, is sitting without support and is still exploring everything with his or her mouth. This is a time to introduce finger foods, that is, anything the baby can pick up and

I know it goes in somewhere around here!

eat with the fingers, e.g. lumps of cheese, apple pieces, small sandwiches. Weaning is not just about eating different foods; it also develops independence in feeding, promotes fine motor skills, and develops the mouth muscles involved in speech. Let them experiment with safe finger foods, and put their hands in the food and test the textures. Mealtime can be play time for a young baby, and is a very healthy approach to take.

A vital piece of equipment at this stage is a sheet of plastic to protect the floor if it is not washable. A suggested day's menu as a baby progresses towards a normal family diet could be like the one shown below, with adaptations for family preferences.

Time of day	Daily diet 6–9 months	Daily diet 9–12 months	Daily diet 12+ months
On waking	Breast or bottle feed	Breast or bottle feed	Drink of milk
Breakfast	Baby breakfast cereal with puréed fruit	Porridge made with 90 ml (85 g) infant/follow-on milk	1 slice of toast, 1 Weetabix with milk, well-diluted orange juice
Mid-morning	4 satsuma segments	2 breadsticks and cheese cubes	Carrot sticks and chickpea purée (houmous)
Lunch	3 tbs broccoli and potato with cheesy sauce, 90 ml (85 g) infant/follow-on milk, chopped melon pieces	1 hard boiled egg with soldiers, 1 fromage frais, 90 ml (85 g) water or well-diluted orange juice	Scrambled egg on toast, baked banana and custard, 90 ml (85 g) water or well-diluted orange juice
Mid-afternoon	Half a small mashed banana or mango, water as a drink	Toast fingers, water as a drink	90 ml (85 g) fruit smoothie, 1 pitta bread or bread with cheese or ham
Tea	3 tbs creamy tomato sauce with 1 meatball and pasta shapes, 90 ml (85 g) infant/follow-on milk, 1 small yoghurt	4 tbs shepherd's pie made with meat or lentils (potato can be mashed with follow-on milk), 1 tbs broccoli, 1 tbs carrots, 1 banana	Portion of fish pie and vegetables, 1 handful of seedless grapes or stewed fruit
Evening	Breast or bottle feed	Breast or bottle feed	Breast feed or milk

Feeding difficulties

It is rare for a child to make the transition to everyday family meals without a few tears and tantrums on the way. Many children are seen to have a food problem at some time. The approach that carers take is an important part of dealing with this. Refusing food at a designated mealtime is not a problem. Any child who has food offered in a relaxed, thoughtful manner will eat as much as he or she needs if opportunities are provided. This continues throughout childhood; eating and not eating only become a problem if the child's carers see them as a problem. A baby has every right not to eat if not feeling hungry, in the same way as you have. Why would a toddler want to sit down and eat when he or she is in the middle of an exciting play activity, or investigating what is in the cupboard in the hallway? Sometimes a child is simply too busy, too tired or still full from the last meal to want to eat. If a parent understands this, it can take away a lot of the pressure at mealtimes. Simply removing the plate and letting the child go back to play is the best approach.

DID YOU KNOW?

Many people who are overweight or suffer from eating problems, e.g. anorexia, bulimia etc., relate that mealtimes were a battle zone in childhood.

Occasionally a baby may have an allergy to a particular food, and react with sickness, skin rashes or breathing problems. In serious cases urgent medical help may be needed. Usually the baby will have already shown this tendency with milk feeds if there is an allergy to cows' milk, or through the mother eating certain foods when breast feeding. Babies can be allergic to certain foods and as they start to wean this becomes apparent. However, great care needs to be taken before deciding a baby is allergic to a certain food, as it is easy to deprive a baby or child of vital nutrients. The appearance of a rash after eating something may be a coincidence. If an allergy is suspected avoid that food until advice is taken from the child's doctor or health visitor.

From time to time items appear in the media suggesting that certain foods, either too many or not enough, are the cause of conditions in children. One such example was artificial food colorants resulting in behaviour problems. Large amounts of certain fish oils are thought to contribute to improved behaviour. A response to some of these may seem sensible, and as a child carer you should keep yourself up-to-date with such news items and advise parents to seek advice before restricting or supplementing their child's diet.

Supporting parents' wishes

Feeding a baby can be a difficult and emotional topic for parents. Many people see a thriving child as the sign of 'good' parenting. A child who does not eat well could be regarded as not being cared for properly. We develop our attitudes to food from a very early age, from our parents and our own experiences. Parents can become upset about what their child is or is not eating, and many parents come under pressure from grandparents. Despite being aware of the latest healthy diet issues, they may find it hard not to follow their own parents' suggestions. As a child care worker, you can offer support to parents in encouraging healthy eating in their babies.

When a child is at nursery this is fairly easy, but if you are working in a child's home it may be less so. It is important to remember that the final decision is that of the parents. Disagreements with them in front of the child will only make the situation worse. You may be able to have an informal chat with the parents about eating and diets, or show them an article you have read, but you cannot force your opinion on them.

THINK IT THROUGH

Survey the menus of all the babies at your placement. Do they all eat the standard menu of the nursery? If they do, find out what provision there is for following parents' wishes where they have different requirements for their child's diet. How would the nursery support those parents?

As a worker in a care setting, you should as far as possible follow the wishes of parents in all aspects of care unless there are health and safety issues at stake. This applies particularly to food. Parents are the most informed about their children's needs and requesting they do not eat a certain food may have a reason you are not aware of. Cultural variations should always be respected when you are designing menus for young children. Always avoid offering 'forbidden' foods such as pork to Muslims, or meat to vegetarians.

ASSESSMENT ACTIVITY

Describe the dietary needs of a baby aged 0–12 months and demonstrate how to prepare bottle feeds and weaning foods.

1 Collect up-to-date information about the national dietary guidelines for a baby in the first year of life. Produce a set of easy to follow guidelines for the parents of a new baby.

2 Either a) Give a demonstration of making up a bottle feed or preparing fresh and packet weaning foods. If you choose this option you should prepare a 'script' or tape of your demonstration outlining the key points.

Or b) Design and produce an illustrated sheet showing the important safety points to consider when preparing bottle feeds and weaning foods.

To achieve a **merit grade** you will need to explain how the feeds you have prepared will meet the dietary needs of babies.

To achieve a **distinction grade** you will need to explain how good nutrition is linked to babies' development.

Creating a safe and stimulating environment for babies

Bonding, attachment and communication

All babies need to develop close links with at least one important adult within the first year of their life. This is the start of a person's emotional security. John Bowlby (1907–90) was made famous by his research findings that if a baby has long separations from the main carer, or does not form an attachment to a main carer, there would be serious problems for the child in later life. It is unusual for this to happen, as all child care professionals are aware of the need to encourage the development of close bonds with consistent carers. It is usual for most people to have close emotional links with several people.

The first close emotional bond is usually with the baby's mother. Before birth, the baby has been listening to the mother's voice, hearing her heart beat, and generally becoming familiar with the rhythms of the mother. In a normal delivery, the mother often holds the baby while the placenta is being delivered, and a breast-feeding mother may start to feed at this point. If there are complications in the birth, every effort is made to ensure that the mother can hold or touch the baby as much as possible, even if the baby has to be in an incubator.

All this helps with the process of 'bonding', which is strengthened by:

- skin-to-skin contact
- eye-to-eye contact
- familiar sounds of voices
- familiar smells.

It is important for a baby to develop relationships with significant others. This not only allows more flexible caring, but is part of the process of primary socialisation. We cannot learn to develop relationships and mix with people in society generally until we have developed a range of relationships in our early months with different family members and other close carers. Ideally, a baby needs one or more constant caring figures, usually mother and father or grandparents. A good bonding relationship can and does develop with non-family members; you will see this yourself as you progress in your work with babies. If a baby is cared for outside the home, then the carer should not be constantly changing. Many settings now use a key worker system, where one person has the prime responsibility for a child.

THINK IT THROUGH

■ *Louie, aged nine months, attends a day nursery every day from 8 am to 6 pm. The baby room is staffed by whoever is available from the main nursery. Louie's mother is concerned because she never seems to see the same person when she drops Louie off or picks him up. Louie seems to be losing interest in nursery and cries or is miserable most of the time.*

■ *Leila is also aged nine months and also attends nursery from 8 am to 6 pm. The baby room has its own team of staff, with two key workers responsible for each baby. They are never on duty together, but have a good communication system to inform each other of how the babies are progressing. There is also a meeting once a week for the key workers to discuss 'their' babies. Leila's mother feels confident that she is leaving Leila with the same people all the time, and Leila greets her carers with a big smile every morning.*

Why do you think Leila and Louie react so differently to their day care?

Separation anxiety

Forming close attachments to a person means that when a baby is separated from that person he or she will probably be distressed. This will start to be obvious at around five or six months of age. If you are the new carer in a baby's life, there are ways of making this change easier for the baby:

■ approach slowly

■ talk gently to the baby before you try to pick him or her up

■ make sure that the baby can look at the parents as you take him or her from them.

From a very early age babies will show that they prefer the company of some people rather than others, usually by crying if they do not like a person. If you find that a baby does not respond well to you, speak to a supervisor about it and arrange for someone else to care for that baby. It may be a matter of time before the baby gets used to a new carer.

More usually, the problem you encounter will be how to deal with the ending of your care for a baby. It may be at the end of a short placement, or once you are qualified, or as a baby moves to another nursery, or you change jobs. Always remember that you will have played an important role in the life of that baby. If possible, try to keep in touch with the family. Continuing to visit a family where you were a nanny is perfectly acceptable, and will help the new person who is taking over. In a nursery, encourage the mother to bring the baby back for visits if possible, or if the baby has moved on to the next stage in nursery, there should be a transition stage during which you take the baby into the next room and stay for a time. All good child care settings accept the principle of bonding.

The role of the carer in language development

Apart from the security that consistent care gives to a baby, continuity of care is important in developing a baby's communication skills. From birth, you can see a baby trying to communicate with his or her main carers. Watch and listen to a new baby and mother. The mother will usually be talking in a language that to you may sound like nonsense, but this 'motherese' way of talking is an important part of initial communication for a baby. In response to talking, cooing, etc. from the carer, a baby will make noises back and then wait for a response; this is the start of 'turn taking' in communication. This is not restricted to mum and baby. One of the delights in caring for any child is the interaction and communication that happens, but to see the response of even a very small baby to talking and facial expressions is especially rewarding. It is easy to identify a baby who has had a lot of experience of being talked to; the baby will be constantly 'talking' on his or her own, experimenting with sounds.

Carers have a heavy responsibility in the development of language in a child. There are several theories about language development, but what is clear is that children learn to speak by hearing speech. A child who cannot hear well learns to speak the distorted words they are hearing. A child who hears a lot of swearing will soon start to repeat that swearing. The speech that a child hears needs to be directed to them.

DID YOU KNOW?

Research has shown that babies who spend long periods of time in a room with the TV or radio on do not develop their language skills as quickly as a child who has lots of face-to-face communication.

A child's identity, self-esteem and self-concept starts to develop from birth; some would say before that. Constant communication, good bonding and relationship forming for a baby starts the process of how a child will see him or herself. A variety of people, e.g. adults and children who are clearly interested in you and want to spend time talking, playing and caring for you, make a baby feel wanted and valued. Think about the opposite scenario: a baby who is not wanted, left alone for long periods, and rarely, if ever, played with. Apart from poor bonding with the carers taking place, the baby will not feel valued and cared for.

As a baby starts to learn new skills, reinforcement that the baby is doing well is essential. It is very easy to praise and encourage a baby as the baby starts to roll over, shake a new toy, crawl and start to walk. Think about other everyday activities that can be praised and encouraged. We all like to be told how good we are and this starts form birth. Studies again show that a baby who has not had enough praise and encouragement from parents can be timid and easily discouraged when things go wrong. There is an obvious cause and effect here; if parents have not had the praise and encouragement needed from babyhood, how do they know how to offer that to their own children? As a carer you can add to inadequate encouragement from parents to benefit the child, and by your example may encourage parents to do the same.

ASSESSMENT ACTIVITY

Describe the importance of bonding, attachment and communicating with babies.

1. In a small group, share your experiences of care for babies under 12 months, focussing on how consistent the carers in the child's life have been. This might be from a nursery, from discussions with parents who have changed the care for their baby on several occasions, or from your observations. Chart your findings with a list of good practice and poor practice, giving examples and reasons for the effect on a child.

2. Now using the information from the group and your own knowledge, describe the importance of the quality of early bonding and attachment on a young child, as well as the quality of the carer's communication with the child.

To achieve a **merit grade** you will need to explain how your work in caring for babies takes account of bonding, attachment and the importance of communicating with babies.

To achieve a **distinction grade** you should reflect on your practice and devise a personal development plan to improve your bonding or attachment and communication skills in working with babies.

UNIT SEVEN

WORKING IN PARTNERSHIP WITH PARENTS

Working in partnership with parents and carers will be an integral and important part of your role as a child care worker. By working together with parents, you can help to support the social, emotional and intellectual development of children, and help them to feel secure and happy. A friendly and professional relationship with parents and other carers is essential, and this unit will help you work towards that aim.

In this unit you will learn about:

- working in partnership with parents and families
- the boundaries of responsibility when working with parents
- sharing appropriate information
- the role of the carer as a member of the caring team.

Working in partnership with parents and families

Promoting a positive relationship with parents

Whatever type of family setting a child lives in, he or she will usually relate principally to the carers in that setting. The term 'parents' is used in this chapter to refer to the main carers of the child, regardless of the actual relationship. A child's parents are central to a child's life. It is usually the parents who decide which playgroup, nursery or school their child will attend. You are acting only as temporary custodian of their child for a limited period; at the end of the day the child goes home with the parents. As a child care worker you have a responsibility to work with parents and build up an effective, trusting relationship with them, for the benefit of the child.

Since the 1970s, parents' and children's rights have been enshrined in various charters and regulations placing a legal responsibility on child care workers to co-operate with parents in the care of children. Some of the reasons behind this are shown below.

- A child needs the feeling of being at the centre of a group of concerned adults, all with his or her well-being at heart.

- A child may be cared for during the majority of the day by adults other than the parents. All those involved need to pass information to each other about the child's day and night.

- A child may require some intervention such as work on behaviour. This will only work if all adults collaborate.

- The child care setting needs the co-operation and permission of parents for outings and activities.

- Some schemes such as home reading schemes will not work without parental involvement.

- Parents have a right to be involved in and consulted about their child's care setting, because they are responsible for their children.

- Parents can and do challenge decisions as a result of their rights under the Parents' Charter, which lays down a framework within which professionals involved with families must work in partnership with parents.

A positive relationship is crucial. Parents must feel they are part of the team caring for their child, never just tolerated.

DID YOU KNOW?

Parental involvement is eight times more important for a child's academic success than social class. Children whose parents are involved in their learning have better language and numeracy skills than those whose parents are not involved.

THINK IT THROUGH

Does your placement have a clearly displayed charter? Ask to see it and obtain a copy of the Parents' Charter, your placement should have one, or your local education authority will. Read it carefully. Now devise your own version of a parents' charter, making it appropriate for the settings in which you work.

The benefits of parental participation

Parents can bring skills and experiences to a group that can greatly enrich your work with the children. Not only do they have detailed knowledge and understanding of their own child, but they may also have specific skills, for example playing an unusual musical instrument or carpentry skills.

Usually, the first involvement a parent will have is in helping his or her child to settle. A move to a new nursery, or even a new room, the change to primary school, or the very first start in group care, are all potentially traumatic for both parent and child. Parents should always be encouraged to stay with a child during a defined settling-in period, which will vary with each setting and the age and stage of the child. The benefits to children of a parent being with them at this stressful time include:

- the presence of a familiar and loved figure in a strange setting
- security
- an opportunity for the parents to learn about the routine and activities in the setting, which is reassuring to them
- a focus for conversation at home to discuss the setting.

Many child care settings have an active programme of parental involvement, including:

- regular parent volunteers in schools assisting with reading, the home corner, putting up displays, routine tasks such as photocopying, or work in the school library

- occasional involvement, e.g. when baking, on outings, or on special occasions such as the Christmas play, when parents may help to make the costumes and scenery

- parents who are central figures in the organisation, e.g. in playgroups or mother-and-toddler groups

- assisting a child who may have some disability or special needs with which the parent prefers to help, such as a child with speech difficulties

- fund-raising, e.g. through a support group, parent–teacher association or parents' committee.

All parents can offer something to their own child and others, through listening to readers, helping with the painting area, reading stories, or just being a useful extra pair of hands. Parents who have not always had a very positive experience of child care settings can benefit from making valued contributions by building their own self-esteem. A child's self-esteem is also improved by the input of his or her parents. You should guard against the risk that children whose parents cannot participate, due to work or other commitments, may feel at a disadvantage.

By participating in their child's care, parents can often learn new skills and knowledge that will benefit the child at home. For example, they may learn:

- ways of initiating play

- improved communication skills

- new recipes for playdough

- new ways of dealing with unwanted behaviour

- more about child development.

Sometimes involvement has advantages for parents because they are spending time outside the home interacting with other people, as well as their child. This is especially the case for parents who are in isolated situations.

THINK IT THROUGH

Find out the level of parental involvement in your placement. Do staff feel that parents are involved as much as they could be? How could this be improved? Create a booklet for your placement, written for the parents, to encourage parents to come and be involved with their child's care in the setting. Include the advantages to them and to their children. Remember to make it sound fun!

Why parents may find it difficult to participate

DID YOU KNOW?

Almost half of all parents do not talk to their children's teachers even once a term because they are lacking in confidence about their own knowledge and ability or have bad memories of their own school days.

Parents coming into a nursery or school for the first time may feel nervous or anxious before they start. Added to all the natural nervousness involved in a new experience, parents are concerned about the feelings of their child, and do not wish to appear inadequate in front of them or let them down. There are many other reasons why parents may find it difficult to become part of the group, as outlined below.

- Parents may have had a bad experience of education during their own time at school, and find it difficult to go into a school or nursery to help in their children's education. They will need reassurance that they are valued as partners in the care of their children.

- Parents may fear not having adequate skills to be of assistance in the child care setting. Parents need encouraging to see that they have a wide range of skills and experiences that are of value, e.g. cooking, story reading, musical skills or talking about their culture.

- Parents may feel intimidated by staff as a result of attitudes and the use of jargon. It is easy to forget that terms such as DLOs, SATs or assessments may mean little to parents, and indeed can make them feel shut out. Giving parents very unimportant tasks, not offering them a cup of coffee or showing them where to put their coats sends a message that can result in parents feeling very unwelcome.

- Parents can feel intimidated by other parents, especially if there is a clique of parents who are already involved in the setting and have developed working relationships with each other and the staff.

- Parents may lack time because of work commitments. This can be very difficult for a child to understand, especially if the parents of their friends spend a lot of time in the school or nursery. Often, there is not an easy solution to this problem.

- Care of other children can impinge on the time parents have available to help in school or nursery. With some thought this can be overcome, perhaps by allowing younger siblings to come into the setting while parents are helping. This can have the additional benefit of allowing the younger child to become accustomed to the group child care setting.

- Language problems may prevent adequate communication between staff and parents, and may deter parents from offering their services. Bilingual parents can be very helpful to a school or nursery. They can interpret, provide information about their culture, tell stories, make music and offer an alternative experience to that available from the staff.

- Sometimes cultural issues may prevent involvement; it may not seem appropriate to be involved. A lot of work must be done encouraging parents, breaking down barriers and making parents feel they are partners. Hostility is often due to a lack of understanding of recent changes in education and care, and previous negative experiences at the hands of care professionals.

- If parents have a sense of being tolerated in school or nursery, rather than being welcomed as true partners in their child's care and education, they will soon stop offering their services.

- Parents need to feel a real sense of purpose during their time in nursery or school. Although parents are usually happy to undertake routine jobs, always doing menial tasks such as washing the paint pots will not help them maintain a sense that their time is valued.

THINK IT THROUGH

Think of a time when you have felt very nervous because you have found yourself in a new situation. It could be starting on your college course, starting school or joining a new club. Do you remember the nervous questions: will I fit in? will anyone talk to me? where do I go? what do I do? will I understand what is going on? and so on?

THINK IT THROUGH

Brainstorm a list of all the ways that you can think of to encourage parents to become actively involved in the child care setting you are most familiar with. How many of these ideas are used in your placement?

Shared care

Both parents and carers are very important members of the team in a child's shared care, but parents are ultimately the most important adults in a child's life. They have to make the ultimate decisions about what is best for their child's welfare. Parents usually know their child best, and do not take decisions about their child's care lightly.

Parents need to be confident in the care their child receives when in the chosen child care setting. There are many different styles of parenting and families. Finding a care setting that most closely reflects the approach at home is important for successful care. It is highly unlikely that even in the best of situations, there will be an exact match of all aspects of the parents' views and culture in relation to their children and their expectations of them. It is important to respect differences of opinion that parents express about the care you offer. Every effort should be made to accommodate their wishes, providing you are not offending other parents or staff. This is not always possible, especially where outside circumstances have meant that the parents did not choose the setting, but were directed to use it, e.g. through a care order.

Handing a child over to someone else can be a difficult experience in any circumstance. How this is carried out is very important in forming a positive relationship for all involved in the child's care. Early years workers have a responsibility to find out as much as possible about a child before he or she enters a child care setting. Look at the following case study to see what can go wrong.

Case study – John

Week 1

John, aged two and a half, is to start at nursery. His mother is planning to return to work in a month's time. On his first visit, John stays very close to his mother, who looks around the nursery, asks a lot of questions about it and after half an hour of watching the activities leaves with John to consider if this nursery is suitable for her child.

Week 2

After a telephone conversation with the owner, John and his mother return with the plan that John will spend an hour at the nursery. He clings to his mother for about 20 minutes, but eventually becomes interested in the activities that are going on. He sits down to join in with story time and songs. His mother stays throughout. Later in the week, John returns with his mother. After about 20 minutes his mother goes out of the room and talks to the owner in her office about fees, etc. John plays quite happily.

Week 3

John starts nursery full time. All the staff have been moved round, and no one knows John. He wails miserably as soon as his mother goes, and some days he does not stop crying for some time. It takes a lot of persuading for John to join in any activities. By the time his mother collects him in the evening he is often very tired, and falls asleep in the car. Whenever she asks how John is settling and whether she can come in to see him, his mother is always told he is fine and so does not need to visit. She puts his quietness down to tiredness and a change in routine.

John's mother begins to be concerned when he starts waking a lot at night and refusing to use his potty. Mentioning this to the nursery staff, she gets very little response. Whenever she asks what John has been doing during the day, all she gets is a vague answer that he has been 'playing', and she starts to realise that she knows very little about John's days. After careful thought John is removed from the nursery and temporarily spends time with his grandparents. His mother decides to look for another nursery where she feels that she will be able to share in her son's time.

THINK IT THROUGH

In the case study above, at first the nursery seemed to be acting in an appropriate manner to help John settle in. What went wrong? Try to identify how the staff should have behaved to help him settle.

Benefits of exchanging information

In the previous case study, the staff had not given much thought to checking with John's mother about his favourite toys, comfort objects or routines. Instead of just allowing his mother to sit in the room with John for a short time, the staff should have been active in seeking out information about John's routine and habits. Look at the table below for details of a possible day in the nursery for John.

Time/routine/activity	Information needed before child starts in the setting	Information needed on a daily basis
Arrival at nursery	Pet names for John, comfort object, how he reacts early in the morning, usual breakfast. Stage reached in potty training. Usual home routines. Level of independence in tasks such as hand washing, going to toilet, feeding.	How he slept last night, what he had for the previous evening's meal, breakfast. How potty training is going. Anything out of the ordinary in home circumstances or his routine.
Free play	Favourite toys, games, activities.	Any new activities, etc. at home.
Snacks and lunch time	Favourite foods, dislikes, allergies. Cultural influences on diet – vegetarian, religious influences. Way of drinking – cup, feeder cup, etc. Usual level of appetite.	Any digestive upsets, change in appetite.

Time/routine/activity	Information needed before child starts in the setting	Information needed on a daily basis
Story time, TV time	Interests, favourite stories, experiences.	New interests, current favourite book, favourite TV programme at home.
Rest time	Routine and timing for daily routine. Preferred type of bedding, any allergies to feathers, etc. Whether frightened of the dark. Comforters used at sleep times.	Any changes to rests.
Nappy changing, toileting	Type of nappy used, creams, potty routines.	Any nappy rash, changes in toilet habits, any diarrhoea.

If you regularly exchange information with parents they will feel that you have a genuine interest in their child as a whole person, and that he or she is not just another child who happens to be in your group in the nursery or class.

There are benefits for everyone in exchanging information on a child.

■ Parents know what has been happening to their child during their absence.

■ They can talk to the child about his or her day.

■ Some activities can be carried through at home providing continuity for the child, e.g. songs at bath time that have been sung in nursery.

■ Carers get to know more about the child and the family, helping to develop a more useful relationship.

■ There is less obvious separation between home and the care setting for the child.

■ Important milestones are promoted and supported for both parties, e.g. toilet training, weaning.

DID YOU KNOW?

Recent research shows that only 12% of fathers become involved in their child's education. More work needs to be done to encourage fathers to understand they have an important role to play in their child's education.

THINK IT THROUGH

Choose two different children in your group at your placement. Try to choose two at a slightly different stage of development. Without breaching confidentiality, devise a chart similar to the one in the table above, personalising it with the information you have about each child and the consultations that you or your colleagues have with the parents on a daily basis. Do you think you are consulting with the parents as much as possible? If not, what is missing?

ASSESSMENT ACTIVITY

The manager of your child care setting has asked you to work on a leaflet for new parents who will soon be sending their children to your setting. Produce an easy to read, attractive booklet that covers the following criteria.

■ Give reasons why child care workers should work as partners with a child's parents.

■ Describe a range of ways in which child care settings can work in partnership with parents.

To achieve a **merit grade** you will need to include an explanation of the benefits for children of parents and children working in partnership.

To achieve a **distinction grade** you will need to include examples of the most effective ways of promoting partnership between parents and child care worker.

The boundaries of responsibility when working with parents

Respecting parents' wishes

When parents take their child home at the end of the day, they will continue to care for the child in their way, not yours. If this is widely different, the child may be confused by the inconsistency. Differences may arise for a number of reasons, for example some parents may not mind if their children eat with their fingers or run around at mealtimes, whereas you may need the children to sit down. There may be cultural differences concerning clothes, food and age of weaning.

Through effective communication, any potential difficulties about differences of approach can be prevented. A clear explanation of the child care setting's policies and procedures, given before a child is admitted, will offer parents the opportunity to decide if the philosophy of the setting fits in with their ideas on caring for children. Meetings with parents before admission should encourage parents to provide details about care routines and specific issues of concern.

Some issues are not negotiable. If a parent holds religious convictions that involve dietary restrictions, you would be wrong to challenge them; many Jewish people do not eat pork, for example. Restrictions may also be based on medical conditions; it would be very wrong to allow a child who is diabetic to eat the wrong foods. The only occasions on which you should consider contravening parents' wishes are those concerning health and safety. For example, allowing a child to play unattended near a pond, or on swings, is unacceptable. If the parents say it doesn't matter, that their child is 'sensible', tell them 'I'm sorry, but it's against health and safety regulations'. If you knowingly allowed a child to be injured by neglecting health and safety, you would be held responsible, even if you were obeying a parent's apparent wishes at the time.

It is also not possible to concur with a parent's wishes when they contravene equal opportunities policies. This is a serious issue that may make the parents reconsider their child's placement, but it is not negotiable.

Case study – Leila, Luke, Sarah and Joel

- Leila, aged three, is about to start at the nursery class in her local primary school. Her family are strict Muslims and Leila wears a shalmar chemise at all times. The head of the nursery likes all children to wear shorts for their time in the gym. Leila's mother is not comfortable talking to the male nursery nurse, as mixing with men other than those in her family is not allowed unless a male relative is present. She is concerned that Leila may not be given a suitable diet, avoiding pork and non-halal meat.

- Luke is eight months old and is joining the baby room at a nursery attached to his mother's workplace. He is still fully breast-fed, and his mother intends to come in every four hours to feed him. One of the staff has already commented that he should be on solids.

- Sarah, aged 18 months, is the only child of older parents. She is attending your nursery for a short period while her mother goes into hospital. When she came to look around, Sarah's mother was insistent that Sarah was not to be allowed out of the nursery on trips or outings. A regular feature of the toddlers' care is to go out at least once a week to the park or supermarket.

- Joel is five and his best friend is Liam. Liam has some difficulty in tasks requiring fine motor skills, and also some degree of learning difficulty. Staff in school are distressed when Joel's father comes to school asking that his son should not be allowed to play with Liam, 'because he is handicapped'.

Work in pairs through the case studies above. For each child, make a list of the potential problems that may result from the parent's wishes. For each point, state why the parent's wishes should be respected and why the parent may feel that way.

Could you talk through any of these issues with the parents? If so, what approach could you take? Try role playing one of the situations.

Seeking professional advice

Parents are usually committed to the best interests of their child. Often, they may ask your opinion about an issue of concern, for example their child's hearing, health issues such as a rash or failure to put on weight, or problems with their child's behaviour. Whatever your opinion, always advise a concerned parent to seek appropriate professional advice, for example take the child to the doctor, or ask a solicitor or health visitor. If you are concerned about some aspect of a child's care or development, it is important that you pass this information on to the parents with a suggestion as to how to follow the matter up. Be careful about referring a child to a professional without the parent's knowledge; this is not within your responsibilities, except in very rare circumstances that we will discuss below. You must always check with your supervisor first before discussing a child with the parents. Read the case studies below and think about what you should do next.

Case study – Ashra, Sarah and Jay

- Ashra is three, and has been in your group for three weeks. You are worried because he often seems to ignore you when you call his name or ask him to do something. His speech is not easy to understand, and he seems to have a constantly runny nose.

- Sarah is five and in the reception class. Sarah seems to have few friends, and is often the cause of disruptions in the home corner. You have seen her thumping and nipping another child, and she seems incapable of sitting still.

- Jay is six. He is very thin and withdrawn, and often comes to school smelling of urine and appearing dirty. At changing time for PE, you notice some very odd bruises on his back that seem to be in the shape of buckle marks.

What do you think you should do about each of these cases?

- Ashra would appear to have a hearing impairment, and it would be helpful to ask his parents if they have noticed it, and suggest he should be taken to his GP.

- Sarah's problems should likewise be discussed with her parents, and the carer might suggest that she is referred to a psychologist.

- Jay's situation should be discussed with your supervisor and a referral made to social services, without discussing the situation with the parents first.

A simple rule is that if you are in doubt, you should advise parents to seek a professional opinion. The nursery or school may sometimes arrange the referral, but usually the parents need to do this. In cases of suspected abuse, for example strange bruises on the child, it is essential that immediate steps are taken to protect the child. As a junior member of staff you should speak to your supervisor, who will then follow local policy. Most professionals associated with children are happy to give informal advice. It is very useful to build up contacts with speech therapists, social workers, health visitors, psychologists, etc. to whom you can turn for informal advice and guidance.

Sharing appropriate information

Sharing information with parents and others

Before a child starts in nursery or at a school it is important that the child's parents have received all the relevant information. This includes practical details such as:

- address and telephone number of the setting
- the staffing structure: names, roles, qualifications
- the name of the child's main worker
- the opening, closing and holiday times
- fees, and effects of absence on fees
- a contact to be informed if the child is ill
- what parents have to provide, e.g. nappies, food, money.

Details of the way the setting is organised and the 'spirit' of its way of working should be included, for example:

- how play and learning are organised
- whether there are outings for children, and who is involved in them
- any rules
- how parents can become involved in the setting.

Parents have a right to receive information from the nursery or school once their child is established there. Information should always be given about:

- changes in circumstances, e.g. moving to a new class or room, a change in start or finish times
- planned outings or trips away from school or nursery
- a child's progress or concerns about a child's behaviour
- holidays, teacher or staff training days

- schemes to promote children's learning, e.g. reading at home

- opportunities to view a child's work.

Equally, parents have a responsibility to provide the setting with information about their child. Before the child starts at the setting, parents should provide information to help you gain as full a picture of the child's life as possible. This information will include that shown below.

Child's name, date of birth and address

Family information – position in the family, who lives with the child

Reliable daily contact numbers for use in emergency or illness

Details of the child's doctor

Medical information on illness or allergies

List of people allowed to collect the child from school or nursery

Details about the child's interests, food preferences, toys, or comforters (if appropriate)

Involvement of any other professionals, e.g. social workers, speech therapists.

THINK IT THROUGH

Design a form that could be used to share information about a child. It should contain the information you and the parents need to share about the child. It could be designed to be filled in at a child's entry to nursery or school, with a copy kept by both parents and carers. Show it to a parent. Does it contain everything the parent wants included?

Think about the importance of verbal and non-verbal communication skills. These apply to all types of communication in the child care field. Remember the important points.

- Maintain appropriate eye contact.

- DO NOT interrupt when the other person is speaking.

- Show you are listening by nods and smiles.

- Give feedback in summary form of what has been said.

- If you are asked a question to which you do not know the answer, say so. Do not try to cover up lack of knowledge.

- Do not shout back if a parent or child starts to shout at you. Talk quietly and calmly, show you are listening, and try to move the conversation to a private place.

- Think about your body language. Do not stand talking with folded arms, or appear distracted by other activities.

- Be sensitive to communication barriers, for example an accent that is difficult to understand or someone with poor hearing. Have an interpreter present if needed, or use pictures and visual aids.

- Never belittle the other person.

- If in doubt, refer to your supervisor.

- Never gossip, either to or about a parent, child or colleague.

Another important rule is always to tell the truth. Parents need to be informed, confidentially, if their child is behaving in a manner that causes concern. Think about how and where you talk to parents. Most settings have a staff room or interview room to which you can invite parents for a private chat, always do this with your supervisor. Important information should always be easy to understand, clear, and if necessary repeated in some way. The following list shows some ways in which information can be given to parents and other carers:

- posters in the collection area

- notes sent home with the children

- use of an interpreter to speak to parents

- discussions when parents collect their children

- booklets of information

- a meeting

- articles in the local newspapers

- messages through community representatives

- information on the local radio or TV.

Information to pass on to parents

Young children learn and do something new every day. Even though their parents are not with their child all day, they will want to know what their child has been doing. Has a little one taken a first step or said a first word? You have a valuable role in passing on information at the end of the day. Information that could be passed on to parents includes that relating to physical care, activities and achievements, and any changes or new information.

Physical care information

■ Any accident or illness that occurs to the child during his or her time with you.

■ When a child is on regular medication, e.g. for asthma, how often it was used.

■ Food eaten during the day, and any problems with food that might have occurred.

■ The amount of sleep taken.

■ Issues involving physical care such as nappy rash with a baby, or the success or otherwise of toilet training.

Activities and achievements

■ Visitors to the setting, or outings.

■ New achievements, such as a first step or being able to read at a higher level.

■ Activities done by the child, e.g. painting, models, etc., which should be taken home if possible.

■ Anecdotes about incidents during the day, such as how the child helped other children or staff.

Changes and new information

■ Any changes in behaviour.

■ Any concerns about the child.

■ Information relevant to the next day in the care setting, so that parents can ensure children are prepared and suitably equipped.

This type of information transfer is particularly important in settings with the under-fives. Their memory span and communication skills may not enable them to tell their parents everything. Even with older children, however, it is important to make sure that parents are kept fully informed.

THINK IT THROUGH

When you are next in your placement, make notes on the information that needs to be given to parents at the end of the day. Were you able to pass it on to them? How useful was the information you gave and the way you gave it?

ASSESSMENT ACTIVITY

Describe effective ways to communicate with parents and other team members.

I   Look at the many different ways of communicating with children, their parents and other professionals.

Make a list of ways of communicating with each of these groups. Try to include examples of leaflets, letters, etc. that have been produced in your placement.

2   Look for ways of communicating that are common to all three lists and describe how they are used with each group.

3   Describe the methods that are left in each group and explain why they may be best suited to one of the groups rather than all of them.

No extension to merit or distinction is possible for this assignment.

Building up trust with parents and teams

Confidentiality is essential in any care setting. When parents are in a school or nursery, they may confide personal information to staff. You would not disclose information about a child unless it was professionally necessary, and the same applies to confidential information about parents. Personal information about parents should not be the topic of gossip in the staff room, and should never be repeated to other parents. In an early years setting you have to exchange information with other members of staff to help each other operate effectively. Because life is busy in a nursery or school, this exchange of information may take place in the room with children. Ensure that parents are not able to overhear such conversations, or you will be guilty of breaching confidentiality.

Information that is divulged by parents is confidential to those who need to know, e.g. care staff caring for the child. You need to be aware of the pressures many parents are under in bringing up their children; these pressures that can affect how they view the early years setting and indeed which they choose. Life events such as illness, moving house, divorce, death or redundancy can have a profound impact on parents and their children. Having to work very long hours to support yourself and your children may not be the choice of a single parent, but he or she needs support from you, not silent criticism because he or she leaves the children so late at the nursery.

You will often receive very personal information from parents. Some information has to be shared with others, even if the parent has indicated that he or she does not want the information to be passed on. Some examples of this are given below.

- If a parent confides that her partner is hitting their children, who are already on the child protection list, you cannot keep the information a secret. You must make it clear that you will have to pass the information on to your manager.

- If a parent confides that he or she intends to leave her partner, this poses a different dilemma. This information may not involve the child being put directly at risk, but it will have an emotional impact on the child. You may feel that you have to discuss this confidentially with your supervisor.

- Information about health problems in a child that may affect his or her performance or give rise to a medical emergency in school or nursery must be passed on.

- Changes in the child's circumstances that may affect his or her behaviour, e.g. a death in the family or a parent losing a job, should also be communicated to the necessary people.

Consider the guidelines given below about confidentiality in a child care setting.

Good practice: confidentiality

- Parents need to feel that confidentiality is respected when they are working in close partnership with carers.

- Everyone concerned must be aware of the rules of 'professional confidentiality', that is, which information must be shared with a line manager, such as issues relating to child protection.

- Let parents know that you may have to share some information with your line manager, before they start to talk about confidential issues.

- Never gossip about parents, children or other members of staff.

- Never discuss one parent with another parent.

- Do not make value judgements about a child or a family, but always respect a person's culture and identity.

- Remember to share information about a child's dietary needs, allergies, who collects the child, and any concerns with the rest of the care team.

Most child care settings hold a lot of personal information about their charges. It is important that everyone concerned is aware of the requirements of the Data Protection Act. This allows people to view the information that is held on file about them or their children. Remember this when you are committing your thoughts to paper or computer; you must report facts and events objectively, factually and accurately. Parents should be made aware that they have rights under the legislation, and reassured that all files are kept in a secure environment.

ASSESSMENT ACTIVITY

Outlines guidelines for maintaining confidentiality while working alongside parents.

Find out how your placement ensures confidentiality and the protection of information. Make notes, and discuss the matter with your tutor and supervisor and then produce a simple charter of guidelines on confidentiality when working with parents.

To achieve a **merit grade** you will need to suggest reasons why child care settings must maintain confidentiality at the same time as working closely with parents.

To achieve a **distinction grade** you will need to evaluate the effectiveness of methods of maintaining confidentiality while not excluding parents.

The role of the carer as a member of the caring team

General principles relating to roles and responsibilities

There are several golden rules that should underpin your work in the child care field. The basic principles can be summarised into the following ten commandments.

1   You have a responsibility for the care of the children, shared with their parents. Always remember that all children have parents or guardians who are the final decision-makers about their child.

2   Always consult about care needs, with the child if possible, and always with the parents. Respect the wishes of parents and child.

3   Always behave in a manner that shows your respect for the child and his or her culture and background.

4   Always challenge discrimination and stereotyping behaviour.

5   Have a child's safety foremost in your thoughts when planning for his or her needs.

6   Always keep information that is given to you confidential, if that is the wish of the parents and it is appropriate to do so. Know when you must pass on information.

7   Be willing and ready to seek help, either from your line manager or outside agencies, especially if you see other staff behaving inappropriately.

8   Never force a child to do anything against his or her wishes.

9   Always try to praise a child's positive behaviours and minimise the negative.

10   Enjoy your work with young children; your enthusiasm will be infectious.

The basic role of any child care worker or parent is to help the children in their care to develop to their full potential. A prime responsibility of all such people is to ensure a child's safety and to see that all their basic needs are met.

The role of the parents

Parents' roles in a child care setting have been discussed in the earlier parts of this unit. Parents do not give up all responsibility to their child's carers when they leave the child at the door. They have a duty to inform the carers about issues relevant to their child and his or her safety and welfare. Parents have a responsibility to make sure, to the best of their ability, that their child is being cared for in a satisfactory manner.

The role of the child care worker in a group setting

If you work as a child carer in a group setting, you have different roles and responsibilities. You have a responsibility to:

- the children in your care
- the children's parents
- your fellow team workers
- the organisation that employs you and pays your wages.

Sometimes it can be difficult to fulfil all these responsibilities, as there is potential for conflict of loyalties. The following list shows the main responsibilities of a care worker in a group setting:

- to follow the organisation's policies and procedures
- to carry out instructions from supervisors and managers
- to report accurately on the progress of children
- to contribute to the evaluation and change of procedures
- to try to minimise conflict in the team by working effectively with other team members
- to adhere to rules about confidentiality and the boundaries of responsibility at all times
- to pass on all appropriate enquiries or referrals to the relevant person
- to respect all parents and children
- to respect all other team members.

THINK IT THROUGH

Using the list of responsibilities given above, discuss with a colleague the best ways to promote good teamwork in child care workers. Present your ideas to the rest of your group.

The role of a nanny or childminder

Working in a child's home as a nanny or looking after children in your own home as a childminder has even more responsibility than working in group day care. For much of the time you will be in sole charge of one or more babies or young children. Parents who choose this type of care for their child usually want a more home like setting for their children.

THINK IT THROUGH

What do you think the advantages are of a home care setting for a child, parents and carer? What possible disadvantages might there be?

Home care workers have more shared responsibility with parents than care workers in a group setting. This is due to the closer working relationship between them and you. Working in a child's home, or your own, places a greater responsibility on you to be independent and able to deal with most issues. Parents employing a home care child worker naturally expect that their child will be cared for exactly as they wish and so must discuss and share these expectations with you. Key areas for agreement include:

- observing parents' wishes for care, including sleeping, type of hygiene routines, type of nappies, toilet training
- safe practice including child's freedom to explore, taking children out in the car, use of safety equipment
- mealtimes: timing, diet, approach to mealtime 'rules'
- discipline: house rules, management of behaviour
- language: use of 'baby' talk, avoiding bad language
- activities, outings, time watching TV, visiting friends.

It is important that you are all comfortable with the expectations. It is not a good idea to try to care for a child if you do not agree with the parents' wishes, and very foolish to try to go against them. It is likely that you will soon be looking for another job, one where you have greater job satisfaction in working in partnership.

Case study – Sasha

Sasha was working as a nanny for two children aged 12 months and three and a half. When she went to the clinic for the baby's hearing test he did not appear to be hearing very well. She agreed with the health visitor that he needed to be referred for further tests and told her to go ahead. When she mentioned that a referral had been made to his parents that night they were very angry and warned her that if she took matters into her own hands again she would be dismissed. Sasha was surprised at the parents' reactions.

What had gone wrong in this situation?

What should Sasha have done?

As a rule you should never take action that involves a child's health and well-being being assessed by an outside agency without the express permission of the parents. They will obviously wish to discuss the matter themselves and with appropriate people, and probably choose where any investigations or treatment are done. It is important not to let parents think you have been discussing issues with other professionals without their involvement or consent, especially if it includes reference to personal circumstances. A golden rule to follow is 'How would I feel if this was my child?'

As you have seen, confidentiality is a vital priority in your work in any child care setting. In a home care setting this is as, if not more, important. You will be party to very personal information about the child and the family. If working as a nanny in the child's home, you will be surrounded by a lot of personal and private information about the family. Always remember you are there to look after the children, not to be involved in the parents' personal lives.

As a nanny you are likely to have sole charge of a child or children. Although there are no legal controls as to who can become a nanny, you have a duty to be realistic about your abilities. Being a nanny can be a very isolated job; you may be in someone else's home, alone for most of the day, and with little contact with the outside world. Working overseas as a nanny can be even more isolating, as you will be living in a different culture, even if it is an English-speaking one.

You have a responsibility to be realistic about your role and its boundaries, and the personal skills and abilities you need to cope. It is also important to ensure that your contract is clear about your duties, pay and conditions, and that you are happy with them. Before accepting a post as a nanny, do a lot of research, asking other nannies about their jobs, talking to nannies previously employed by the family, and applying for jobs through reputable agencies who will back you if things do go wrong. You might like to think about cases that have been highlighted in the media when things went dreadfully wrong.

Childminders have some similarities to nannies in that they are based at home. However, they are in their own homes, and as you have seen they are covered by strict regulations. Very often, childminders care for a mixture of children, some of their own, and others from two or more families. There are several possible areas of conflict for a childminder:

- the risk of neglecting their own children in favour of the others

- the risk of favouring their own children

- resentment from their own children about lack of full attention

- refusal of their own children to share toys, etc.

- parents having opposing views on aspects of care.

Just like nannies, childminders may feel isolated, but they do have the advantage of being in their own home, in their familiar community with friends and neighbours nearby for support. Many local authorities encourage support groups of childminders, and many offer training groups.

DID YOU KNOW?

More than 300,000 children in England and Wales are cared for by registered childminders. Some childminders also provide overnight care for families where the parents have shift working arrangements.

THINK IT THROUGH

Think about the roles and responsibilities of different child care workers. Using the title of each role as headings, make a list of the different responsibilities. What sort of issues and incidents might make carrying out these roles and responsibilities difficult?

Regulatory requirements

Unit 3 discussed regulatory authority requirements for the registration of child care settings. You will remember that all child care settings have to be inspected by Ofsted, to ensure they are meeting the needs of the children in their care. Ofsted inspects both group and home child care. To help them meet the requirements of their inspections, Ofsted produces guidelines for child care settings. The guidelines state what the Ofsted inspectors need to find out about in the inspection, and cover the following points.

Home care workers have to show that they:

- are suitable people to look after children

And are able to:

- work in partnership with parents
- act with integrity and confidentiality when dealing with the family
- use the space and resources of the home effectively and do not exceed the agreed number of children they may care for
- ensure the children are well cared for and provide activities and play opportunities that contribute to their learning and development
- be aware of hazards and keep children safe at home and on outings
- promote good health for children
- provide drinks and food that are adequate for children's needs and conform to parents' wishes
- promote equality of opportunity for all children
- are aware that some children may have special needs and work with parents to take appropriate action to meet them
- manage children's behaviour in a way that promotes their welfare and development
- know what to do if concerned about the welfare of a child
- keep any records that are necessary for the welfare of children and share them with parents.

The frequency of visits varies depending on circumstances, but will be at least every two years. Parents are informed when an Ofsted inspector is due to visit, and may be interviewed by the inspector.

THINK IT THROUGH

What do these guidelines really mean? In groups, choose some of them and discuss them. Report back to the whole group what you think they mean and give examples.

THINK IT THROUGH

Has your placement experienced an inspection by Ofsted? Try to read the report; you will find it on Ofsted's website www.ofsted.gov.uk. Do you recognise the child care setting you are working in? Why?

Being a good team member

Most people enjoy working as part of some sort of team. There are many benefits to this, including:

- having someone to share responsibility with
- having people to ask about things and to learn from
- working together for one purpose
- making friends.

Being a member of a team has responsibilities including:

- knowing and understanding your role
- knowing and understanding other people's roles
- recognising your own strengths and weaknesses and seeking support for weaknesses
- carrying out your responsibilities to the best of your ability
- being thoughtful about other team members
- arriving at work on time and always letting your line manager know if you cannot be there
- attending meetings, open evenings and other team activities
- being a good team member, willing to help others out when needed
- being ready to ask for help if you need it
- respecting the organisation's policies and procedures.

Improving your performance

Throughout your training as a child care worker you will have been receiving feedback on your performance. This will have come from:

- college tutors, about your written work and practical performance
- supervisors in placements on a daily or weekly basis, both informally and formally
- a combination of both in the form of a report on your performance in placement
- parents and children, in the manner in which they respond to you
- yourself, as you have evaluated events and activities throughout your training.

It is important to recognise that no one is perfect, or ever will be! But it is very useful to develop the skill of constantly reviewing your performance. After a major activity, and at least at the end of every day, ask yourself the questions in the following checklist.

Good practice: recognising strengths and weaknesses

- What have I done today that went well? Why did it go well?

- What has gone less well? Why did this happen?

- Did I ensure that I met the needs of all the children I worked with today? How could I have improved this?

- Have I communicated effectively with everyone, e.g. other carers, professionals, parents and children? How could I have improved?

Following this checklist and listening to feedback from formal and informal reports should help you to identify your strengths and weaknesses. Admit that you have areas for development, but even more importantly recognise and value your strengths.

THINK IT THROUGH

In a group of four (ask your tutor to divide you into groups according to personality, to achieve a balanced group) compare the qualities you feel you each have, and your weaknesses in relation to child care. Does your opinion of your own weakness match that of your colleagues, or do they see your weakness as a strength?

It is useful to ask other people for their honest, objective opinion of your methods of working with children and parents. It is perfectly acceptable to ask a colleague in your placement what he or she thinks of planned activities. In fact, while you are training you should always be doing this, and afterwards asking what the person thought of your progress. Ask the children what they thought, too, but be prepared for some less than welcome answers.

Having identified your strengths and weaknesses, it is important that you do something with that knowledge. As a student, you should be drawing up an action plan to discuss with your tutor about ways you intend to overcome your weaknesses and build on your strengths. Look at the example overleaf.

Area for development	Action needed	Where to get help	By when
Difficulty keeping interest when reading stories to a large group	More practice, and ideas to maintain interest	Observe class teacher Ask to try with smaller group	End of the month
Ideas for working on themes	Read relevant material Attend planning meetings in nursery	Supervisor, head of placement	Before the end of term
Tend to run out of ideas to encourage children to tidy away at the end of a session	Observe experienced practitioners	Supervisor	Ongoing
Enjoy working with children with communication problems; seem to have a special skill in this	Develop more methods of working	Read relevant material Observe other 'experts'	Ongoing

ASSESSMENT ACTIVITY

Describe the role of the childcare worker in working alongside parents.

1 The careers teacher at your old school is promoting child care as a career choice. He has asked you to come into school and talk to pupils about the job. You decide to concentrate on the importance of working in partnership with parents Prepare, and write the script for, a ten-minute talk for the group on this topic.

2 To achieve a **merit grade** review all your reports, work, evaluations, etc. that refer to your role in working with parents and draw up an action plan similar to the one shown above. It will be helpful to brainstorm areas of strengths and weaknesses first, and ask your colleagues, friends and supervisors for their views. When you are developing your action column, be realistic, and do not try to achieve too much at once!

No extension to distinction is possible for this assessment.

UNIT EIGHT

POST-NATAL CARE

For a variety of reasons, often health related, a mother sometimes needs assistance to provide some or all of the care for her new-born baby (neonate). It is vital that she and the rest of the baby's family are in control of the care given by health and care workers. After a period of time, the mother or other members of the family will be totally responsible for the care, without your assistance. The key principle, therefore, is to avoid taking over entirely, even for a mother who is very ill or unable to perform tasks. This unit provides the knowledge you need to develop the necessary skills. You will also need to refer to Unit 6 as you work through this unit as this has additional material about feeding and caring for babies and about the importance of bonding.

In this unit you will learn about:

- principles of development of the baby and mother
- key principles of infant care and feeding
- the relationship with the child's mother.

Principles of development of the baby and mother

The normal neonate

New babies are born totally helpless, requiring support and protection from caring adults. This care starts well before delivery, with a series of ante-natal procedures and checks. The delivery period is carefully monitored, with the mother receiving care from a midwife, and occasionally an obstetrician if there are complications.

Careful observation of the baby at birth is essential to provide a baseline of its state of health to measure against in the future. As soon as a baby is born the midwife scores it against an APGAR score. This means that five vital signs are observed:

- heart rate
- breathing
- muscle tone
- reflex response to stimulation
- skin colour indicating oxygen distribution.

A score is given for each point, to a maximum of 10 as shown in the following table.

Sign	0	1	10
Heart rate	Absent	Slow (below 100)	Fast (above 100)
Breathing	Absent	Slow, irregular	Good, crying
Muscle tone	Limp	Some movement of hands and feet	Active
Reflex response	No response	Grimace	Cry, cough, sneeze
Colour	Blue, pale	Body oxygenated, hands and feet blue	Well oxygenated to extremities

- A score of 10 shows the baby is in prime condition.
- A score or 8–10 is good.
- A score of 5–7 gives some cause for concern, particularly about the breathing condition.
- A score of 4 or less suggests a poorly baby, requiring urgent care.

The majority of healthy babies have a score of 8 or above at birth, rising to 9 about five minutes later, with the extra point often reflecting a tendency to have slightly blue extremities at birth. A baby's APGAR score is carefully recorded, as it is a good indicator of future developmental progress.

Normal variations

If you compare a number of new-born babies they may seem very different in outward appearance. This is despite the widely held view that all new babies look the same. They do have many features in common, however. Babies are measured and weighed to determine their basic length, weight and head circumference and to test future progress.

- **Weight:** Most babies fall within the range of 2.5 to 4 kg. A weight under 2.5 kg suggests a baby is of low birth weight and may need special care.

- **Length:** Most babies measure around 50 cm, though it is difficult to make an exact measurement.

- **Head circumference:** The average is around 35 cm.

DID YOU KNOW?

Britain's smallest surviving baby was born in 2003. She was 23 cm long and weighed only 340 g. She was born 12 weeks early, after failing to grow properly in the uterus.

Primitive reflexes

Babies are all born with 'primitive reflexes'; they appear to be capable of some quite extraordinary skills that disappear in the first months of life. The primitive, involuntary movements are replaced by voluntary responses as the brain develops. If a baby does not have these reflexes at birth, or they persist too long, this may be an indication of problems.

- **Rooting reflex:** Gently stroking a baby's cheek will make the baby turn towards the finger to try to suck.

- **Sucking and swallowing reflex:** A finger gently placed in the mouth will be sucked, and the baby will make swallowing actions.

- **Grasp reflex:** A finger placed in the palm of the hand or under the big toes will be grasped tightly.

- **Stepping or walking reflex:** Held upright with the feet on a firm surface, the baby will make forward stepping movements.

- **Asymmetric tonic neck reflex:** Turning the baby's head to one side results in the arm and leg on that side straightening, and the opposite limbs flexing.

- **Startle reflex:** A sudden noise or bright light will make the baby fling out the arms with fists clenched.

- **Moro reflex:** Gently releasing support of the baby's neck results in arms being thrown out with open hands, followed by the arms folding back over the chest.

New babies appear helpless, and until recently it was thought that they had few skills at birth. Research has shown this is not the case, and in fact a neonate can possess many skills.

- **Sight:** The new-born can focus the eyes within 20 to 25 cm, the distance of the carer's face during feeding. Colour and three-dimensional objects attract interest.

- **Hearing:** Very soon after birth, babies learn to recognise their main carer's voice. They respond to sounds by blinking or jerking their limbs.

- **Smell and taste:** By ten days, a breast-fed baby can identify his or her mother by smell, and shows a preference for sweet tastes.

- **Touch:** A new baby is very sensitive to touch and enjoys close physical contact. The mouth is the focus of these tactile sensations.

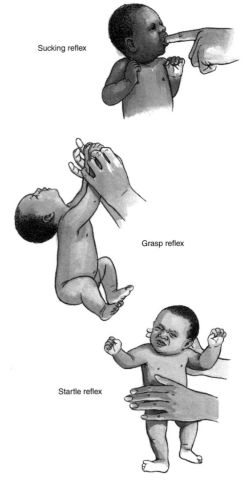

Sucking reflex

Grasp reflex

Startle reflex

Figure 8.1 Some of the 'primitive reflexes' of new-born babies

- **Motor skills:** A new baby lies prone with the head to one side. If pulled up to sitting, the baby's head lags, the back curves and then the head falls forward. Eyes and head turn towards the light. Hands are tightly closed.

- **Emotional and social skills:** New babies need close physical contact to follow on from their time in the mother's uterus, and to develop their emotional attachments to their carers. Cuddling and feeding are a neonate's main activities.

Factors affecting early development

Development throughout life is affected by influences before birth and during delivery. At birth and in the first ten days, these effects are usually apparent and fall into the categories shown in the table below.

Factor	Example	Possible effects
Genetic	Extra or missing chromosomes, mutations Combining of two recessive genes	Down's syndrome Congenital heart defects Cystic fibrosis
Environmental	Macro-pollutants in the atmosphere, living near chemical works Micro-pollutants in the home	Range depending on stage of pregnancy at time of exposure – e.g. limb deformities
Maternal illness in pregnancy	Rubella, toxoplasmosis Sexually transmitted diseases	Deafness or hearing impairments Heart defects or damage
Drugs taken in pregnancy	Alcohol Nicotine Prescription drugs Illegal drugs	Foetal alcohol syndrome Low birth weight Limb deformities Addicted baby
Radiation	Routine X-rays Atmospheric radiation	Limb deformities Physical deformity
Diet and nutrition	Lack of essential nutrients Presence of harmful bacteria, e.g. listeria	Spina bifida (lack of folic acid) Nervous system problems, low birth weight
Emotional stress in the mother	Relationship problems Worry about managing with baby	May be 'jittery', irritable baby
Delivery	Delayed birth causing lack of oxygen to brain Umbilical cord round neck Forceps delivery Foetal distress	Developmental delay Cerebral palsy Paralysis of limbs

An important focus of ante-natal care is to try to avoid or minimise the risk of any of these factors. Screening tests and advice to expectant mothers from a wide range of health professionals aim to ensure that babies are as healthy as possible. A new-born baby has several examinations and checks to identify any concerns in the first few days of life. The APGAR test referred to above is the first of these. Sensitive handling of the parents is essential if problems are discovered, and any concerns you have should be passed immediately to your supervisor, not communicated to the parents by yourself.

The way that any infant is handled in the first ten days can influence how that child develops in the future. In the first few days, a welcoming experience for a baby can be provided by remembering the following:

■ always speak in a gentle voice

■ ensure a baby is never left exposed without any clothes for longer than a few seconds

- keep bathing to a minimum

- feed on demand

- ensure there is frequent cuddling and holding, especially by the mother

- the temperature of the environment should be kept at approximately 20°C.

Weight gain

In the first few days after birth most babies loose a few grams of weight, especially breast-fed babies, as the milk supply settles in. A new-born baby's body contains extra fluid to tide the baby over the first few days when he or she is only taking small amounts of colostrum. Most babies lose around 6 per cent of their weight, sometimes as much as 10 per cent. The majority of babies regain their birth weight within the first week, but this varies and is not a cause for concern if the baby is feeding well.

After that babies gain weight at a steady rate and this progress should be checked on a regular basis. A baby who starts to lose weight for no obvious reason, or who does not gain weight for a few weeks, is cause for concern. If this happens, the health visitor will refer the baby to the doctor for a check as the weight loss could be a sign of some health problem.

A baby's weight can be tracked on a centile chart. This helps to compare a baby's growth to an average. It also helps to measure long-term weight gain. The centile, or 'percentile', line on a chart shows the percentage of babies whose weight falls beneath that line. For example, a typical chart would show that at birth 98 per cent of babies weigh less than 4.5 kg, but only 2 per cent weigh less than 2.5 kg. The 50th centile is the line that falls in the middle of the chart, showing the average for the particular population being measured. The line is drawn so that out of any randomly selected group of 100 babies, 50 will weigh or measure more, and 50 will weigh or measure less. Centile charts are useful because they can track the overall growth of a baby and help reassure parents about variations in weight gain.

ASSESSMENT ACTIVITY

Describe the development of the neonate in the first ten days of life.

A friend who is 36 weeks pregnant is keen to find out what to expect from her new-born baby. Produce a poster or leaflet for her,

explaining what she will see in the development of her baby in the first ten days after birth.

No extension to merit or distinction is possible for this assessment.

Anatomy and physiology of breast feeding

Breast feeding produces the ideal food for a new baby, and milk is automatically produced by the majority of new mothers in a production system that starts before delivery. Many women feel they may not be able to breast feed because they have small breasts, inverted nipples or breasts that are too large. However, breast size, shape or appearance rarely prevents successful breast feeding. Large breasts are usually an indicator of a greater amount of fat deposit, not of the size of the milk production equipment. It is not common for a woman to be unable to breast feed due to any physical problem.

DID YOU KNOW?

Government statistics show that more women are choosing to breast feed their babies. Breast-fed babies are five times less likely to be admitted to hospital with gastro-enteritis and 20 per cent less likely to develop obesity as adults.

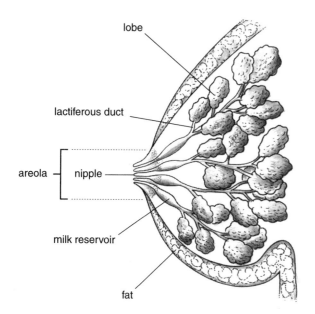

Figure 8.2 *How the breast produces milk*

Each breast is divided into lobes, like bunches of grapes, where the milk is produced. Each of these lobes contain 15 to 25 ducts or tubes. Each duct widens on the way to the areola (the coloured area around the nipple) where the milk gathers before it is expressed. Breast milk is produced in the lobes, travels into the milk reservoir and then leaves via one of 15–25 lactiferous ducts. Montgomery tubercles (small glands in the areola) produce a fluid that helps to keep the nipples lubricated and soft.

Milk is released to the baby through the 'letdown' reflex. This is when blood rushes to the breasts, bringing blood sugars to the milk glands. With sucking, oxytocin is released into the bloodstream, causing the cells around the milk glands to contract and squeeze out sweet-tasting milk. This squeezing is known as the letdown reflex.

1 Infrared photographs of lactating breasts show that they grow hot in response to a baby's cry.

2   Sucking at the nipple stimulates messages to the brain from the nerve endings. This can also occur in response to a crying baby, the approach of the usual feed time or just holding the baby.

3   The pituitary gland in the brain releases hormones on receiving the message.

4   The action of hormones on the breast muscles causes the release of milk from the lobes into the ducts.

Some mothers feel the letdown reflex as a strong sensation, while others hardly notice it. In the first few weeks of feeding it is the letdown reflex that can cause breasts to leak, until the supply and demand situation is sorted out. Even before the letdown reflex occurs, some milk is waiting for the baby. This is called foremilk and it is both thirst-quenching and rich in protein. But the hindmilk that comes later has more fat and therefore more calories and satisfies the baby better.

The letdown reflex must be stimulated for the milk supply to build up. Once breast feeding is established baby and breast work in harmony, with the milk supply matching the baby's hunger. By letting the baby feed on demand, the mother's body responds by producing the correct supply. Limiting the length of feeds or topping up with a formula feed affects this supply and demand, and milk production will fall eventually leading to the need to supplement more with bottles.

The composition of breast milk changes in the first few weeks of feeding. For the first few days a substance called colostrum is produced. Colostrum has a very high protein content, packed with the mother's antibodies for protection against illness. It looks very rich and creamy. By the third or fourth day milk is produced and mixes with the colostrum, with the balance changing so that by ten days the milk does not contain colostrum and appears thinner and watery, but all the required nutrients for the baby are produced.

Support from an experienced midwife and/or health visitor, and the mother's family, is important to establish breast feeding. For a mother who is unable to care for her baby by herself, this support is even more vital. A mother who is breast feeding should be encouraged to have a good fluid intake, as well as a balanced diet, to encourage milk production. Milk is produced on demand; the more a baby feeds, the more milk the mother will produce. Plenty of rest is important in the early weeks of breast feeding to promote the supply. Time and care taken in the first few weeks, with good support from family and friends, pays dividends in establishing breast feeding. After the early weeks when mum has settled into feeding, breast feeding is far easier than bottle feeding.

Some common difficulties associated with breast feeding are described in the table opposite.

Problem	Possible cause	Support/solution
Baby wants to feed all the time.	A delay in supply building up, poor position for feeding (baby not properly latched on).	Baby may be building up the milk supply, should settle again in 24–48 hours. Let the baby feed on demand. If nipples are sore as well, baby may not be positioned correctly. Check that the baby is latched on properly.
Sore/cracked/bleeding nipples.	Poor positioning, or the baby sucking on the nipple rather than the breast.	Take the baby off (breaking grip with little finger first), and try again, making sure that the baby's mouth is wide open when he or she goes on. Try a different feeding position, such as mum holding the baby under her arm, or lying down to feed. If there is soreness, some milk should be expressed and spread around the nipples. Feed from the least sore side first.
Sore nipples with white marks on them that do not heal. The baby may have white spots in the mouth and nappy rash; deep breast pain after feeds.	Thrush, which can sometimes occur after either mum or baby has a course of antibiotics, or it may come out of the blue.	Both mum and baby need treatment with an anti-fungal cream. Occasionally tablets are needed.
Full, hard, lumpy breasts, or flat nipples.	Primary engorgement, which often takes place when the milk first 'comes in' on the third or fourth day. Secondary engorgement, which happens when the baby drops a feed, e.g. when he or she first starts sleeping longer through the night.	Applying warm flannels helps the milk to flow, or having a bath or shower before feeding. Expressing a little milk before offering the baby the breast, so that it is easier for the baby to latch on. Feeding baby frequently to reduce fullness.
Small tender lump in the breast.	A blocked duct: something that has stopped the milk from flowing freely. This can happen if a bra is too tight, if mum has sat for some hours with a seat belt across her breasts, or maybe slept awkwardly.	Massage and warmth to help the milk to flow and disperse the lump. Let the baby feed by positioning him or her with lower jaw nearest to the lump if possible so that the strong action of the jaw can 'feed it away'. Feed from the sore side first. Massage and express after a feed if the breast still feels full and lumpy.

Problem	Possible cause	Support/ solution
Red, inflamed areas on breasts; flu-like symptoms.	Mastitis: an inflammation of the breast, which happens when breast milk leaks into breast tissue.	Mum should go to bed and rest and continue to feed baby, offering the sore side first. Feed frequently. Ask the midwife to recommend a painkiller. Warm and cold compresses to reduce swelling. If no better after a few hours, the doctor should be contacted as antibiotics may be needed.
Baby won't take the breast.	Change of taste of the breast milk, caused by change in diet or a course of tablets. Use of a nipple cream. Stopping using nipple shields; different texture. Periods starting/ dental treatment/even hard exercise!	Encouragement not to give up. Try feeding in a different way, e.g. standing up, in the bath, when baby is half-asleep, when lights are dim. If stopping using a nipple shield, trim it down with scissors, snipping out the centre first a little more each day. If breast refusal continues, mum may need to express milk to keep up the milk supply.

ASSESSMENT ACTIVITY

Describe the anatomy and physiology related to breast feeding.

Your elder sister is pregnant and is now asking you about breast feeding. She is curious about how milk is produced. In order to explain this, draw a labelled diagram to show the structure of the breast. In short sentences, describe how milk is produced in the breast.

No extension to merit or distinction is possible for this assessment.

Common difficulties for a new mother

It does not take much imagination to see that many mothers will experience some degree of difficulty in the first weeks after delivery. Many of these difficulties are minor, but there may be significant difficulties that require more than just support and encouragement by her carers. The huge responsibility that has been taken on can seem overwhelming to some mothers.

Pregnancy causes huge changes in the body, and after the effort of birth it is little wonder that a woman can experience a variety of problems as her body returns to normal. Many mothers experience both physical and emotional difficulties. The table below shows some of the potential problems.

The post-natal period is an emotionally demanding time. Mothers often feel out of control of their bodies, and can find the changes alarming. Care is needed, therefore, in supporting mothers and their families in the first ten days. Always pass on concerns to the midwife responsible for the family.

Type of problem	Cause	Possible solutions
Breast feeding difficulties	Engorgement – overfull breasts Blocked milk ducts Cracked or sore nipples Mastitis or infection Poor milk supply	Demand feeding Correct positioning of baby Exposing breasts to fresh air Attention to fluids and diet Support and encouragement
Tender or infected perineum	Difficult delivery Sutures (stitches) to area near vagina	Cushions to sit on Frequent use of bidet and warm baths Attention by midwife or doctor
'Baby blues' within 10 days – lasts up to 48 hours	Hormonal changes Sore breasts Family or external pressures Worry about baby or self Poor initiation of bonding	Reassurance that this is normal Support, listening, explanations to family Dealing with physical issues that need attention Usually stops, but health workers should be informed if continuing beyond 10 days – risk of developing into post-natal depression
Failure to return to pre-pregnancy body weight	Normal progress of post-natal period	Explanation to mother that it takes six weeks for body to return to normal, and that much of the weight gain is not just the baby, but general

Midwives can support the family until 28 days after birth, with the health visitor having responsibility from ten days.

Baby blues and post-natal depression

About half of all new mothers suffer a period of mild depression called the 'baby blues'. This may last for a few hours or, at most, for a few days and then it disappears. There are several symptoms of the blues including:

- feeling very emotional and upset

- crying for no particular reason

- feeling very anxious and tense

- feeling very tired and lethargic but having difficulty sleeping.

Baby blues may have several causes, some biological and some emotional, for example:

- sudden changes in the mother's hormone levels

- being unprepared for the exhaustion after a birth

- minor health problems of the baby, e.g. jaundice or feeding difficulties.

You can help a mum with the blues in the following ways.

- Encourage her to cry if she wants to and talk about her changing emotions.

- DO NOT tell her to pull herself together.

- Encourage her to discuss her feelings with a midwife, health visitor or GP.

- Listen and reassure her that the blues are very common, won't last, and that she will soon feel better.

- Help to ensure she has as much rest as possible.

- Make sure that friends and relatives know that affected mothers are often over-sensitive about what is said to them. Tact and empathy are very helpful.

In a few cases the 'baby blues' do not go away and the symptoms become worse. In this case a mother should see her doctor as soon as possible, as this is a common and treatable condition.

Post-natal depression is a very unpleasant illness which often starts after the mother has left hospital and been discharged by her midwife. It affects about 10 per cent of mothers who have recently given birth. Your role is to be aware of the symptoms of it and recognise when the baby blues are more than a passing problem. Reassuring the mother and her family is important, and encouraging her to talk to her health visitor or doctor is vital.

It is not always easy to recognise post-natal depression in the early stages. It has many symptoms including:

- feeling less able to cope with the demands of the baby and home

- feeling very despondent

- feeling very sad and crying frequently

- feeling anxious and fearful, may worry about her own health and that of the baby

- panic attacks and feeling tense and irritable all the time

- feeling guilty that she is not coping

- feeling tired and lacking energy

- inability to concentrate and finding simple tasks too much

- pains for no reason

- difficulty in sleeping

- poor appetite

- no interest in sex

- obsessional and inappropriate thoughts.

A mother with post-natal depression may suffer from many or all of these symptoms. You have an important role to play in identifying the warning signs of depression.

DID YOU KNOW?

The Association for Post-Natal Illness provides support for mothers with post-natal depression. It works to increase public awareness and encourage research into post-natal depression.

Case Study – Pearle

It is two weeks since Pearle went home with her third baby – a boy. She had really hoped to have a girl this time. Her husband has to go away on a business trip next week so she will be alone with the children. Pearle is still very weepy, and on the Sunday evening she begs him not to go. 'do not be silly, you were just like this with the other children. You will be fine in a few days, and I will be back next weekend,' Paul says. However, this time things do not get better. The baby cries a lot particularly during the night, and Pearle is becoming exhausted. She is very reluctant to let the older children touch the baby in case they pass on any germs, and yesterday when they came back from a walk in the park, Pearle washed over the whole pram to ensure that there were no germs to infect the baby. To make matters worse the other children are misbehaving in order to get attention. One day one of them climbed on top of the piano while Pearle was feeding the baby and would not get down. When she finally got him down she was so angry that she smacked him, which was something she had never done before. Pearle sat down in the corner of the room and sobbed bitterly. 'I wish I had never had this baby. I am obviously a hopeless mother if I can not cope with three children…'

1) Make a list of the signs that tell you Pearle may be suffering from post-natal depression.

2) Can you explain why she is feeling the way she does?

3) What could you do to support Pearle?

ASSESSMENT ACTIVITY

Describe the difficulties a mother may experience in the first ten days after the birth of the baby.

Talk to several new mothers and/or women who have recently had babies. What minor problems did they experience in the first two weeks? Produce a booklet alerting parents to these difficulties. Ensure you identify sources of help and advice.

To achieve a **merit grade** you will need to explain the reasons for these difficulties.

Key principles of infant care and feeding

Methods of feeding

Breast feeding is the natural feeding method of choice for any infant. Whenever possible, a mother should be encouraged and supported in choosing this method. Breast feeding has seen variations in popularity in the last 100 years and among different cultural groups in society. In the year 2000 figures suggested that approximately 70 per cent of women in Britain breast feed to some extent. However, many do not feed for more than a few weeks, some giving up in the first few days.

The choice of a method of feeding is one for the baby's parents. Breast feeding is nutritionally and healthwise the best for a baby, but the most important factor is the contentment of the mother with her choice. The reasons for choosing not to breast feed that mothers give include:

- embarrassment
- risk of being tied
- plans to return to work
- friends aren't doing it
- won't know how much the baby is getting
- thinking it will hurt
- not fashionable
- will get saggy breasts
- not sexy
- it's disgusting
- won't be able to do it
- too many broken nights' sleep
- my partner doesn't want me to.

The response to these arguments is obvious and as mentioned before it is the choice of the parents. Research shows that a partner not supporting the idea of breast feeding is the most important reason for a mother not even trying breast feeding, or giving up very early. An unhappy and stressed breastfeeding mother will not be helping her baby. A happy, bottle-feeding mum is far better than an unhappy breast feeder. However, you can play an important role in supporting a mother in breast feeding. Occasionally, a mother may not wish to or find it difficult to breast feed, and will require support in that choice, too.

Breast feeding is the best method for several reasons.

	Advantages	Disadvantages
Breast feeding	Protection against infection. A complete food. No risk of salts and mineral overload. Always available on tap. Effect on mother – baby bonding. Maternal benefits (less body fat, lower fertility, lower risk of breast cancer). No cost. Protection against allergies, eczema, asthma. Some protection against Sudden Infant Death Syndrome. Thought to offer some protection against diseases in adulthood, e.g. diabetes.	Demands on mum's time. Some initial practical difficulties. Difficulty in measuring/sustaining supply. Embarrassment. Jealousy by partner/siblings. Often incompatible with returning to work.
Bottle feeding	Other people can feed the baby. No embarrassment about feeding. Can see what volume of milk taken. Easier to return to work.	Risk of infection. Financial cost. Need for special equipment. Need to prepare and heat feeds. No natural immunity to pass on to baby. No health advantages to mother or baby. Risk of overload of salts and minerals.

ASSESSMENT ACTIVITY

Describe the advantages, to both mother and baby of breast feeding.

You have been asked to give a short talk to a group of expectant mothers who are keen to breast feed. Plan your talk giving a balanced view of the advantages of breast feeding to both mother and baby.

To achieve a **merit grade** you will need to explain the reasons why some mothers choose not to breast feed.

To achieve a **distinction grade** you will need to compare the relative benefits of breast feeding and bottle feeding.

Planning and delivery of feeds

It is obvious that babies need feeding to help them to grow and develop. Food provides:

- energy
- nutrients for growth and repair of body tissues
- nutrients for the growth of bones
- nutrients for the development of the nervous system
- fuel for maintaining body temperature and metabolism.

Babies vary in the amount of feed they need. If you think about the range of birth weight, it is obvious that a 4 kg baby will need more food for fuel than a tiny 2 kg baby. Even though new babies do not appear to do very much, they use a lot of energy in sleeping, breathing, excreting, crying and feeding. The basal metabolic rate is the amount of energy we use merely to be alive.

For a bottle-fed baby, there is a formula to calculate the amount of feed required. The packets of infant feed show this formula. As a guide, however, you will need 75 ml of reconstituted feed for every 500 g of a baby's weight every 24 hours. The total is then divided into the number of likely feeds, usually eight per 24 hours for a new baby or one every three hours.

Breast-fed babies cannot be given a neat formula; they need feeding whenever they are hungry, for as long as they need. 'Experts' used to dictate figures such as five minutes per breast every three to four hours, which is fine for some babies, but not for all.

The important points to remember are:

- all babies are individuals, and some may be hungrier than others, or hungrier at different times

- a baby should not go any longer than four hours without a feed during the day in the first few weeks of life.

Careful attention to hygiene is essential, both in the process of making feeds, and the hygiene of the person making and/or giving the feed. Unused bottles should never be kept for later, even if only a small amount of feed has been taken.

All babies should enjoy close physical contact with the person giving their feed. For this reason it should ideally be the baby's parents who do the feeding. Babies need to hear talking, singing or cooing when they are being fed, and need to enjoy eye contact with their feeder.

ASSESSMENT ACTIVITY

Describe what a mother needs to do to plan, prepare and feed her baby.

You have been asked to help a mother organise her feeding schedule for her new baby. She is using formula feeds.

To achieve a **merit grade** you will need to give explanations for each stage of the process of planning, preparing and feeding a neonate.

Hint: You will need to refer back to Unit 6 for information on preparing formula feeds.

No extension distinction is possible for this assessment.

Assisting the mother

DID YOU KNOW?

It is possible for a new mother to hire a maternity nurse or maternity nanny to help her recover from the birth and to establish a feeding pattern. The maternity nurse may be a former midwife, or a nursery nurse who has a lot of experience with new-born babies. They can provide 24-hour care or simply move in at night-time to allow the mother a good night's sleep.

The key feature of assisting the mother is to help and support without taking over. Wherever possible, the mother or other family members should be carrying out the care of the baby. If this is not possible, then all care of the baby should be done in front of the mother. The most important principle is that care should, wherever possible, be based on the requests of the baby's parents. In the first ten days, any baby needs:

■ regular feeding

■ frequent physical contact with the mother

■ to be kept clean and dry

■ adequate warmth

■ to be kept safe.

When the baby is awake or even when he or she is asleep, encourage the mother to hold and stroke her baby if possible. This is a vital component of the bonding process.

Physical care

Physical care should be kept to the necessary minimum to ensure the baby is clean and comfortable. New babies do not get particularly dirty, other than in the nappy area. Often a new baby will feel very insecure if given a bath, not enjoying the procedure at all. If this is the case, advise the mother that all that is needed is the washing of the hands, face and nappy area. Cotton wool should be used for the hands and face, dampened in warm water. Soap should not be used on a new baby. Always use one piece of cotton wool for each eye, cleaning from the inner eye outward. Never be tempted to poke in a baby's ears or up its nose. The nappy area should be cleaned with cotton wool and warm water. Female babies should have soiled faeces cleaned from the front to the back to avoid contaminating the genitals. Clothing for a new baby should be light, preferably made from cotton, with several thin layers, rather than one thick layer of clothing.

If a mother is unable to carry out any of the care for her own child, she will appreciate seeing daily tasks done for her baby. However, very few mothers are so ill or incapacitated that they are unable to perform some of the tasks involved in care. At the very least, they can hold the baby after you have done the practical jobs. By being as involved as possible, the mother will be getting to know her child and ensuring that her ideas are valued.

Helping with a crying baby

Crying is a baby's way of saying that he or she wants something. It certainly has the desired effect on carers! Usually a carer will try and find out as quickly as possible what it is that the baby wants in order to stop him or her crying. Listening to a baby crying is not easy for most people.

DID YOU KNOW?

Most small babies spend at least 7 per cent of each day crying.

Unfortunately, at first, until a parent or carer has got used to a baby's cries, it is not always easy to work out what the problem is. Possible causes that might make a baby cry include:

- hunger: if a baby is hungry, nothing you can do, apart from feed the baby, will stop the crying

- wind: if a baby has just had a feed, he or she may be crying because of wind

- a dirty nappy that needs changing

- being too hot or too cold

- may just want a cuddle: some babies seem only to be happy when they are being held – putting the baby in a sling can help

- boredom: wanting company and stimulation

- being over-stimulated or tired: in this instance the baby needs to be left alone to rest or go to sleep

- illness: ill babies may cry in an urgent or high-pitched tone, or in a way that is particularly fretful or insistent.

Sometimes you can eliminate all these causes and the baby will still cry. Some babies just do not seem to like being babies. They want to be doing things but they are not yet able to and they cry out of frustration. Others find it hard to cope with life outside the womb; the new sensations, such as hunger and tiredness, and different levels of stimulation, such as loud noises and bright lights, overwhelm them. These babies will cry less as they mature and develop.

DID YOU KNOW?

Cry-sis is an organisation that offers support for families with excessively crying, sleepless and demanding babies. You can reach them on their 24-hour helpline: 020 7404 5011.

THINK IT THROUGH

Imagine you are assisting in the care of a new baby whose mother has very limited use of her limbs (due to severe arthritis). How would you help her to participate to the maximum extent in the care of her baby?

Safety of the neonate

New babies are perhaps the most vulnerable members of our society. They are exposed to a range of potential dangers as soon as they emerge from the uterus. Babies need help with all the factors shown below.

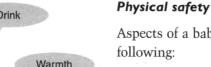

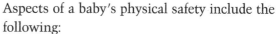

Figure 8.3 *New-born babies need help and protection in many ways*

Physical safety

Aspects of a baby's physical safety include the following:

- correct feeding procedures: how and where the baby is fed. Always have all equipment ready and ensure the person feeding the baby is in a comfortable position.

- a safe place to attend to hygiene needs, e.g. nappy changing, bathing and washing. These are best done in the baby's cot to avoid any risk of falls from beds or tables. Thought may be needed to improve access to the cot for someone in a wheelchair, for example.

- safety of the baby's mother when caring for her child: if the mother has some health or mobility difficulty that makes her unsteady on her feet, look for ways to encourage her to protect the baby from falls.

Protection from other people

In recent years there have been several cases of babies being taken from maternity units by unauthorised people. *All* staff in a maternity unit are responsible for challenging someone claiming authorisation to take a baby for 'tests' or 'check ups'. Ideally a baby should not go anywhere without his or her mother, or another member of the family. Check the procedure in your placement or workplace relating to this.

Another aspect of protection from others relates to people with illnesses. Babies are vulnerable to infection, and visitors with infectious illnesses such as coughs and colds should be discouraged from visiting. As a carer, you should think carefully about being in close contact with babies if you are ill yourself.

Mistaken identities of babies

Very occasionally, babies have been 'mixed up' and the wrong baby has gone home with the parents; you may have read about these cases in the press or seen them on TV. Procedures to prevent this happening are in place in all maternity units. The usual procedure is that every baby is tagged with a wrist and ankle name tag at birth, in front of the parents. This happens before there is any possibility of the baby being removed from the delivery room for treatment, tests, etc. The tag should have the mother's details, name, record number, sex of the baby and time and date of delivery. These tags should *never* be removed before the baby goes home, and then only by the parents. Find out the procedure for this at your placement.

Health and safety issues

Every employee at any place of work has a duty of care under health and safety legislation. This is particularly important where babies are concerned. You should always be on the alert for any possible risks to the babies in your care, for example from:

- slippery floors where someone could slip when carrying a baby
- faults in equipment
- incorrectly functioning fridges that hold baby formula milk
- blocked fire exits.

THINK IT THROUGH

How could you reassure a concerned mother that her baby will be safe in hospital?

The relationship with the child's mother

Limitations of a carer's role

Imagine you were unable to care for your new-born baby. Perhaps you had a very difficult delivery that resulted in your being too weak to do so. Or you might have some illness or disability that will require you to have support in caring for your baby when you get home. Although you require support, you do not want the care of your baby to be totally removed from you. You can certainly hold your baby and you have very clear ideas on how you want to bring your baby up. However, you are a new mum, and you welcome advice and ideas on the best way to do certain tasks such as bathing, dealing with nappies, feeds, etc.

THINK IT THROUGH

Faced with someone else having to do much of the practical care of your baby, what would concern you? Think about it and discuss it with a colleague.

The following concerns may be going through the mother's mind.

- Will the carers be taking over my baby?
- Can I discuss my ideas with them?
- Will they follow my cultural preferences?
- Will they try to change my mind about breast feeding?
- Will they try to do everything for the baby and not let me try to see which aspects I can manage?

As a carer you must always remember the fact that the baby will probably be going home with its mother at some stage. The baby belongs to his or her family; their choices about ways of caring are the important choices. If you are constantly involved in the care of a baby it is easy to become attached to that child. Continuity of care, allowing you to develop a relationship with the mother and family, is an ideal situation in many respects, but it can be difficult for the carer when the time for the baby to go home arrives.

As a carer, in any situation it is important to establish the boundaries of your care relationship. This can be made easier by:

- ensuring that the parents plan the baby's care, and that you follow their plan – remember that different individuals and cultures have different ideas about baby care
- always asking the baby's parents for permission before you do anything, even picking the baby up
- always asking how the parents would like things done for their child, and checking that you are doing the right thing
- always doing tasks for the baby in front of the parents

- whenever possible, encouraging the parents to perform the care, or part of it, themselves

- never assuming that it will be all right to give an extra feed, or give the baby a bath, without following the guidelines above

- reminding yourself that you are there only for support, and for a very short period of time, whereas the parents will be there for life.

The importance of the family in bonding

Research has shown that babies need to develop close links with at least one important adult, and that this is the best way to help a child to mature into a person with emotional security. Usually, we develop close emotional links with several people early in life, as shown below.

The first and most important link a baby will form is usually with the mother. Before birth, the baby has been listening to the mother's voice, hearing her heart beat, and becoming familiar with the rhythms of her body. In a normal delivery the mother may hold the baby while the placenta is being delivered, and she may start breast feeding straight away. Even if the birth has presented problems, it is usually made a priority that the mother holds the baby as soon and as often as possible, even if the baby has to be cared for in an incubator.

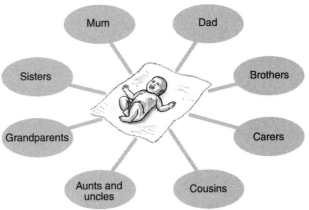

Figure 8.4 *Babies develop close links with several different people early in life*

The process of bonding is strengthened by skin contact, eye contact and the sounds of voices. Bonding does not have to be with the natural mother, however. A baby can develop strong bonds with several people, but what is important is that babies have consistent carers. Ideally a baby needs just one or two constant caring figures.

If a mother cannot look after her new baby completely by herself, it is even more important to ensure that close bonds are formed with other members of the family. Whatever the reasons for other people being involved in the care of the baby, it is vital to the psychological development of the baby that there is a consistent carer in his or her life.

In the first ten days of life, family and friends are often frequent visitors to the new baby and parents. Rather than just viewing them as visitors bringing flowers and chocolates, you should involve some of them from the start in the care of the baby. If the support required by the mother is a long-term issue, the involvement of others will probably have been discussed at some earlier stage. Maternity units should actively encourage families to start this process in the hospital, rather than waiting until the baby goes home.

Case Study – Gemma

Between the age of 18 and 27 Gemma experienced long periods of depression. She is now 29 and has just come home following an emergency caesarian section to deliver twin boys. Her friends decided to have a rota to help her as they were worried that she would not be able to cope. One of her difficulties when she is very depressed is that she needs to sleep a lot, so initially she was quite grateful to have so many people to come and look after the boys and allow her to have plenty of sleep. It seemed that the house was always full of people who were either helping, or had just come to look at the new babies. Even when Gemma was awake her friends encouraged her to rest and she was beginning to feel that the babies were not hers at all. A month later Gemma had still not spent an evening alone with her husband and the babies. One afternoon when she woke up, she heard two of her friends arguing about what to do with one of the babies and whether he was crying was because he was hungry, bored or tired. Gemma lost her temper and shouted at her friends 'I wish you would just go away and leave us alone'.

1) Why is Gemma angry?

2) Why might it be difficult for the babies to have so many carers?

3) Describe what you would have done if you had been asked to support Gemma.

Plans of care for the neonate

When planning care for a neonate the first priority is to draw up a plan with the baby's parents. Different cultures have different views on the care of the new-born. Some cultures do not believe you should bathe a baby in the first weeks of life. There are many different religious rites surrounding new babies, and you should always discuss these with the parents; never assume that your ideas are the same as theirs. By asking, you will learn a lot about other cultures, and avoid offending the parents.

If asked for advice, you can suggest that care should be arranged around feeds. There is little point in waking a baby for a wash in between feeds, for example. A neonate needs:

■ regular nappy changes: bowel movements are very frequent in the first few weeks, as the intestines automatically contract every time the baby feeds; for the first few days stools are dark and sticky, made up of the meconium that has been in the bowels before birth

■ hands and face to be cleaned on at least a daily basis

■ clean clothes daily, to avoid rubbing from sweat or dried milk

■ regular feeds: every three hours on average, but this may be every two hours in some babies or as little as every four hours

■ close physical contact with parents, especially the mother

■ a lot of sleep: many neonates sleep from 18 to 22 hours a day, waking only for feeds.

This pattern of needs fits in well with the needs of the mother. She has had a period of hard work, and also needs to rest and recover from the birth. A useful plan of care could look like the one shown below.

The important point about the care plan is to ensure that the mother is fully involved wherever possible. If she is breast feeding this will be much more obvious, but encourage her to perform as many tasks as possible. In between feeds, encourage the mother to rest, depending on her state of health. Your role in this care could be as simple as ensuring that the mother can reach the cot, and has all the necessary equipment to hand; or it could involve you doing all the activities yourself, with the mother present. Of course you will be constantly talking to her, and checking all your actions with her.

Time	Activity
5 am	Feed followed by nappy change – back into cot.
8 am	As above.
10.30 am	Hands, face and bottom washed or bath. Clean clothes and nappy. Feed, probably with clean nappy after the feed.
2 pm	Feed, change.
5 pm	As above.
8 pm	As above, but change into nightwear.
11 pm	Feed and change.
	Possible middle-of-night feed.

Figure 8.5 *An example of a plan of care*

ASSESSMENT ACTIVITY

Describe the role of the care worker in assisting the mother to care for the baby.

You are to plan a period of care for a new baby. Outline your plan, giving details of your role in assisting the mother or carer to care for the baby. How could you encourage members of a new baby's family to become involved with his or her care.

To achieve a **merit grade** you will need to explain the benefits to child and mother of involving her and her family in all aspects of the care of the baby.

To achieve a **distinction grade** you will need to explain the possible consequences of failing to involve the family in all aspects of the care of the baby. You will also need to analyse the role of the care worker in supporting a mother in the first ten days after birth.

Glossary

Abuse: deliberate injury or harm to another person, particularly vulnerable people e.g. children, older people and people with disabilities. The abuse can be physical, emotional, sexual or neglect.

Adaptations: changes made to the arrangement or design of a building, piece of equipment or an activity ensuring it is inclusive.

Adolescence: the period of development leading to adulthood – starts at puberty. A period of rapid physical growth and development.

Adoption: the legal transfer of a child from their birth family to another family.

Anorexia nervosa: an eating disorder in which severe and potentially dangerous weight loss occurs. Approximately 50 percent of all patients need hospital treatment, with between 5–10 percent dying as result of the condition.

Antibodies: proteins produced by the body in response to foreign substances such as bacteria and viruses (also called antigens). Antibodies circulate in the blood and 'attack' any specific antigens.

APGAR: a scoring system used to assess a newborn baby. Breathing, heart rate, colour of the skin (especially hands and feet), muscle tone and response to stimuli are measured at one minute and again at five minutes after the birth.

Asthma: a constriction or narrowing of the airways that causes wheezing and coughing – often due to an allergen, exercise, pollution or emotion.

Attachment: the very early relationship of a baby with his or her primary carers. Also known as bonding.

Attention Deficit Hyperactivity Disorder (ADHD): a condition in children which affects their behaviour. They are unable to sit still for periods of time, concentrate, are easily distracted and have short attention spans.

Autism: a condition that disrupts the development of a person's communication and social skills, resulting in difficulties in making sense of the world. Some of the common features include difficulties in coping with change, communication and social relationships, lack of creative pretend play in children. Some people with autism can show high levels of skills in some aspects of life such as numeracy. The condition has no known cause or cure.

Bacteria: are very small micro-organisms. Some types of bacteria are essential to maintain good health, but others are harmful and cause disease.

Balanced diet: a diet that contains all essential nutrients, in the right amounts, for good health and development.

BCG: a vaccination used to protect against tuberculosis.

Bedtime rituals: are regular behaviours or activities that children enjoy at bedtimes. These can be useful in settling a child to sleep e.g. a bedtime story or saying goodnight to favourite toys. In some children the activity can be very long and delay bedtime settling.

Behaviour: the way people act and conduct themselves in certain situations. Behaviour is often identified as 'good' or 'bad' depending on the situation and the expectations of those involved. For children appropriate behaviour is linked to their age and stage of development.

Behaviour policies and procedures: set out what sort of behaviour is expected of the children, and what will happen if they do not behave in the accepted or appropriate way

Bilingual: refers to children, or adults, who can fluently speak two languages.

Body language: is a way of communicating thoughts, feelings and attitudes without words e.g. turning away from someone to show that you do not want to speak to them.

Bonding: (see attachment)

Brittle-bone disease: an inherited condition in which the bones are very easily broken. A baby suffering from this condition may be born with broken limbs, and can fracture bones through normal handling.

Bulimia: an eating disorder in which the sufferer constantly over eats and then self induces vomiting. This often occurs in secret and can have the same long-term effects as anorexia.

Bullying: is threatening, intimidating and harassing behaviour by one person towards another. It can involve name calling, aggression, demands for money or acts of violence

Caesarean section (c-section): the delivery of a baby by a surgical operation. The baby is removed through a cut in the mother's abdomen into her uterus. The procedure is used if the baby is in distress in labour or for other medical reasons.

Carbohydrates: are the main energy source in the diet – contained in sugar, pasta, potatoes or rice.

Carpet time: a time when children, usually in primary school – particularly Foundation Stage, sit down and share their news. It used to encourage communication and sharing of worries.

Centile chart: are charts used to record a child's weight and height as compared with standard growth rates of other children.

Cerebral Palsy: a condition caused by damage to the developing brain during pregnancy, birth or early post natal. Movements, posture and communication is affected in varying degrees.

Child protection: a term used to describe the guidelines produced to promote and safeguard the safety of children. It covers child protection conferences, assessment orders, the Child Protection Register and Children in Need.

Childminder: offers care for children in his or her own home. Registered by OFSTED, all childminders are trained and regularly inspected to ensure they are maintaining high standards of care and education.

Circle time: (see carpet time).

Cold cooking: cooking with children that does not require heat – by use of a hob or oven.

Colostrum: the fluid produced by the breast during pregnancy and the first days after delivery. It contains low levels of fat and sugar and high levels of antibodies to provide the ideal first food for newborn.

Commission for Racial Equality (CRE): commission set up following the Race Relations Act (1976) with the aim of working towards the elimination of discrimination, monitoring the act and taking legal action against breaches of the act.

Confidentiality: the respect for the privacy of any information about a child, parent or other client – a founding principle of care. It is supported by the Data Protection Act (1998).

Convulsions: a reaction of the brain to certain stimuli, resulting in uncontrollable shaking, rigid limbs and sometime short-term loss of consciousness. In babies and young children convulsions are a common response to a very high temperature. It is also feature of epilepsy.

Culture: refers to shared rituals and practices that give a particular group – society or family, a sense of identity.

Cystic fibrosis: a hereditary condition that causes problems with the absorption of fats and nutrients from food as well as chronic lung infections.

Disability: a long-term condition affecting a person's physical or mental ability to carry out normal activities of daily living.

Disability Rights Commission (DRC): an independent body established to help eliminate discrimination against people with disabilities and to promote equality of opportunity.

Discrimination: a term used to describe situations in which a person, or group of people, are not treated as fairly as others based on judgements of gender, sexual orientation, lifestyle, religion or culture.

Diversity: recognising and valuing differences between individuals and groups of people.

Desirable Learning Outcomes (DLOs): the minimum curriculum requirements for children aged four years, covering early literacy, numeracy and a range of personal and social skills.

Down's syndrome: a congenital condition that results in delayed development, characteristic facial features and often heart problems.

Dysentery: a bacterial infection of the digestive tract resulting in severe vomiting, diarrhoea and pain.

Dyslexia: a specific learning difficulty affecting literacy and/or numeracy.

Early Learning Goals: targets given in the Foundation Stage curriculum for children to reach by the end of their reception year.

Emergency Protection Order: a court order that gives a social worker the power to remove a child, who is thought to be in danger, from their parents or primary carers. The order lasts for up to 8 days and gives parental responsibility to the social services.

Emotional development: the development of a child's identity, self image and the development of relationships with others.

Equal Opportunities Commission (EOC): an organisation set up to enforce laws relating to sex discrimination, promote equality of opportunity between men and women and propose reviews and amendments to legislation.

Equal opportunities policy: policies and related procedures that ensure equal and fair access to employment, services regardless of gender, sexuality, race, religion, class and age.

Fats: needed for energy, absorption of vitamins: A, D, B and K, to protect organs in the body and provide insulation, are an essential component of a balanced diet.

Fibre: fibrous material found in many vegetables, fruit, wheat and oat products —essential to stimulate the bowel, by providing bulk to the faeces.

Fine motor development: movements of the hand and wrists.

Foster care: the care of a child by appointed foster carers.

Gastroenteritis: (see dysentery).

Genetics: the study of the factors relating to inheritance.

Gluten: a protein found in some cereals, especially wheat. It can cause an allergic response in some people resulting in digestive problems.

Gross motor development: development of movements that involve the use of a whole limb such as sitting, standing or walking.

Haemophilia: an inherited gender-linked condition resulting in an inability for blood to clot. Cuts and bruises can be potentially life threatening and suffers require transfusions of the missing clotting factor to stop the bleeding.

Halal: a particular way of killing animals for consumption as prescribed by the Muslim faith.

Harassment: any unwelcome conduct, verbal or physical, which has the intent or effect of creating an offensive environment or situation.

Health visitors: registered nurses who have undertaken further training in preventative health. Usually based at a GP's surgery, health centre and Sure Start schemes, health visitors monitor and promote the health of babies and young children and older clients. They also work closely with other child agencies in child abuse cases.

Holding therapy: a method to manage a child's outburst of temper. The child is calmly but firmly held by an adult until the child is calmed, followed by a cuddle to reassure the child.

Immunisation: the activation of an artificial immune response by giving someone a very mild or dead form of a disease-causing bacteria or virus. The body is then stimulated to produce antibodies which will protect the body from a live version of the disease.

Incubator: a special crib that controls the temperature and oxygen content around a baby who is very ill or premature.

Independence: the ability to control all ones' own activities and lifestyle without support from someone else. Children gradually move towards independence as they become able to feed, wash and dress themselves and start to make their own decisions.

Infection: a condition caused by contact with a disease-causing organism, such as bacteria, virus or fungus, leading to signs and symptoms of the illness.

Inspection: examination by experienced trained professionals of the practices and services in a particular setting. Early years settings are inspected by OFSTED inspectors who ensure that children in the setting are well cared for and receiving appropriate educational input.

Letdown reflex: the response of a woman's breasts to suckling at the start of a breast feed, or sometimes when her baby starts to cry. Milk production in the alveoli starts and travels 'down' into the milk ducts.

Meningitis: inflammation of the meninges in the lining of the brain caused by bacteria or viruses. It is most common in children under five years and can be fatal or cause serious disability.

Milestones of development: skills that are looked for as children develop, usually linked to age.

MMR: a vaccination to prevent against Measles, Mumps and Rubella.

Nanny: a person employed to care for a child in that child's home. There are no requirements of registration or training for nannies that only care for the children of one or two families.

National Children's Bureau: a charity that promotes the interests of children and young people.

National Curriculum: government standards ensuring all children are taught the same basic curriculum. There are four key age-related stages, each with tests (SATs) to ensure all requirements of that stage have been met.

National Society for the Prevention of Cruelty to Children (NSPCC): a voluntary organisation with powers to act in the care of children and their families. It employs qualified social workers and works closely with the statutory social services and the police.

Natural immunity: the bodies' natural response to illness or disease.

Non-accidental injury: the act of deliberately causing physical harm, can include burns, fractures, bruises, head injuries and poisoning.

Nutrients: the vital components of food that provide the necessary requirements for a healthy functioning body.

Observations: watching a child, or group of children, with the aim of commenting on an aspect of his or her development or behaviour.

Occupational Therapist (OT): a professional working with children and adults with particular needs that requires specialist equipment or support.

OFSTED: the organisation which inspects, monitors and reports on the performance of schools, nurseries and childminders.

Orthoptist: a professional specialising in the treatment of visual defects, prescribing eye exercises and monitoring the progress of the condition.

Otitis media: an infection of the middle ear. Common in young children as the Eustachian tube – tube from the ear to the throat – is often very narrow and easily blocked by mucous.

Post-natal depression: a psychological disorder affecting a new mother in the weeks after her delivery. It involves feelings of worthlessness, sadness, anxiety and being overwhelmed by motherhood. Severity ranges from a relatively mild form (baby blues) treated at home, to severe psychosis needing hospital treatment

Prejudice: making negative judgements about other people based on stereotypes or assumptions

Protein: nutrient in food that helps with the growth and repair of cells. Found in meat, beans, nuts, dairy produce and fish

Puberty: the period between childhood and adolescence. A rapid increase in hormone production results in the development of secondary sexual characteristics such as breasts pubic hair, and the onset of menstruation.

Racism: negative attitudes and behaviour towards people from another racial group. Racism can be both obvious and subtle using behaviour, words or practices which advantage or disadvantage people because of their skin colour, culture, language or ethnic origin.

Reasonable adjustments: changes that have to be made to enable a person with a disability access to a service or facility.

Salmonella: a bacterial infection resulting in severe gastroenteritis.

Sexism: discrimination or unfair treatment on the grounds of someone's gender.

Social workers: qualified professional who work with individuals and families with arrange of problems. They operate in the voluntary and statutory service.

Socialisation: lifelong process starting at birth, of learning about yourself and how you fit into the wider world. There are three types: Primary socialisation – within the family; secondary socialisation – formed with friends and peers and tertiary – relationships with other groups in society.

Special Needs Co-ordinators (SENCO): the person in a setting who co-ordinates and oversees the setting's Special Needs Education policy.

Standard Attainment Tests (SATs): tests that measure the achievement of children at the end of each key stage of the National Curriculum.

Statutory services: health and social care services provided as a requirement by the law of the country.

Sudden Infant Death Syndrome (SIDS): the sudden, unexplained death of an infant between three and twelve months, also known as cot death.

Sure Start: a multi-agency (health, social services and education) programme to improve the start in life available to children from deprived areas.

Turn taking: an obvious pause in 'conversation' when a baby intently watches his or her carer talking to them, the baby will then responds with facial responses and vocalisations.

United Nations Convention on the Rights of the Child: the statement by the United Nations setting out the rights of all children and young people throughout the world.

Vaccination: (see immunisation).

Vitamins: essential for general health required in small quantities and available in a range of foods. Some are fat soluble – Vitamins A, D, B and K– the rest are water soluble.

Weaning: the process by which a child transfers from a purely milk diet to that of a normal family diet. This process takes place over a number of months through various stages of sloppy and mashed foods.

Useful addresses and websites

Barnado's
Tanners Lane
Barkingside
Ilford
Essex
1G6 1QG
Tel: 020 8550 8822
Web: www.barnados.org.uk

British Nutrition Foundation (BNF)
High Holborn House
52-54 High Holborn
London
WC1V 6RQ
Tel: 020 7404 6504
Web: www.nutrition.org.uk

ChildLine
2nd Floor Royal Mail Building
Studd Street
London
NI OQW
Helpline: 0800 1111
Web: www.childline.org.uk

Child Accident Prevention Trust (CAPT)
18-20 Farringdon Lane
London
EC1R 3AU
Tel: 020 7608 3828
Web: www.capt.org.uk

Children's Society
Edward Rudolf House
Margery Street
London
WC1X OJL
Tel: 020 7841 4436

Kidscape
2 Grosvenor Gardens
London
SW1W ODH
Tel: 020 7730 3300
Web: www.kidscape.org.uk/kidscape

National Childbirth Trust
Alexandra House
Oldham Terrace
Acton
London
W3 6NH
Tel: 0870 770 3236
Web: www.nctpregnancyandbabycare.com

National Children's Bureau
8 Wakley Street
London
EC1V 7QE
Tel: 020 7843 6000
Web: www.ncb.org.uk

NSPCC
National Centre
42 Curtain Road
London
EC2A 3NH
Helpline. 0808 800 5000
Textphone: 0800 056 0566
Web: www.nspcc.org.uk

Parentline Plus
520 Highgate Studios
53-79 Highgate Road
Kentish Town
London
NW5 1TL
Tel: 020 7284 5500
Web: www.parentlineplus.org.uk

Professional Association of Nursery Nurses
St James's Court
Friar Gate
Derby
DEl 1BT
Tel: 01332 372337

Save the Children (UK)
17 Grove Lane
Camberwell
London
SE5 8RD
Tel: 020 7703 5400
Web: www.savethechildren.org.uk

Index

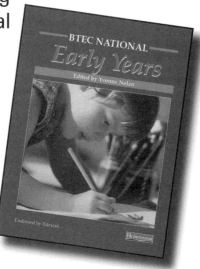

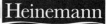